KU-641-707

Housing the Family

ISBN   0 904406 00 8

CONSTRUCTION LIBRARY,
Liverpool Polytechnic.
Victoria Street, L1 6EY

WITHDRAWN

LIVERPOOL POLYTECHNIC LIBRARY

3 1111 00149 6098

MTP CONSTRUCTION
HOUSING THE FAMILY
MP ABE 728.3 MTP 1974

DESIGN BULLETINS

Housing the Family

MTP Construction 1974

© Crown copyright 1966-71. Published in this edition by MTP Construction
in 1974. Reprinted by permission of the Controller of Her Majesty's
Stationery Office.

Published in 1974 by
MTP Construction
P.O. Box 99,
Lancaster,
England.

LIVERPOOL POLYTECHNIC
LIBRARY SERVICE

Accession number
007945/74

Class number
428.3 MTP

Publisher's Note

This book brings together in a bound and indexed form those publications
from the Department of the Environment directly concerned with the problem
of Housing the Family.   The resultant volume is a unique compendium of
authoritative information which will enable architects and builders to place
adequate emphasis on the design requirements of the modern family.

Acknowledgement

We would like to gratefully acknowledge the co-operation of both the
Department of the Environment and Her Majesty's Stationery Office in
granting us permission to publish the material contained in this volume.

Contents

1

HOUSE PLANNING

A Guide to User Needs

Introduction

1. The Parker Morris Report suggested that new patterns of living were emerging which required a radical reconsideration of house design. The effect of the television set, more mechanical equipment, growing car ownership, more higher education, an increasing variety of leisure activities and greater affluence, all had to be recognised in designing homes for today and tomorrow. In addition, new types of layout to separate the car from pedestrians and the need for higher density housing in some areas have altered the context of house design. The Parker Morris Report urged that minimum room size requirements should be abandoned and that the spaces required for activities in the home should determine house design in the future.

2. This new approach to design released the architect simultaneously from his fetters and his props. It was, however, recognised that architects needed tools for designing in the new way and should not have to spend the time and energy required for creative design on fashioning such tools themselves. MHLG Design Bulletin 6 *Space in the home* therefore set out in detail space requirements related to activities and furnishing. This bulletin is a sequel, focussed on the design of the whole house in the context of its immediate environment and on the relationship between spaces for various activities within the home. It consists of a detailed check list for house planning, followed by a discussion of the advantages and disadvantages of terrace houses, patios and clusters. It must be emphasised that the plans used in these sections have been chosen purely to illustrate particular points of house planning and, although some of them are very good plans indeed, they are not included here as models to be copied.

3. The present bulletin deals solely with houses, not with flats and maisonettes. It touches on housing layout by emphasising the balance that must be struck between satisfactory internal planning and the part the house has to play in achieving a satisfactory layout. This aspect of house planning will be developed further in a future design bulletin devoted entirely to housing layout.

4. The bulletin is primarily for those designing houses for the public sector; however it includes plans developed for private builders and housing associations and the general approach it puts forward should be of use to anyone designing houses.

5. With the introduction of new recommended and mandatory standards for the public sector in MHLG Circular 36/67 , some local authorities will have to design afresh or revise some of their house plans. At the same time as standards are being raised, the housing programme is being increased, and it is important now more than ever, to increase productivity in design offices and on site. This means some reduction of variety in house plans as well as standardisation of dimensions and components. It is also important to keep plans in production for a reasonable time and to make revisions which are related to the building programme in a systematic way. The National Building Agency's publication, *Generic plans* , shows that houses can take many different forms within a limited range of spans and dimensions. This bulletin is a further aid which, by setting out the needs of the users, aims to help designers to adopt plans which are suitable for large scale repetition.

6. There are so many demands on resources for housing that it is essential, by cost planning in the early stages of design, to use economical plans for at least the majority of houses in a scheme. No attempt has been made in this bulletin, however, to give detailed comparative costs or to suggest 'best-buys' from the plans illustrated. Costs will vary according to methods of construction, and the comparative economy of using different types will vary according to site conditions and the densities at which they are used.

7. For instance, it might be necessary at some densities to use a comparatively expensive patio plan which gives privacy, in order to use a very economical terrace plan for the majority of houses elsewhere on the site. Similarly, a narrow-frontage three-storey house, which costs more than the two-storey house, would be more acceptable to the majority of large households and more economical than the alternative of a flat.

Part 1:

8. People demand a lot of different things from their home, and the designer's task is to satisfy as many of these demands as possible within the limitations imposed by density and cost, site conditions, technical requirements, and the need to increase productivity. This means that a balance has to be struck between many competing priorities.

9. The purpose of the check list in the following pages is to provide an aid for the designer to use when appraising the advantages and disadvantages of alternative plan arrangements and when establishing priorities with clients, housing managers, and his colleagues in the design team. The check list includes design and survey experience from the Ministry's research and development projects at West Ham, Sheffield and Oldham. This experience will be published more fully in the near future in a series of bulletins covering each project.

10. Development Group survey findings have been consistent with each other and with findings of other surveys, such as those described in the Building Research Station's *Houses and people.*** In this way a picture has been built up of basic requirements for house plans which will meet the needs of most families at various stages in their development.

11. The check list covers a very wide range of requirements and an attempt has been made to pick out, for special attention, those aspects of design which the surveys have shown to be of particular importance to the user. People's needs are not static however, and demands differ according to habits, tastes and incomes. They

also differ according to the size of household and the stage of its development, with needs increasing and becoming more complex as household size increases. The check list is intended to provide the basis for particular briefs for housing in both the public and private sectors. Occasionally some questions may be more important than those given priority in the check list and also there may be local requirements not covered by the check list at all.

12. Some basic provisions, however, are now considered necessary for all houses in the public sector. These provisions, based on the Parker Morris Report, are shown in Appendix I of Circular 36/67. Extracts from this Appendix are given in full in the check list, and reference should be made to the circular itself for further information about the recommendations which have been made mandatory. The intended metric measurements set out in MHLG Circular 1/68, *Metrication of housebuilding***, are also given with each extract from Appendix I, 36/67, for convenient reference. These are not exact metric equivalents of the imperial measurements. Further general comments about the costs of different house types are made in Part 2 of this bulletin.

13. Several questions in the check list are intended to be read in conjunction with the metric editions of Design Bulletin 6, *Space in the home*. Detailed dimensions for furniture and space in Design Bulletin 6 provide a guide to design, and it is important for the designer to design so as to give as much freedom as possible for choice in selecting furniture and arranging it in the home.

A An appraisal survey interview.

**See page 48.

4

14. The check list concentrates on plan arrangements rather than such details as sound insulation or the design of fittings, but obviously these matters are also important to the user. For instance, adequate sound insulation in partitions can sometimes overcome planning disadvantages and make a great difference to the acceptability of living room and bedroom arrangements. Also, an adequate volume of storage in the kitchen will be of little account if most of it is out of reach.

15. Such details are also important for safety, and reference should be made to Design Bulletin 13, *Safety in the home** for a full check list of safety items.

16. Detailed design data for housing for the elderly are given in Design Bulletin 1, *Some aspects of designing for old people**, and standards in public sector housing for the elderly are to be published soon. The more specific needs of disabled people are given in Selwyn Goldsmith's *Designing for the disabled**.

17. In short, the present bulletin can be regarded as one of a collection of desk aids which include the publications mentioned above and will include future bulletins arising from current work on housing layout.

18. All designers are familiar with the problem of meeting every item in a brief within the budget for the job. Two living areas, a separate kitchen large enough for occasional meals to be taken in comfort, individual bedrooms of adequate size for the children, and flexibility for partition and furniture arrangements, are all highly desirable in themselves, but where they cannot be fully attained it is necessary to strike a balance—to get as close to the ideal as possible and to give priority to the more important requirements. It is the intention of this check list and the following chapter to help all those concerned with house design to strike the right balance and give priority to the right things, as well as setting out a full list of points to consider.

*See page 48.

B Furniture is often placed in different positions from those shown on the designer's plans.

The check list

The purpose of this check list is to set out a list of points for the designer to consider when appraising the advantages and disadvantages of alternative plan arrangements and when establishing priorities with clients, housing managers and his colleagues in the design team.

■ Questions marked ■ are those covered by Circular 36/67, Appendix I. Extracts from this circular have been included in the check list for convenient reference.

● Questions marked ● are other items which surveys have shown to be of greatest importance to the user.

P Some questions relating to privacy are marked distinctively with a P. These are important points, but there may be more than one way of meeting them other than by the house plan itself, e.g. by the designer in the arrangement of the buildings or by the user hanging net curtains at the windows.

The metric measurements given in brackets are those set out in Circular 1/68. These are not exact metric equivalents of the imperial measurements.

Areas

Q 1 Do the net floor area of the house and its general
■ storage space conform to the mandatory standards given
in Circular 36/67* (or the metric equivalents set out in
Circular 1/68)?

'*A home for occupation for the number of people shown in
the Table below shall be designed to provide areas of Net
Space and General Storage Space not less than those set out
in the Table and fulfilling the conditions in the Notes
following the Table.*'

TABLE		\multicolumn{14}{c}{Number of people (i.e. bed-spaces) per dwelling}												
		\multicolumn{2}{c}{1}	\multicolumn{2}{c}{2}	\multicolumn{2}{c}{3}	\multicolumn{2}{c}{4}	\multicolumn{2}{c}{5}	\multicolumn{2}{c}{6}	\multicolumn{2}{c}{7}
		sq. ft.	m²	sq. ft.	m²	sq. ft.	m²	sq. ft.	m²	sq. ft.	m²	sq. ft.	m²	sq. ft.	m²
1 Storey	N	320	30	480	44,5	610	57	720	67	810	75,5	900	84		
	S	30	3	40	4	45	4	50	4,5	50	4,5	50	4,5		
2 Storey (semi or end)	N							770	72	880	82	990	92,5	1,165	108
	S							50	4,5	50	4,5	50	4,5	65	6,5
(intermediate terrace)	N							800	74,5	910	85	990	92,5	1,165	108
	S							50	4,5	50	4,5	50	4,5	65	6,5
3 Storey (excluding garage if built-in)	N									1,010	94	1,050	98	1,210	112
	S									50	4,5	50	4,5	65	6.5

N=Net space (Note 1)   S=General storage space (Note 2)

Tolerance: Where dwellings are designed on a planning grid and not otherwise, a maximum minus tolerance of 1½% shall be permitted on the Net space.

Note 1: Net space *is the area on one or more floors enclosed by the walls of a dwelling measured to unfinished faces. It includes the space, on plan, taken up on each floor by any staircase, by partitions and by any chimney breast, flue and heating appliance and the area of any external w.c. It excludes the floor area of general storage space (S in Table) and dustbin store, fuel store, garage or balcony and any area in rooms with sloping ceilings to the extent that the height of the ceiling does not exceed 5 ft 0 in (1,50 m) and any porch, lobby or covered way open to the air.*

In the case of a "single access house", any space within a store required to serve as access (taken as 2 ft 3 in (700 mm) wide) from one side of a house to the other shall be provided in addition to the areas in the Table.

Note 2: General storage space *is the space which shall be provided exclusive of any dustbin store, fuel store, pram space located in a store and, in the case of a "single access house", any space within a store required to serve as access (taken as 2 ft 3 in (700 mm) wide) from one side of a house to the other.*

Some of the storage space may be on an upper floor but at least 25 sq ft (2,5 m²) shall be at ground level,
—where some of the storage space is provided on an upper floor, it shall be enclosed separately from linen or bedroom cupboards; it shall be accessible from the circulation space or from a room if conveniently accessible in relation to furnishing,
—where there is a garage integral with or adjoining a house, any area in excess of 130 sq ft (12,0 m²) shall count towards the general storage provision.'

*These minima are those recommended in the Parker Morris Report with the addition of standards for seven-person houses.

Site layout implications

Q 2 Is the plan:
(a) suitable for single access?
or
■ (b) does it require access from both sides?

'Most house layouts now provide for public access to both sides of the house, but where public access to a house of three or more persons is from one side only, a way through the house from front to back shall be provided and this must not be through the living room. In such cases the dustbin compartment shall be on the front.'

Q 3 Does the plan itself give reasonable privacy:
P (a) to its living rooms and bedrooms from people calling or passing by?
P (b) to its private garden from overlooking from other houses?
P (c) to the gardens and living rooms of other houses?

Q 4 Does the plan allow:
(a) for the car to be kept within the curtilage e.g. by a built-in garage, an attached garage, or a parking space?
P (b) for this space to be used by others without intruding upon the householder's privacy if the household does not own a car, i.e. not built-in or with doors leading into the house?

Q 5 What orientations are best suited to the plan?

The entrance

Q 6 Is there a reception lobby or hall to provide a buffer against callers intruding on the privacy of the living areas, and to minimise heat loss:
● (a) which is large enough to receive visitors and to allow a pram and furniture to be brought indoors?
■ (b) with space for hanging outdoor clothes?

'A dwelling shall have an entrance hall or lobby with space for hanging outdoor clothes.'

Q 7 Is there at or near an entrance:
■ (a) provision for storing a pram without entering the living areas?

'For three-person and larger houses and three-person and larger dwellings served by a lift or ramp a space shall be provided for a pram (4 ft 7 in x 2 ft 3 in) (1 400 x 700 mm).'

● (b) a w.c. and wash-hand basin, accessible without going through the living areas? (See also Q.38 and Q.39.)

Q 8 Is there shelter from the rain for callers waiting at the entrance?

Q 9 Is there a covered route from the house to:
(a) the garage?
(b) the refuse store?
(c) the fuel store?

Q 10 Is the refuse store:
● (a) accessible to the refuse collector without his entering the house, its store or its garage? (See also Q.2.)
(b) inconspicuous from the main entrance?

Q 11 Can meters be read:
(a) from outside the house?
or
(b) without entering the living areas?

Q 12 If prepayment meters are fitted, would there be
● convenient access to them from inside the house?

C A convenient relationship between kitchen and dining areas with a counter and venetian blind between them to screen any untidiness.

D A convenient relationship between the main living room, dining area and kitchen, all with views out into the garden.

E The kitchen has a view of and close access to the garden, for supervising children's play, hanging out washing, etc.

Circulation and relationship between spaces

E

Q 13 Is there a convenient route for the pram and for children
● through the house to the garden, without entering the main living area? (See also Q.2.)

Q 14 Can members of the household get from the entrance to their bedrooms without disturbing:
(a) any living area?
or
● (b) at least the main living area?

Q 15 Can visitors get from the main entrance to the main living area without entering:
● (a) the kitchen?
(b) the dining area?

Q 16 Can members of the household get from bedrooms to the bathroom and a w.c. without:
■ (a) entering any other room?

'Except in one- or two-person dwellings access from bedroom to the bathroom and a w.c. shall be arranged without having to pass through another room.'

(b) crossing the entrance hall?
(c) going up or down stairs to another floor?

Q 17 Are the circulation spaces:
● (a) adequate in size for larger items of furniture to be moved about the house?
(b) suitable for other purposes, e.g. cupboards, telephone?

Q 18 Is there a convenient relationship between the kitchen, the living areas and the outside spaces so that:
● (a) the kitchen has direct access to the dining area and reasonable access to the main living area?
● (b) the kitchen has a view of, and close access to, the private open space for supervising children's play, putting washing on the line, etc.?
(c) the kitchen has some view of the outside world, callers and passers-by, etc.?
(d) the kitchen has convenient access to the refuse store without going through the main living area?

Q 19 Do the living areas have:
(a) a view of the garden and easy access to it?
P (b) privacy from callers approaching the main entrance?

Q 20 Is the general storage provision:
● (a) conveniently distributed, e.g. so that bicycles and gardening tools do not have to be taken through the house? (See also Q.1, Note 2.)
● (b) likely to be free from damp—for storing the vacuum cleaner, trunks, etc.?

F An internal kitchen in use, with ironing airing by the warm-air grille and a settee in the dining area.

G An internal kitchen between dining and main living areas in a narrow-frontage house.

H Work sequence in a galley kitchen.
Worktop – cooker – worktop – sink – worktop.

The kitchen

Q 21 Is there adequate space in the kitchen for:
■ (a) built-in storage for cooking utensils, foodstuffs, cleaning materials, etc.?

'Kitchen fitments comprising enclosed storage space in connection with:
(a) preparation and serving of food and washing-up;
(b) cleaning, and laundry operations and
(c) food,
shall be provided as follows:
three-person and larger dwellings 80 cu ft (2,3 m³)
one- and two-person dwellings 60 cu ft (1,7 m³).
Part of this provision shall comprise a ventilated "cool" cupboard and a broom cupboard. The broom cupboard may be provided elsewhere than in the kitchen. Where standard fitments are used the cubic capacity shall be measured overall for the depth and width, and from the underside of the worktop to the top of the plinth for the height.'

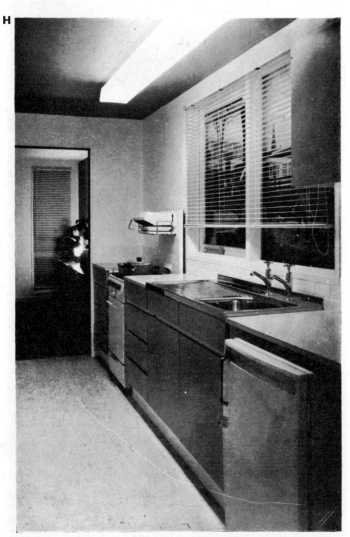

H

■ (b) the basic items of equipment, e.g. cooker, washing machine, spin dryer and refrigerator?

'In addition to kitchen storage, the sink and space for a cooker, a minimum of two further spaces shall be provided in convenient positions to accommodate a refrigerator and a washing machine. The latter may be in the kitchen or in a convenient position elsewhere. These spaces may be provided under worktop surfaces.'

(c) items likely to be bought in the future, such as a dishwasher, deep freeze and tumbler dryer?

Q 22 Are the working arrangements adequate, i.e.:
(a) is the total work surface adequate in area?
■ (b) is there an unbroken work surface between, and either side of, the sink and cooker?

'Worktops shall be provided on both sides of the sink and on both sides of the cooker position. Kitchen fitments shall be arranged to provide a work sequence comprising worktop/cooker/worktop/sink/worktop (or the same in reverse order) unbroken by a door or other traffic way.'

(c) is the relationship between the sink, cooker, refrigerator and ventilated 'cool' cupboard:
(i) compact?
(ii) free from through circulation?
(d) is there a utility room, or space in the kitchen for washing and ironing clothes, a clothes-drying rack, etc.?

Q 23 Is there space in the kitchen for some members of the
■ family to eat occasional meals?

'The kitchen in a dwelling for two or more persons must provide a space where casual meals may be taken by a minimum of two persons . . .'
'Furniture . . . Kitchen—A small table unless one is built in.'

Q 24 Do doors which open into the kitchen clear working
● areas and cupboard door-swings?

Q 25 Are there adequate means to prevent cooking smells reaching:
(a) the main dining area?
(b) other parts of the house?

I A main living room which is free from through circulation and can be kept tidy.

J The second living area with space for children's play as well as meals. This area opens through double doors into the main living room.

K The dining area used as a second living room.

L The same kitchen and second living area in use in two different houses.

Living areas

Q 26 Is the main living space large enough to accommodate the necessary furniture:
■ (a) for the whole family and occasional visitors?

'*Furniture . . . Living Space—*
2 or 3 easy chairs
A settee
A TV set
Small tables
Reasonable quantity of other possessions, such as:
Radiogram
Bookcase.'

● (b) to provide for alternative furniture arrangements?

Q 27 Can the main living space be shut off from the rest of
● the house?

Q 28 In houses for four persons or more:
● (a) is there a separate second living space (dining room, dining hall, kitchen with dining area, or study)?
(b) can both living spaces be thrown into one for special occasions?
or alternatively
(c) are they well separated on plan to contribute to sound insulation?

Q 29 Is the main dining area large enough for the whole
■ family and occasional visitors?

'*Furniture . . . Meals Space—Dining table and chairs.*'

Q 30 If the dining area is separate from the main living space
● is it large enough to accommodate a sideboard and an easy chair as well as the dining table and chairs?

Q 31 Can the working area of the kitchen be screened from view from the main dining space?

14

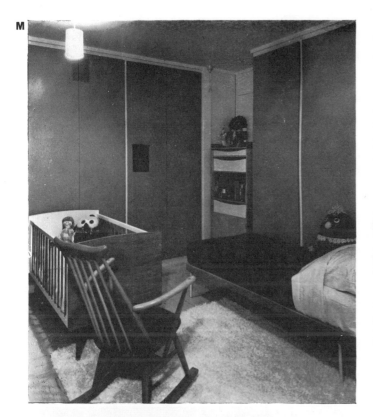

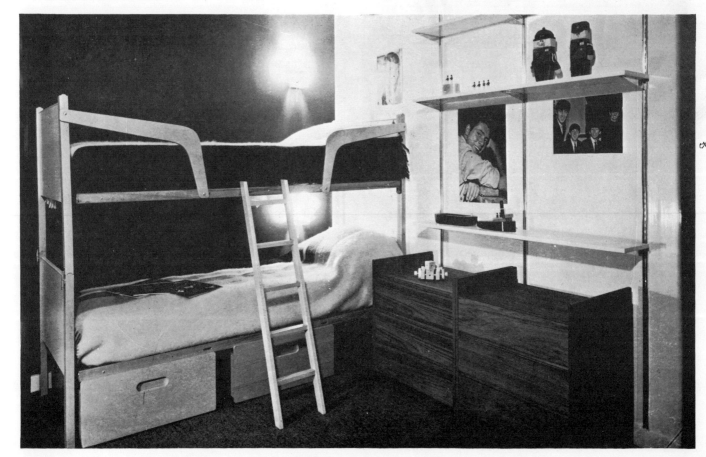

15

Bedrooms

M Bedrooms with changing uses
  (a) when the children are very young (this is a subdivisible double bedroom without the partition; a cupboard has been placed in front of the second door);
  (b) a small separate bedroom occupied by one older child;
  (c) when the children are a little older.

N A ground-floor bedroom linked to the main living room
  (a) used as a hobbies room by a young family;
  (b) used as a bed-sitting room.

*Where single beds are shown they may abut or where alongside walls must have a space of 2 ft 6 in (750 mm) between them.

†May be provided within easy access outside the room.

Q 32 Can each member of the family other than the parents
  ● have a single bedroom to himself?

Q 33 Is there space in each bedroom to:
  ■ (a) accommodate the required furniture?

'*Furniture . . .*

Single Bedrooms
Bed or divan (6 ft 6 in x 3 ft 0 in) (2 000 x 900 mm)
Bedside table
Chest of drawers
A wardrobe or space for cupboard to be built in

Main Bedrooms
A double bed (6 ft 6 in x 4 ft 6 in) (2 000 x 1 500 mm)
(and where possible as an alternative)
Two single beds* (6 ft 6 in x 3 ft 0 in) (2 000 x 900 mm)
Bedside tables
Chest of drawers
Double wardrobe or space for cupboard to be built in
Dressing table

Other Double Bedrooms
Two single beds* (6 ft 6 in x 3 ft 0 in (2 000 x 900 mm)
each)
Bedside tables
Chest of drawers
Double wardrobe or space for cupboard to be built in†
Small dressing table

Note: Spaces for wardrobes, or space for cupboards to be built in later should be on the basis of 2 ft 0 in (600 mm) run of hanging space per person. The space provided for a cupboard depth should be not less than 1 ft 10 in (550 mm) internally.'

  ● (b) allow of sensible alternative arrangements?

Q 34 In addition to the furniture required above is there:
  (a) space for a cot to be put occasionally in the main bedroom of houses for three persons and above?
  (b) space for a desk or dressing table in single bedrooms?

Q 35 When the house is not fully occupied or when the children are young and sharing bedrooms:
  (a) can at least one of the unoccupied bedrooms, by folding doors or a demountable partition, be used to enlarge the living areas or another bedroom?
  (b) can two of the single bedrooms be used, by the same means, as a double room? (See Q. 32.)

Q 36 Does the plan contribute to sound insulation between
  ● the bedrooms and between bedrooms and the living areas?

Bathroom and w.c.

Q 37 Is the bathroom and w.c. provision adequate?
■

> '*The w.c. and wash-basin provision shall be as set out below:*
> (*a*) *In one-, two- and three-person dwellings, one w.c. is required, and may be in the bathroom.*
> (*b*) *In four-person two- or three-storey houses and in four- and five-person single-storey houses, one w.c. is required in a separate compartment.*
> (*c*) *In two- or three-storey houses at or above the minimum floor area for five persons, and in single-storey houses at or above the minimum floor area for six persons, two w.c.'s are required, one of which may be in the bathroom.*
> (*d*) *Where a separate w.c. does not adjoin a bathroom, it must contain a wash-basin.*'

Q 38 In houses with a second w.c. and wash-basin, are the compartment and its basin large enough to be used by an adult for washing, as an alternative to the bathroom?

Q 39 Is there adequate space in the bathroom and w.c. compartments:
● (a) around the fittings?
● (b) to open the door and enter easily?
(c) to accommodate a stool in the bathroom in addition to the fittings?

Q 40 Does the plan contribute to sound insulation between the w.c. and:
(a) the main entrance?
(b) the living areas?
(c) the bedrooms?

Storage

Q 41 Is there a store or utility room inside the home with space for a work bench and storage for hobbies and household maintenance? (See also Qs. 1 and 20.)

Q 42 Is there adequate covered storage provision for:
■ (a) fuel where required?

> '*12 sq ft (1,5 m²) where there is only one appliance, 20 sq ft (2,0 m²) where there are two appliances or in rural areas.*'

● (b) refuse—with adequately ventilated space for at least one dustbin and occasional boxes?

Q 43 Is the linen cupboard adequate for the size of the
■ dwelling?

> '*A cupboard shall be provided giving 20 cu ft (0,6 m³) of clear storage space in four-person and larger dwellings or 15 cu ft (0,4 m³) in smaller dwellings.*'

Services

Q 44 Is the heating system adequate to serve:
■ (a) living spaces?
■ (b) kitchen?
● (c) bedrooms?
■ (d) circulation spaces?
(e) bathroom and w.c.?

> '*The minimum standard shall be an installation with appliances capable of maintaining kitchen and the circulation spaces at 55°F. (13°C.) and the living and dining areas at 65°F. (18°C.), when the outside temperature is 30°F. (—1°C.).*'

Q 45 Does the plan form enable whole or partial house heating from a single source to be provided economically?

Q 46 Is the house planned to minimise heat loss from the
● living spaces to other parts of the house and outside?

Q 47 If warm air duct outlets or radiators are used, are they
● positioned to allow furniture to be arranged satisfactorily?

Q 48 Is the hot water cylinder placed so that pipe runs to draw-off outlets are short? (Not more than 15 ft 0 in (4,57 m) to the kitchen sink and 25 ft 0 in (7,62 m) to other fittings.)

Q 49 Can all waste pipes be connected economically to one soil stack?

Q 50 Does the plan avoid:
(a) waste drainage outlets on both sides of the house?
(b) excessive lengths of drainage under the ground floor slab?

Q 51 Have sufficient electric socket outlets been provided?
■

'*Electric Socket Outlets shall be provided for as follows:*
Working area of kitchen 4
Dining area 1
Living area 3
Bedroom 2
Hall or landing 1
Bedsitting-room in family dwellings 3
Bedsitting-room in one-person dwellings 5
Integral or attached garage 1
Walk-in general store (*in house only*) 1'

Q 52 Are the electric socket outlets, lighting points and switches in convenient positions in relation to:
● (a) fittings such as the cooker and worktops?
● (b) possible alternative furniture arrangements?

Q 53 Are lighting points easily accessible for replacing light
● bulbs, e.g. on stairs?

Q 54 Are windows and doors positioned:
● (a) to allow the best possible arrangements for furniture and equipment, e.g. beds in relation to windows?
● (b) to avoid dangerous obstructions in circulation areas within the house and at the entrance?
● (c) to give easy access to windows from inside and outside for cleaning by the occupant, e.g. windows to bathrooms and staircases?

Q 55 Are the stairs designed to avoid:
● (a) winders at the top?
● (b) one riser on a half landing or elsewhere in an unexpected place?
● (c) a handrail which is not continuous?
● (d) a top tread which encroaches into the landing?
(e) a projecting tread at the bottom?

Q 56 Are windows positioned to give the best possible privacy
P to the household from overlooking by passers-by and callers?

Part 2: Characteristics of different house forms

19. The variety of houses being designed today cannot be divided into hard-and-fast categories, but some characteristics (e.g. of frontage or number of storeys) have such a strong influence on internal planning and cost that some generalisations can be made.

20. It will be seen that some plan forms have inherent disadvantages but will still be worth using to meet different layout conditions—density, access, prospect, privacy, orientation and car accommodation. This is implicit in the balance that has always to be struck between layout requirements and the internal arrangement of the house.

21. This section discusses the general characteristics of five groups of plans. The discussion brings in a number of existing house plans, and it is emphasised that these plans have been selected to illustrate particular points about each group and are not in any way put forward as model plans. The plans shown were designed for local authorities, new towns, housing associations and private developers. Almost all were designed after the Parker Morris Report was published, but standards vary from one to another according to the requirements of different clients and sites.* Basic information about each plan is given in the Appendix to show how they compare with the recommendations of Circular 36/67 for net dwelling and storage areas.

22. These plans give some indication of the wide range of solutions being used today to meet the needs of different clients, site conditions and densities. Some solutions are obviously much more expensive than others because of differences in floor area, and costs will vary according to numbers, the comparative costs of external, internal and party walls, roofs, floors and methods of construction. Also, what is an economical plan will depend upon site peculiarities and density. However, despite these qualifications there are some cost factors which are intrinsic to the plans in each category.

23. The most economical houses of all are likely to be found in the medium-frontage terrace range; they are usually the nearest to square in shape and have the lowest perimeter wall/floor ratio. Of these, the two-storey terrace houses without external projections such as porches and stores are likely to be the most economical for four-person families and above. One- and two-storey patio houses, narrow-frontage three-storey, and wide-frontage terrace houses all have a higher perimeter wall/floor ratio. Also, from the point of view of layout costs, the wide-frontage and patio types incur greater costs for external works such as drainage, public footpaths and roads. Usually, their extensive use will only be sensible if complex site problems have to be met or if the only alternative would be a more expensive and less satisfactory flat. The grouping of houses in terraces, with few gable walls and steps or staggers, is obviously cheaper than grouping in small clusters, and changes in level outside the dwelling will usually be cheaper than the use of split-level types.

*Most of the plans illustrated were, however, designed before the Building Regulations 1965 came into effect.

24. These comments are obviously subject to many qualifications and there will be exceptions to such a highly simplified picture. Cost planning at the earliest stages in design will ensure that the most economical plans compatible with user requirements are chosen. For houses in both the private and public sectors, it must be emphasised that there are so many demands from the user for better quality, for example fittings inside the home and children's play areas outside, that care must be taken to choose the most economical house designs compatible with other requirements.

25. The challenge which faces all concerned with housing is to strike the best possible balance between cost, the requirements outlined in the check list and the part the house has to play in achieving a satisfactory layout.

key

B	bedroom
D	dining room
K	kitchen
L	living room
P	patio
h	heater
st	store
⊙	bin
▯	wash-basin
▯⊙	w.c.
⌒	bath
▯	sink
∘	soil pipe

Narrow-frontage terrace houses: 12-18 ft

Main characteristics

26.   Narrow-frontage plans are particularly useful when a high density is required. Against this major advantage in layout, the narrow-frontage plan cannot fulfil as many requirements of the check list as most other plans in this bulletin. Privacy, satisfactory through-access, versatile orientation, space for the car, natural lighting to two living areas, kitchen and bathroom, compact services and circulation, are all difficult to achieve economically. Many of these problems are caused by the small proportion of external wall in relation to the area of each floor. When the area of one floor is small because the house is planned for a small household, or because the house has three storeys, the problem is not too acute. But it is particularly difficult to design an economical single-storey narrow-frontage house for a large household.

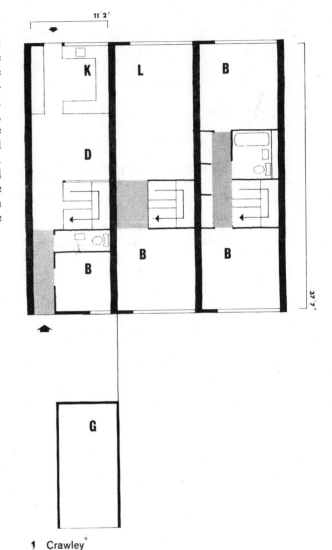

1   Crawley

Density and privacy

27. Narrow-frontage plans make maximum use of road and footpath frontage and the space required for daylighting between blocks. This makes them particularly suitable for use at high densities, where they may make it possible to house far more families with young children at ground level than in the alternative of blocks of flats or maisonettes. The density advantages of this type are, however, somewhat reduced by the distance required between blocks to give privacy.

28. External walls are usually extensively glazed, and privacy from passers-by and callers can be a problem, particularly if there is a bedroom on the ground floor as in the Crawley plan (Figure 1). If footpaths are consequently kept well away from windows this again offsets some of the density advantages of the narrow-frontage type. Projecting stores and entrances, however, can often make some use of this space, as shown in the Guildway plan (Figure 2).

29. As the gardens are usually narrow and easily overlooked from the sides, substantial screening is essential to give privacy at ground level. Some privacy for adjacent gardens can be achieved by staggering the terraces, as in the S.S.H.A. plan (Figure 3), though this is more expensive than a straight terrace with garden screen walls.

30. The S.S.H.A. plan, however, also illustrates one way of achieving closer spacing of narrow-frontage plans by using the stagger to light rooms from the side, achieving a 'blindside' house. The S.S.H.A. house also has complete privacy from callers at the main entrance. The first-floor living room, however, could easily overlook the windows and gardens of houses opposite unless special care were taken in the layout to avoid this happening.

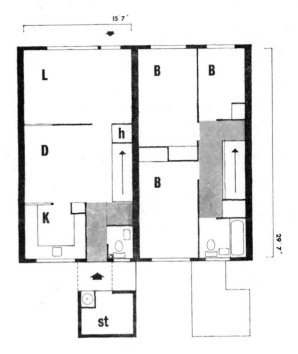

2 Guildway

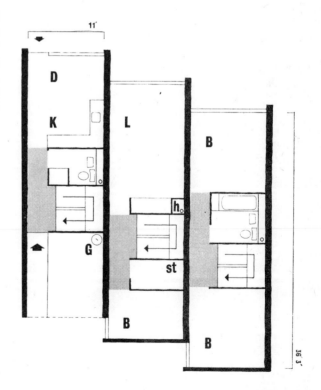

3 S.S.H.A.

Access

31. Access to the garden has often to be through the main living room, as in all except one of the two-storey plans shown. An exception is the Boston Manor plan (Figure 4) which has a passage right through the house. This is achieved, however, at the expense of the living area, and the main living room is also very narrow. A lobby on the garden side, as shown in the Gateshead plan (Figure 5), can help to keep the living room free from muddy shoes, but it is still necessary to go through the main living room from the garden to other parts of the house. Thus, fully satisfactory dual access is very difficult to achieve in narrow-frontage plans for one- or two-storey houses.

32. The more expensive three-storey narrow-frontage houses avoid most of these problems as the main living room can be on the first floor, as in the S.S.H.A. and Crawley plans. The problem of access from the garden in these houses is largely solved by direct entry into the dining kitchen.

Car space

33. In one- or two-storey narrow-frontage houses it is difficult to attach a garage to the house because external wall area is limited. The Guildway plan is the only one illustrated which could allow a garage without obscuring too much light. The S.S.H.A. house has a car-port on the main entrance side, and the inclusion of the car within the curtilage is some compensation for the inconvenience of two flights of stairs. The Crawley plan provides an additional bedroom in this position.

Orientation

34. Narrow-frontage plans do not have as much choice of orientation as wide-frontage ones, as it is difficult, if not impossible, to provide a through living room.

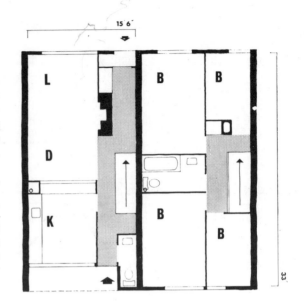

4 Boston Manor

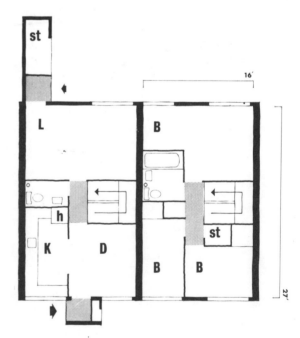

5 Gateshead

Internal arrangements

35.   Internally, the main problem in designing narrow-frontage houses is the central area of the house which is far from any windows. Families of more than three persons need two separate living areas, as well as a kitchen in which it is possible to take occasional meals. Ideally, all three spaces need direct natural lighting, but internal kitchens, as in the Oldham plan (Figure 6), often have to be used as well as internal bathrooms, w.c.'s, and staircases. Sometimes it is possible to provide more natural lighting and a better outlook in the central area by borrowing light from adjacent rooms or by combining the kitchen and dining area. The former arrangement in the Guildway plan provides some useful natural lighting but reduces sound insulation between the two living areas. The kitchen in the Oldham plan is placed conveniently between the two living areas and gets some natural lighting and views out through the dining area.

36.   Another intrinsic problem with the narrow-frontage house is that the depth of plan produces long narrow spaces, increasing circulation areas both within rooms and between them, compared with wider-frontage types.

37.   Only the Guildway plan has a bathroom on an external wall. The others have internal bathrooms and w.c.'s, with a soil stack in the centre of the house or split drainage as in the Crawley plan. All the plans except Boston Manor and Guildway have internal ground floor w.c.'s requiring artificial extract ventilation.

38.   Warm-air heating systems often have longer and more complicated ducts in the narrow-frontage houses than in medium-frontage types.

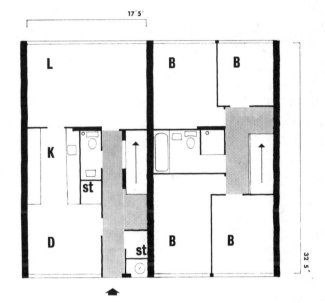

6 Oldham

Medium-frontage terrace houses: 18-24 ft

Main characteristics

39. Medium-frontage terrace houses generally satisfy more of the check list requirements than the narrow-frontage types discussed in the last section. Low perimeter wall/floor area ratios can produce very economical solutions, and privacy, through-access, space for the car, natural lighting to living area, kitchens and bathrooms, and compact services and circulation, can all be readily achieved. Medium-frontage plans are, however, less versatile in orientation than wide-frontage ones.

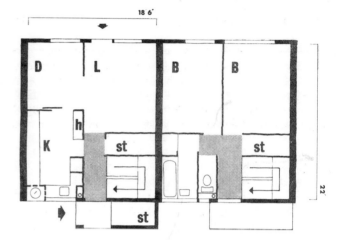

7 East Dulwich

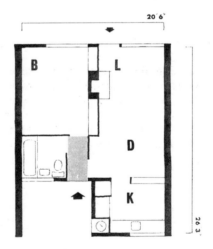

8 Preston

24

Density and privacy

40. It is usually more difficult to achieve high densities with medium-frontage plans than with any other type. They take up more road and footpath frontage and more daylighting space between blocks than the narrow-frontage types. It is also more difficult to achieve a 'blindside' plan for close spacing of blocks than with either wide-frontage or patio houses. Medium-frontage houses for small families, however, can sometimes provide a 'blindside' at first floor level—as illustrated by the East Dulwich plan (Figure 7).

41. The East Dulwich plan also shows that it is possible to place two living rooms side by side facing the garden. This arrangement avoids intrusion on the privacy of living areas by callers at the front door.

42. The Preston single-storey house (Figure 8) provides an entrance courtyard giving privacy at the front door as well as allowing a view from the kitchen window, which most housewives appreciate.

Access

43. In two-storey houses at medium rather than narrow frontage it is easier to provide a route to the garden which does not pass through the main living area. The West Ham two-storey (Figure 9), N.R.O. (Figure 10) and East Dulwich plans provide such a route. The N.R.O. plan is the only one illustrated which has through-access avoiding the kitchen and both living spaces, but this is achieved at the expense of living area.

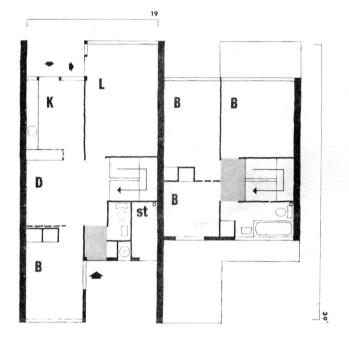

9 West Ham 2-storey 6P

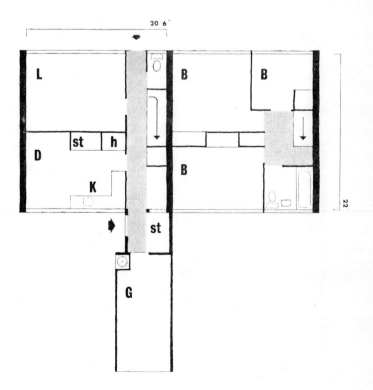

10 N.R.O.

Car space

44. It is also possible for two-storey medium-frontage terrace houses to have an attached or integral garage. The N.R.O. and the West Ham three-storey (Figure 11) plans show this arrangement and the East Dulwich and West Pennine (Figure 12) plans could easily be adapted. Both the West Ham three-storey and the N.R.O. plans illustrate the additional advantage of being able to get to the garage and refuse store under cover.

Orientation

45. With two living rooms side by side facing the garden as in the East Dulwich plan, advantage can be taken of a good orientation south or west. It is still difficult, however, with two-storey houses at this frontage to provide a through living room to give more versatile orientation. One solution is the three-storey house with main living room at first-floor level extending right through the house, as in the West Ham three-storey plan.

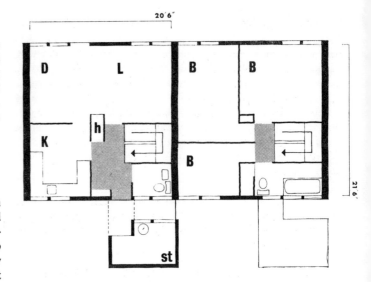

12 West Pennine

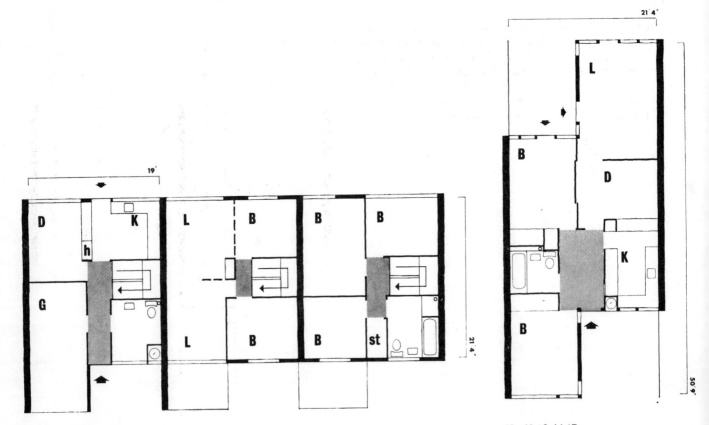

11 West Ham 3-storey

13 Hatfield 4P

Internal arrangements

46. Internally, the two-storey medium-frontage plans often have natural lighting to all rooms as well as compact circulation and services. This latter advantage results from a lower perimeter wall/floor area ratio than is found in either narrow- or wide-frontage plans. The West Pennine plan illustrates these points.

47. At medium frontage it is also possible to get two living areas and a kitchen separate from each other as in the East Dulwich plan and a view from the kitchen to both the front and back of the house, as in the East Dulwich and West Pennine plans.

48. The West Ham two-storey house has one bedroom downstairs. A partition separating it from the dining hall can be removed to extend the dining area if the downstair bedroom is not being used. This arrangement gives flexibility but at the expense of direct natural lighting when the partition is up. In the same house there is a removable partition between the two single bedrooms, another advantage which becomes easier to achieve in two-storey houses at medium frontage.

49. The only six-person plan illustrated is three-storey and, though two flights of stairs are inconvenient, the West Ham three-storey plan does allow four members of the family to sleep in separate bedrooms as well as providing an integral garage. There is also flexibility in the arrangement of the rooms on the first floor. A demountable partition can be removed or put in a different position to extend the living room and reduce the sleeping space or change the shape of the living room. One major problem, however, with this kind of flexibility is that the heating installation has to be similarly flexible.

50. The single-storey plans in this section show that dual use of living space for circulation is usually needed at this frontage when all accommodation is on one level. However, for small households in particular, as in the Preston two-person and Hatfield four-person (Figure 13) houses, it is not essential to have independent access to all rooms. The Preston plan shows a combined living room and kitchen which would probably be acceptable to such a small family. In the Hatfield four-person and the Preston plans, access from the garden is into the living room or bedroom, but at this frontage it would be possible to associate a dining kitchen and a living room on the garden frontage with a bedroom and bathroom on the other.

51. A medium-frontage single-storey house for large families can suffer from the same problem of natural lighting as a narrow-frontage house for smaller families. An important feature of the Hatfield five/six-person house (Figure 14) is the use of an internal courtyard to give natural lighting to a study and bedroom.

52. Both Hatfield plans take advantage of natural lighting through the roof—another possibility in single-storey housing. One of the double bedrooms in the five/six-person house is divisible and relies on roof lighting when divided. The dining area in the four-person plan also has a roof light.

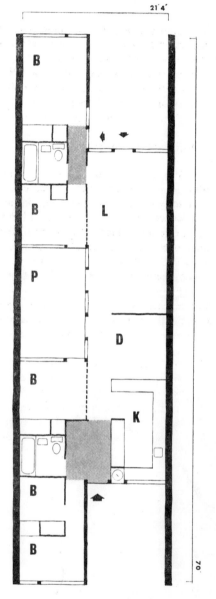

14 Hatfield 6P

Wide-frontage terrace houses: over 24 ft

Main characteristics

53. Wide-frontage terrace houses can satisfy more check list requirements than any other terraced type. They are usually also more expensive than any other terraced type and circulation areas are sometimes high, but privacy, through-access, space for the car, natural lighting to all spaces and versatile orientation are all relatively easy to provide.

Density and privacy

54. Wide-frontage houses take up more road and footpath frontage and more daylighting space between blocks than any other terraced type, but high densities are still possible. This is because many plans are 'blindside' at first-floor level (apart from the bathroom window). Complete privacy on one side of the house can also be provided by wide-frontage plans. A shallow house allows all rooms, as in the Westgate plan (Figure 15), or all rooms except the kitchen as in the Andover (Figure 16) and Hull City (Figure 17) plans, to face one way only. These houses can then be approached by a footpath against the dwelling, thus avoiding the extra space which is needed to give privacy when a living room is lit from the main access side.

55. The Westgate single-storey plan allows a back-to-back lay-out with a walled entrance garden on each side of the block. Equally it would be possible to enter from the 'blindside' only and have gardens abutting without secondary access. Residents, however, would probably prefer to have some outlook on to a public footpath, especially from the kitchen.

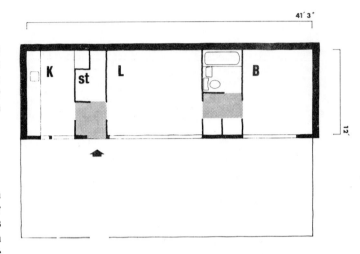

15 Westgate

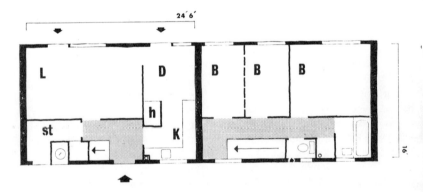

16 Andover

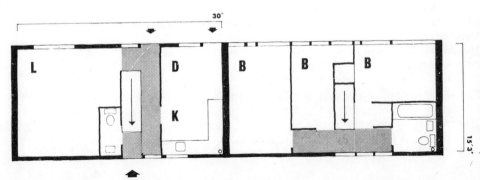

17 Hull City

Access

56.   There are three houses in this section with full dual access by a through-hall or two lobbies. These are the Hull City, Skelmersdale (Figure 18), and M.H.C. (Figure 19) plans. A store is used for through-access in the CAWL house (Figure 20). The space occupied by the through-hall in the Hull City plan has, however, taken away useful living area. (An alternative version of this plan has also been built with a larger dining area and without a through-hall.)

57.   Wide-frontage plans also allow room for two entrances ('clean and dirty') on the same side as in the CAWL and Andover plans.

58.   All the plans illustrated show that wide-frontage plans can easily avoid access to the garden through the main living area. Plans with 'blind' or 'one-eyed' frontages are therefore useful in layouts with pedestrian routes on both sides of the house and also when road access is provided to one side.

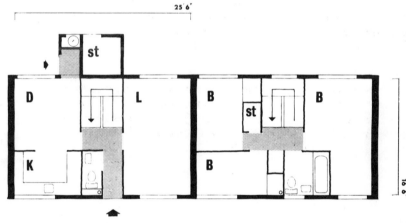

18   Skelmersdale

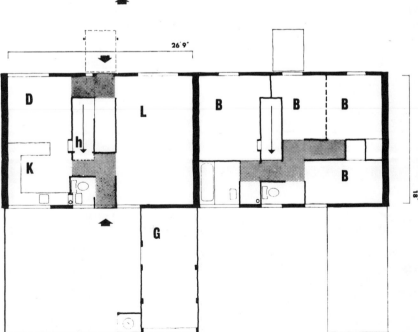

19   M.H.C. Mark 1

Car space

59. It is usually possible to attach a garage, and often to allow an open parking space as well; it is possible at this frontage to provide a built-in garage in two-storey housing as shown in the West Ham plan (Figure 21). This garage also provides a good route through the house.

Orientation

60. A wide and shallow house can have a through living room with a window at each end, as in the Skelmersdale and M.H.C. plans. This makes the house suitable for most orientations if care is taken to prevent intrusion on privacy by passers-by.

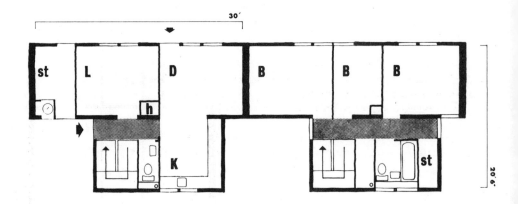

20 C.A.W.L. 5P

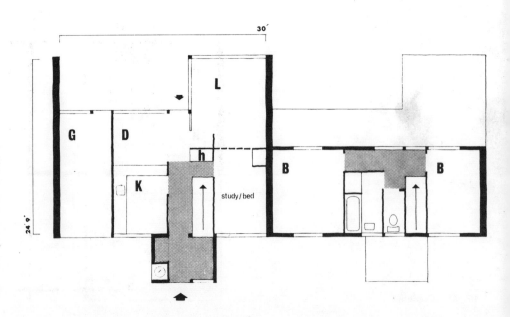

21 West Ham 2-storey 4P

30

Internal arrangements

61. Internally, a good relationship between the kitchen and dining areas is achieved on nearly all the plans, the most typical arrangement being a kitchen/dining area taking up the full depth of the house on one side of the plan, often divided by a counter and with a window for each. A living area free from all through-circulation is achieved by all the plans except the Westgate. However, the Westgate is only designed for two persons and the arrangement would usually be acceptable to a family of this size.

62. A ground-floor bedroom in two-storey houses becomes possible in wide-frontage plans without taking natural lighting away from kitchen and living areas. The West Ham plan illustrates this.

63. Every plan except the Westgate allows access to bedrooms from the main entrance without passing through the main living area. Every plan except the West Ham has a direct route from all bedrooms to the bathroom and w.c. which does not cross the entrance hall or dining area.

64. Circulation space at first-floor level in wide-frontage houses is often greater than in medium-frontage two-storey houses, but it is often possible to put this space to good use for access to cupboards outside bedrooms, as in the Anglia plan (Figure 22).

65. At this frontage it is particularly easy to provide sufficient external wall area to allow one double bedroom to be subdivided as in the M.H.C. and Andover plans.

66. Heat losses, however, can be greater than in other terraced types, and warm-air heating systems can have long duct runs similar to those in narrow-frontage houses.

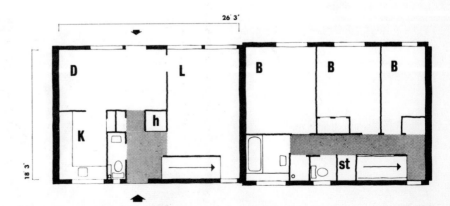

22 Anglia

Patio houses

Main characteristics

67. A major feature of one- and two-storey patio houses is the privacy given by the shape of the house itself. This enables them to be grouped very close together in medium/high density layouts, when privacy is crucial. Patio houses can also be joined together in a variety of ways to suit different conditions of access and orientation. Adequate through-access, space for the car, and natural lighting to kitchens and living areas are all relatively easy to provide, but patio houses are usually more expensive than the terraced houses previously discussed, and circulation and services are often less compact.

68. Single-storey patio plans are more suitable for small households than for large because ground coverage and internal circulation become excessive if five or more people are accommodated. The two-storey patio, though costly, is usually more suitable for large families.

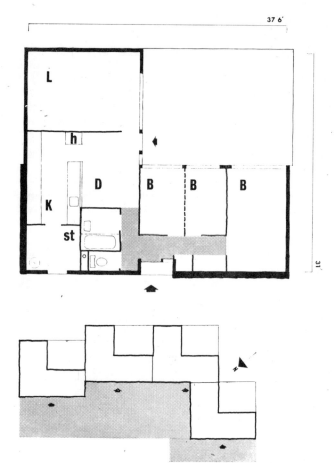

23 Sheffield

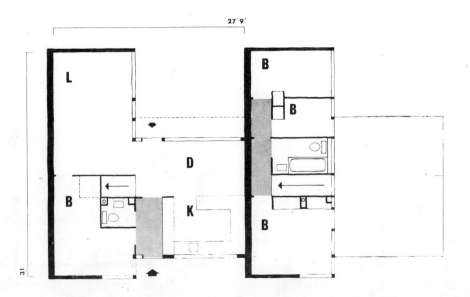

Density and privacy

69.   Patio plans take up more road and footpath frontage than narrow- or medium-frontage terrace houses and their ground coverage is usually greater than that of terraced houses. Despite these disadvantages, however, it is possible to achieve high densities.

70.   One- and two-storey patio houses have adequate privacy thanks to the shape of the house itself, and it is this in particular which makes them suitable for very close grouping.

71.   All the plans illustrated give adequate privacy from over-looking by passers-by and all except the Sheffield plan (Figure 23) have a kitchen with a view on to a footpath.

72.   Sideways-facing first-floor plans are illustrated by the two-storey Adaptable House (Figure 24) and the Sawston plan (Figure 25). First-floor windows need not overlook adjacent houses and the single-storey wings can be used to provide a private terrace at roof level. The Aldershot (Figure 26) first floor does not overlook adjacent patios but would overlook houses or gardens on the main entrance side. In this plan the roof over the single-storey wing could not be used for sitting out without overlooking adjacent patios.

73.   The L-shaped patio house gives privacy to two sides of its own private open space but at the expense of privacy between its rooms, which face each other diagonally across the patio. It is possible to see from one room into another and noise between living rooms and bedrooms could be disturbing.

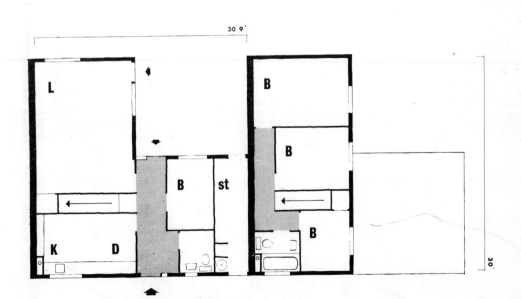

25 Sawston

Access

74.   Entrance positions can be varied, particularly in the West-gate (Figure 27) and Sawston plans. The Sawston, CAWL (Figure 28) and Aldershot plans each have a through-hall and could be used for layouts requiring full dual access. The Sawston plan has the additional advantage of two routes from one side of the house to the other, although this results in a very high circulation area.

Car space

75.   With road access available all the plans illustrated could have attached garages and parking spaces. Built-in garages could be provided in all the plans if additional frontage was acceptable.

Orientation

76.   Single-storey plans can be made even more versatile in orientation if roof lighting is provided to catch the sun in living areas. Two-storey patios, however, overshadow their own and their neighbours' private open space more and are less versatile in orientation than most single-storey plans.

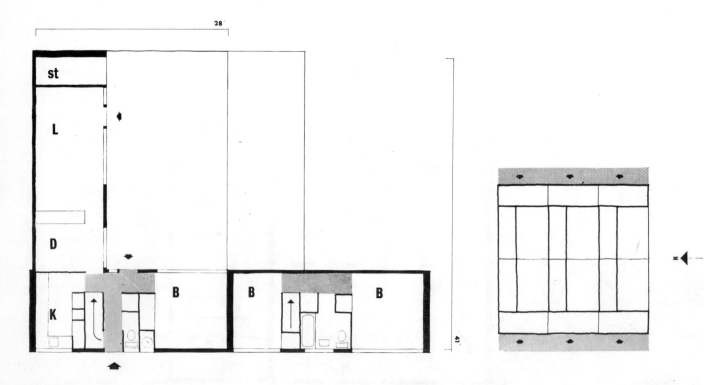

26   Aldershot

Internal arrangements

77. Internally, the main disadvantages of L-shaped single-storey patio houses are illustrated by the Sheffield and the Westgate plans. These disadvantages are extended circulation, long ducts if both wings are heated by a warm-air system and the use of one living space as a through route. Access to the kitchen in the CAWL plan is through the living room; an acceptable arrangement for such a small household but less satisfactory for a larger one. Both the CAWL and Sheffield single-storey plans have centralised plumbing services, but access from bedrooms to the bathroom is across the entrance hall. This disadvantage is overcome in the Westgate plan at the expense of splitting the plumbing services.

78. It is possible to provide sufficient external wall area in patio houses for a subdivisible double bedroom as shown in both the Adaptable House and Sheffield plans.

79. A two-storey patio house has extra space on the ground floor, and in all the two-storey plans illustrated this extra space is used for a downstair bedroom. This room can be very satisfactory for an older child or an adult relative, besides providing additional living area on the ground floor when the house is under-occupied, but it might not suit families with young children only. Access from the downstair bedroom to the w.c. in all three plans entails crossing the entrance hall.

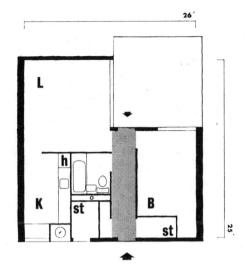

28 C.A.W.L. 2P

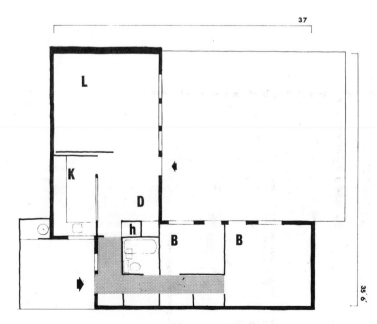

27 Westgate

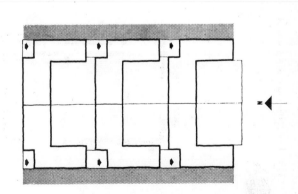

Cluster houses

80.   Two kinds of cluster block are illustrated in this section as examples of complex house forms which do not fit easily into the previous categories of terraced and patio houses. Both kinds of cluster are similar to forms used for multi-storey flats—the isolated 'point block' (the Kemsing plan, Figures 29(a) and (b)) and the central pedestrian 'corridor' (the Killingworth plan, Figures 30(a) and (b), and the N.R.O. plan, Figure 31).

81.   Some of the patio and terrace houses shown previously can also be grouped into clusters, but the houses in this section have been designed especially to take advantage of the opportunities presented by the cluster form.

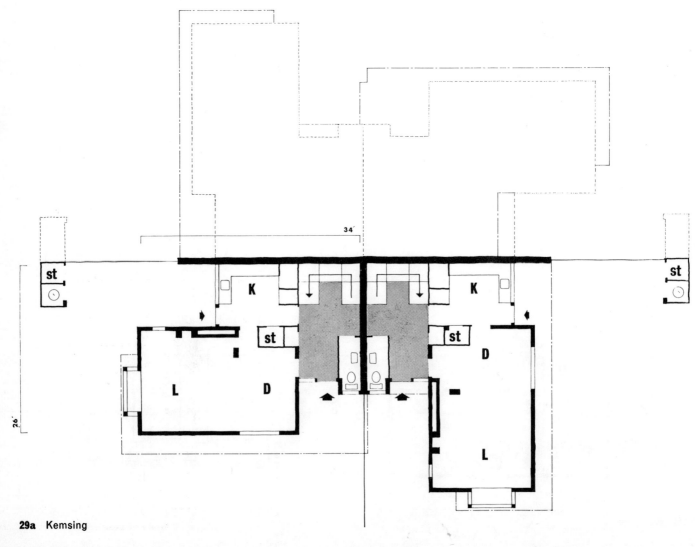

29a   Kemsing

Density and privacy

82. The Kemsing plan is considerably larger than the general run of houses in either the public or private sectors, but it has been included here to illustrate an unusual building form. It has the advantage of point blocks in being suitable for spacing flexibly in relation to contours and in allowing circulation and landscaping to flow freely around the block. But each of the cluster houses illustrated occupies a lot of space on the ground.

83. Plans in this section are mainly suitable for low to medium density layouts or for small areas of high density layouts where access, contours or prospect demand forms of this kind. If high densities are required it might often be better to 'cluster' some of the 'blindside' and patio plans shown in previous sections.

84. A high degree of privacy from adjacent gardens can be provided, but all the plans illustrated have the inherent problem of achieving privacy between one cluster and the next. Space and screening between clusters need to be greater than between patio houses if the same degree of privacy is to be achieved.

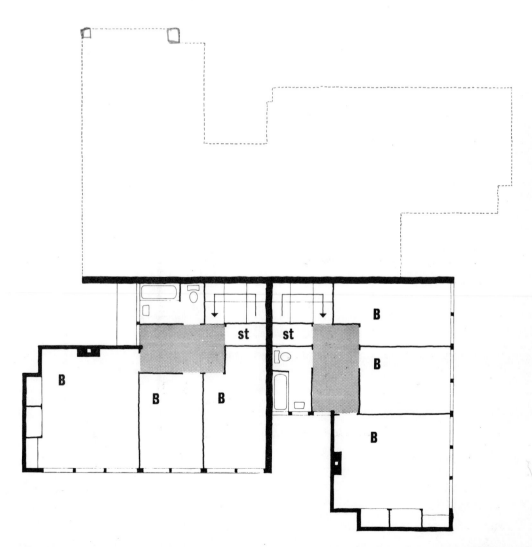

29b Kemsing

30 Killingworth

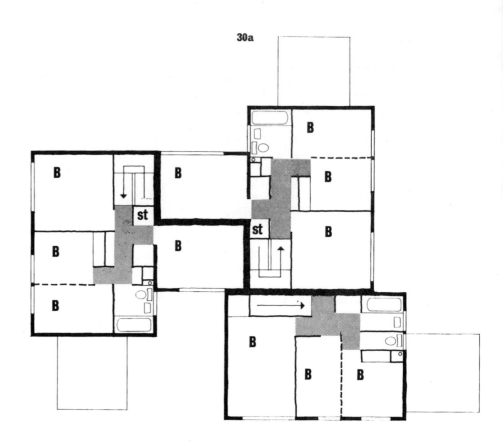

30a

30b

17´ 3´

35

N

Access

85.   Both the Killingworth and N.R.O. plans provide a sheltered pedestrian route, a central 'corridor', which is covered in places by bedrooms at first-floor level. Both plans have the same advantages as detached and semi-detached houses, with direct access to the garden from the pedestrian route. They are therefore very suitable for single-access layouts.

Car space

86.   The plans illustrated are not suitable for attached or integral garages, but the Killingworth and N.R.O. plans could provide a sheltered route to grouped garages at the end of each pedestrian corridor.

Orientation

87.   The N.R.O. plan has living rooms facing in different directions to take advantage of the sun at different times of the day and the single living room in the Kemsing plan has windows facing in several directions. All the cluster plans illustrated are thus more versatile in orientation than normal terrace housing.

Internal arrangements

88.   Internal arrangements vary considerably according to the type of cluster and therefore they do not have any obvious general characteristics.

31 N.R.O.

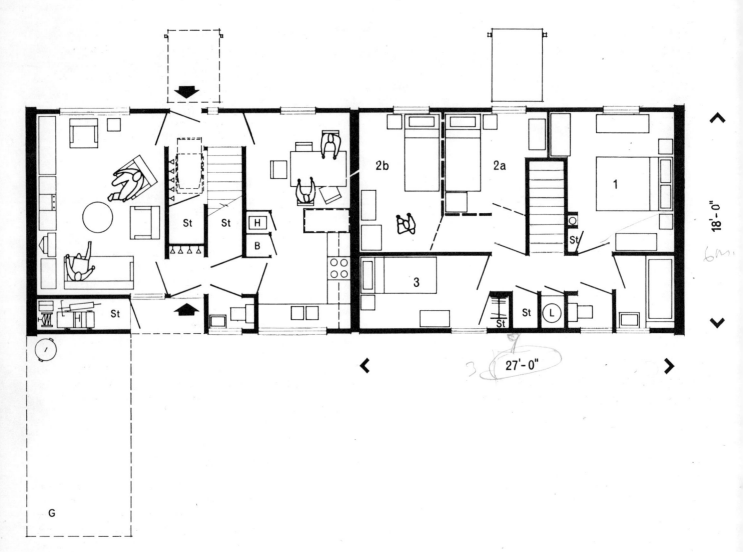

32 M.H.C. Mark 2

PART 3: The check list applied

89. In this section the check list is applied to a plan which is typical of the better wide-frontage terraced houses being designed today—the M.H.C. Mark 2 five-person house. This plan was designed before Circular 36/67 was issued and without reference to the check list contained in this bulletin, but it is the product of systematic development work including a technical and user appraisal of the Mark 1 version, and is being widely used by local authorities in the Consortium.

90. This plan reflects the layout requirements, cost limits, technical disciplines and priorities for internal planning which have been agreed by members of the M.H.C. It is up to each reader to make his own assessment and to decide whether these would be applicable to his own circumstances.

91. As an illustration of the practical use of a systematic desk-appraisal of this kind, comments at the end highlight the major advantages and possible disadvantages of the plan, and suggest lines that future development might take after an appraisal of these houses in use.

Midlands Housing Consortium two-storey/five-person/ three-four bedroom type

Areas (Q.1)

92. The net floor area of this plan is 910 sq ft—exactly at the new mandatory minimum for a five-person centre terrace house. The general storage area is 50 sq ft—also at the mandatory minimum.*

Site layout implications (Q.2 to Q.5)

93. This house has been designed to meet the needs of a fully segregated, dual-access layout; with an open garden on the pedestrian access side and a walled garden on the vehicle access side. It would be suitable, however, for either dual- or single-access and could have an enclosed garden on either side. The plan is not 'blindsided' and does not make any special contribution to privacy. Callers can easily look into living room windows, but passers-by would be kept away from windows on the vehicular side by a projecting garage or screen wall. Screening or planting would be needed to give similar privacy on the pedestrian side. A garage can be attached to the house and would be suitable for

*Gross area between finished wall surfaces is 951 sq ft. Finishes account for 9 sq ft and bring the gross area up to the mandatory minimum area which is measured between unfinished surfaces.

1.5 sq ft of general storage is in the wardrobe cupboard in bedroom 3 and this is not separate as required by the mandatory standards. It would, however, be possible to allocate the whole of this cupboard for general storage as there is space in this bedroom for a wardrobe. The consequent reduction in net floor area would be within the 1½% downward tolerance for houses designed on a planning grid.

subletting if necessary. There is sufficient frontage to provide a parking space by the side of the garage as well. The living room window on the vehicle side is narrow and set back, so the best orientation for this plan would be with the dining area facing between S.E. and W. If used without an attached garage, and if the store were taken outside, the plan could be more suitable for all orientations. This change would involve an increase of 22 sq ft in net floor area and the additional cost of an external store.

The entrance (Q.6 to Q.12)

94. Two entrance lobbies are provided; rather small in size to receive visitors, but with space for hanging outdoor clothes, a pram space on the pedestrian side and a w.c. on the vehicle side. The success of this arrangement would depend upon the actual use of the entrance, which would be influenced by the layout. If a mother with a pram used the vehicle access, her way to the pram space would be inconvenient; if children used the pedestrian side, as intended, the w.c. would be inconveniently situated. A canopy is provided on the pedestrian side and there is a recessed porch on the vehicle side. There would be no covered access to the garage door or refuse bin. The bin is convenient for the collector, but as shown it is in a conspicuous position. The meters are placed in the store off the porch on the vehicle side, with access under cover for the occupier and are easily read without entering any part of the house.

Circulation and relationship between spaces (Q.13 to Q.20)

95. The main living room is free from all through-circulation and there is a convenient route through the house via the dining area and kitchen. Access to bedrooms is possible from either entrance without entering the main living room and visitors can go into the main living room from each lobby without entering any other room. The bathroom and w.c. at first-floor level are accessible from all bedrooms without entering any other room. Circulation space is rather restricted for moving large furniture around but probably adequate. There is a very good relationship between the kitchen, living areas and private garden. The refuse bin is on the kitchen side of the house, and the kitchen and living areas both have a view of the garden and the outside world. Privacy from callers at the vehicle entrance is, however, not so good. All general storage space is within the shell of the house and is very conveniently distributed.

The kitchen (Q.21 to Q.25)

96. 80.75 cu ft of storage is provided and space for appliances is adequate. A ventilated food cupboard is situated beneath the worktop beside the sink. A counter open underneath and with cupboards over is available for casual meals. In addition to the 80.75 cu ft of storage space there is room for the vacuum cleaner under the stairs. There is, however, little space for equipment likely to be bought in the future. Work surface areas are generous, the sequence of fittings is correct, and the layout is compact and

free from dangerous through-circulation. The entrance door is away from working areas but is likely to interfere with access to the ventilated food cupboard. There is enough space to put up an ironing board but a drying rack would be inconvenient in a kitchen this size. Kitchen smells could easily reach the dining area but would be prevented from reaching other parts of the house.

Living areas (Q.26 to Q.31)

97. The main living room is large enough, can provide for a variety of furniture arrangements, and can be shut off from the rest of the house. A separate second living/dining area adjoins the kitchen. This dining area is well separated from the main living room for sound insulation and is partially screened from the kitchen. The dining area is large enough for the family and visitors, but space for items of furniture other than the dining table and chairs is restricted.

Bedrooms (Q.32 to Q.36)

98. Bedrooms are on the first floor and each child can have one to himself. The required furniture can be accommodated and two of the single bedrooms could take a small desk or dressing table as well. The main bedroom, however, is too small to take a cot comfortably and very few alternative furniture arrangements are possible in any of the bedrooms. Bedroom 2a would only just take the required furniture. When the house is under occupied or when the children are young, the demountable partition can be taken down, giving an arrangement of one large double, one small double and one single bedroom. Bedrooms which are shown on the plan as being for children are all above the main living room, but the entrance lobby will prevent some noise from going directly up the staircase.

Bathroom and w.c. (Q.37 to Q.40)

99. Bathroom and w.c. provision is adequate, with easy access and comfortable space around all fittings except the wash-hand basin in the ground-floor w.c. This w.c./wash-hand basin compartment is too small to be a really adequate alternative to the bathroom for washing in. The first-floor bathroom and w.c. are well located to minimise noise disturbance in the living rooms and bedrooms but the ground floor w.c. window is close to the entrance door on the vehicle side.

Storage (Q.41 to Q.43)

100. Storage for hobbies and household maintenance is very well distributed around the house but there is not one space large enough to take a work bench. Space for one would be provided in an attached garage. The refuse bin is in the open, but a full-height store with additional space for boxes etc. above could be provided. 20 cu ft of storage is available in the linen cupboard. The cold water storage tank is in the roof space.

Services (Q.44 to Q.53)

101. Living areas, kitchen and circulation spaces are heated by a warm-air system. Bedroom 1 also could be readily heated. Duct lengths are not excessive, but ducting from the heater position to the main living room has reduced planning flexibility: this duct is above the ground floor slab, so it is not possible to change the position of a pram space or to have a through hall. Entrance lobbies allow good control of heat losses from the living areas to other parts of the house and to the outside. All duct outlets are as sensibly situated as possible but could restrict furniture arrangement along one wall in the main living room. The plumbing layout is very economical: waste drainage can be connected to one stack, and the drainage outlet is on one side of the house only. There are short hot water supply runs. Electric socket outlets and lighting points are not shown here but, satisfactory provision has been made.

General (Q.54 to Q.56)

102. Windows and doors are well positioned on plan in relation to likely furniture arrangements, and the windows can be easily reached for cleaning. Door-swings are generally satisfactory, but there could be difficulties in the small entrance lobbies and, in particular, from the outward-opening door to the ground-floor w.c. The staircase is adequate in all respects. Windows are as well positioned as possible to give privacy to the household at the pedestrian entrance, but there is no choice of position to improve privacy to the main living room from the vehicle entrance.

Comment

103. This house illustrates many of the advantages to be gained by using a wide-frontage plan: space for an attached garage, two entrance lobbies to suit dual access layouts, two living areas with good views out to both sides of the house, a flexible arrangement of bedrooms with the possibility of single bedrooms for each child, and a high standard of natural lighting to all rooms. Additional features not commonly found in wide-frontage terraced houses are extremely compact circulation areas which give comparatively spacious living areas and bedrooms, and well-distributed general storage space economically provided within the house itself.

104. The major criticisms of the plan highlighted by this desk-appraisal are few but important. First, the location of the pram space would not be very convenient if the plan were not used strictly in accordance with the designer's intentions. Secondly, the entrance lobbies are small: they could be inconvenient and even dangerous because neither has a route across that is free from door-swings. Thirdly, and not quite so important, the size and shape of bedroom 2a are such that many families would prefer to keep bedroom 2 undivided.

105. There appear to be a number of possible modifications which would meet these criticisms. It would for instance be poss-

ible to sacrifice the small window into the main living room and include the inset porch within the area of the entrance lobby on the vehicle side. Similarly, it would be possible to have an enclosed porch on the pedestrian side to enlarge that entrance lobby. Also, the method of heating could be changed or the duct could be run beneath the ground-floor slab. The space beside the stairs would then become suitable for several alternative uses; as a through-hall, as a large store with space for the pram, with the present arrangement or reversed. The size of bedroom 2 could probably be increased only by a radical revision of the plan which, in view of its many other advantages, would be unreasonable. Most of these changes, however, would involve either additional cost or a redistribution of cost.

106. What further development work does this discussion suggest? Firstly, it has located some of the problems which are likely to occur and which should be explored further in a live appraisal of the houses when occupied. Secondly, it has located those aspects of the design which might have a claim on any money that becomes available in future from further cost planning and technical development. Cost cannot be ignored, and the development of this plan from the Mark 1 version* has shown that it is possible to make improvements economically. This plan also shows the advantages of keeping a basically sound plan and improving it in a systematic way.

*The Mark 1 version is illustrated in Part 2 (Figure 19) of this bulletin. Current improvements include well distributed storage within the house rather than outside, substantially increased kitchen storage, and relocation of the ground-floor w.c. to prevent its door interfering with the entrance door. These improvements have been made at the same time as the net area has been reduced by 53 sq ft.

Appendix : Areas of plans illustrated

House Type	Fig. No.	Plan Name	Developer	Designer
Narrow	1	Crawley	Crawley Co-Partnership Housing Association Ltd.	Peter Phippen and Associates
	2	Guildway	Guildway Ltd.	Scott, Brownrigg and Turner
	3	S.S.H.A.	Scottish Special Housing Association	Scottish Special Housing Association
	4	Boston Manor	Boston Manor Competition	David Gregory-Jones of Shankland Cox and Associates
	5	Gateshead	County Borough of Gateshead	M.H.L.G. Northern Regional Office
	6	Oldham	County Borough of Oldham	M.H.L.G. Research & Development Group
Medium	7	East Dulwich	London Borough of Southwark	London Borough of Southwark
	8	Preston	County Borough of Preston	J. Stirling & J. Gowan
	9	West Ham 2-S	London Borough of Newham	M.H.L.G. Research & Development Group
	10	N.R.O.	M.H.L.G. Northern Regional Office	M.H.L.G. Northern Regional Office
	11	West Ham 3-S	London Borough of Newham	M.H.L.G. Research & Development Group
	12	West Pennine	West Pennine Consortium	West Pennine Consortium
	13	Hatfield 4P	Cockaigne Housing Group	Peter Phippen and Associates
	14	Hatfield 6P	Cockaigne Housing Group	Peter Phippen and Associates
Wide	15	Westgate	County Borough of Gloucester	County Borough of Gloucester
	16	Andover	Greater London Council	Greater London Council
	17	Hull City	Hull City Council	Hull City Council
	18	Skelmersdale	Skelmersdale Development Corpn.	Skelmersdale Development Corporation
	19	M.H.C.**	Midlands Housing Consortium	Midlands Housing Consortium
	20	C.A.W.L. 5P	Cheshire & West Lancs Consortium	Cheshire & West Lancs Consortium
	21	West Ham 2-S	London Borough of Newham	M.H.L.G. Research & Development Group
	22	Anglia	Greater London Council	Greater London Council
Patio	23	Sheffield	Sheffield City Council	M.H.L.G. Research & Development Group
	24	Adaptable Hse.	Ideal Home Exhibition 1962	M.H.L.G. Research & Development Group
	25	Sawston	Sawston Concrete	Colin Davidson
	26	Aldershot	The War Office	Ministry of Public Building & Works
	27	Westgate	County Borough of Gloucester	County Borough of Gloucester
	28	C.A.W.L. 2P	Cheshire & West Lancs Consortium	Cheshire & West Lancs Consortium
Cluster	29	Kemsing	Peploe Developments Ltd.	Peter B. Bond—formerly of Fry, Drew and Partners
	30	Killingworth	Longbenton U.D.C.	Killingworth Development Group Northumberland County Council
	31	N.R.O.	M.H.L.G. Northern Regional Office	M.H.L.G. Northern Regional Office

NOTES

Internal general storage excludes cupboards required to provide 2 ft 0 in run of wardrobe hanging space per person, linen storage, heater, kitchen and broom cupboards.

* This general storage space is not shown on the plan but it either has been or could be provided by an additional external store.

**This is the Mark 1 plan. The Mark 2 version (Figure 32) with a reduced area is fully appraised in the last section of this bulletin.

Size	Areas				
	Nett	Parker Morris	Internal Storage	External Storage	Parker Morris
6-7P 3-4B	1254	1210	—	14+36*	65
5P3B	922	910	—	42+ 8*	50
5P3B	1027	1010	42	8*	50
6P4B	974	990	11	39*	50
4P3B	854	800	10	26+14*	50
6-7P4B	1111	1165	20	45*	65
4P2B	814	800	62	—	50
2P1B	451	480	—	40*	40
6P4B	981	990	28	22*	50
5P3B	902	910	15	35*	50
6P4B	1135	1050	34	16*	50
5P3B	882	910	—	38+12*	50
4P2B	807	720	—	50*	50
5-6P 4-5B	966	900	—	50*	50
2P1B	495	480	—	40*	40
4P2-3B	762	800	22	28*	50
5P3B	915	910	—	50*	50
4P3B	845	800	8	28+14*	50
5P3-4B	963	910	—	6+44*	50
5P3B	913	910	21	49	50
4P3B	869	800	—	50*	50
5P3B	962	910	9	41*	50
4P2-3B	755	720	43	7*	50
5P3-4B	973	910	—	50*	50
6P4B	1024	990	—	76	50
5P3B	845	910	—	37+13*	50
3P2B	702	610	14	36*	45
2P1B	481	480	37	13*	40
5P3B	1335	910	14	36*	50
6P4B	1010	990	12	49	50
5P3B	898	880	—	34+16*	50

References

Building Research Station

Houses and people: a review of user studies at the Building
Research Station, by W. V. Hole and J. J. Attenburrow
HMSO: 1966

Goldsmith (Selwyn)

Designing for the disabled, 2nd edition
Royal Institute of British Architects: 1967

Ministry of Housing and Local Government

Central Housing Advisory Committee
Homes for today and tomorrow (The Parker Morris Report)
HMSO: 1961

Circular No. 36/67
Housing standards, costs and subsidies
HMSO: 1967

Circular No. 1/68
Metrication of housebuilding
HMSO: 1968

Design Bulletin No. 1: Some aspects of designing for old people
HMSO: 1962

Design Bulletin No. 6: Space in the home
Metric edition
HMSO: 1968

Design Bulletin No. 13: Safety in the home
HMSO: 1967

National Building Agency

Generic plans: two and three storey houses
The Agency: [1965]

2
SPACE IN THE HOME

Part 1 The background to design

In addition to the general instructions which will be provided by the client, whether a private individual, builder, developer or local authority, the designer needs also to build up the background to design for himself. He will need to study the design problems in some depth until he has succeeded in defining his objectives and grasped the pattern of activities to be provided for. The following sections discuss some of the more important topics which the designer should consider during this preliminary work. There is first the wide range of individual and group activities in the home and the ways in which they group themselves, thus imposing certain demands in terms of the use of space. Next the time and place of activities needs to be considered and the fundamental changes which affect individual and family requirements as a family grows to its maximum size and then contracts. As well as looking at the requirements of individuals and families it is necessary to take account of current social and economic trends, trying to estimate what implications they have for design. Finally thought must be given to the environment of the home, its relations and links with the area outside it. This leads on to the problems of access and layout, which will of course vary greatly, depending on the particular sites on which the designer is working.

The range of home activities

The design of a home has to cater for an enormous number of activities, and the designer should start from an awareness of the main ones. For example, the members of a family are continually coming and going, and callers of all kinds come to the house. The housewife is for much of her day engaged in some sort of housework – cleaning, washing, ironing, cooking, clearing up after meals – and looking after children. The family come together and separate for different activities. Formal meals, television, entertaining friends, usually bring them all into one room; homework, reading or pursuing a hobby, tend to disperse them. Personal care and hygiene and activities like home decorating or gardening or cleaning the car also need to be considered.

These references to activities provide a starting-point from which designers can work forward, developing their own assessments of the full range of activities likely to be encountered in the different types of household for whom they may be designing. At the same time it must not be forgotten that a house is more than a place in which people do things. They also want to rest and relax, to enjoy their leisure time and bring up their children in attractive and comfortable surroundings.

Grouping of activities

As designers evolve their plans against a background of functional requirements so they must assess how activities are likely to be grouped together within the frame-work of a particular house plan. This will reveal how far the design will allow activities to be conveniently grouped in ways likely to be preferred by those living in the house, and it will also indicate some of the alternative plan arrangements. Compromises will nearly always be unavoidable, especially in the smaller house, but care should be taken to ensure that the compromise chosen does the least violence to the expected groupings of activities.

When considering how activities can be grouped in different spaces or rooms in a house, they can usefully be divided into the categories of primary and occasional. No rigid demarcation line between the two can be drawn, and how the activities are fitted into the available spaces, whether as primary or occasional, will depend very much on the way in which the total living space is divided up. But usually, certain activities take place mainly in a particular room or area where they can be treated as primary, and around them cluster a wide variety of activities which take place only occasionally. The primary activities in the living area generally engage several members of the family, and therefore tend to make the living room a 'noisy area'. Looking at T.V. is an obvious example of this. Many of the occasional activities will be quieter, such as homework or sewing. As some of them will not coincide in time with primary activities, the living area can often be used without difficulty for both. But where 'noisy' and 'quiet' activities are likely to coincide, as for example looking at T.V. and study or homework during the evenings, the house plan should enable both kinds of activity to be carried on at the same time. This can be done in various ways. For example, if the plan allows for the dining space in a separate room, this may also be used for quiet activities. Alternatively, if more convenient, noisy activities could be transferred to the dining space, thus freeing the living space for quiet activities. Another possibility, if the dining space and kitchen are combined, is to ensure that some bedroom space is suitable for quiet activities. This has various design implications both for how and where the bedrooms are arranged, and for heating and the arrangement of furniture.

Apart from trying to assess which activities should be treated as primary and occasional or as noisy and quiet in particular cases, it is also necessary to ask whether they are 'tidy' or 'untidy'. The separation of 'tidy' from 'untidy' is always difficult and more so in a small house. Practically all activities create some untidiness, especially having meals and looking after young children. If there is a small but well-arranged working kitchen, some untidy activities will have to be carried on in dining space or living room, e.g. children playing. If the dining space is separate (or separable) from the living room, untidy activities of this kind can be concentrated in one of them. On the other hand, the provision of a larger kitchen might make it possible for the children to play there under their mother's eye.

The points which have just been put forward are merely examples of the likely groupings of activities which the designer must take into account. There are others he will think of for himself according to the type of household, local habits and the pattern of living.

Time and place of activities

The two sets of diagrams in Figs. 1 and 2 illustrate, for a family at two different stages in its development, how activities coincide in the home at successive periods of the day. They also give an indication of 'place' as well as showing a pattern of movement about the house. They show the separating out of individual members, and the coming together of the family as a whole. Together they indicate particular points of stress when the home is being most intensively used. The exact nature of these stresses, and of the patterns of movement, will vary with the way of life of the household, but this kind of analysis based on local knowledge can be a useful way of guiding the designer to recognise that family homes –

. . . have to accommodate individual and different group interests and activities involving any number, or all, of the family, with or without visitors; and the design must be such as to provide reasonable individual and group privacy as well as facilities for family life as part of a community of friends and relations.' ('Homes for Today and Tomorrow', para. 24)

Time and place of activities

Fig. 1. The younger family
(Parents and three children: a boy of school age (7) and girls of 3 and 1)

0700 In the early morning rush, instant hot water and warmth are needed.

0710 Breakfast has to be served quickly, the school child got ready and the other children looked after as they wake up.

0830 Father and school child are off. Mother gives the other children their food and has something herself. A place where food can be eaten near the work area is useful.

0930 Mother puts the baby out in the pram and the toddler plays outside. The toddler wanders in and out of the house. Mother needs to be able to see the children easily while she works.

1130 Coming back from shopping loaded up, Mother needs space to put the pram and the shopping and elbow room to take off the children's outdoor clothes, and somewhere convenient to put them.

1200 When the children play indoors Mother needs to be able to see them from the kitchen, but they should be away from the kitchen equipment and not under her feet.

1230 When the family comes home to dinner on week days they have to wash and eat quickly. The dining space should be conveniently reached from the work centre.

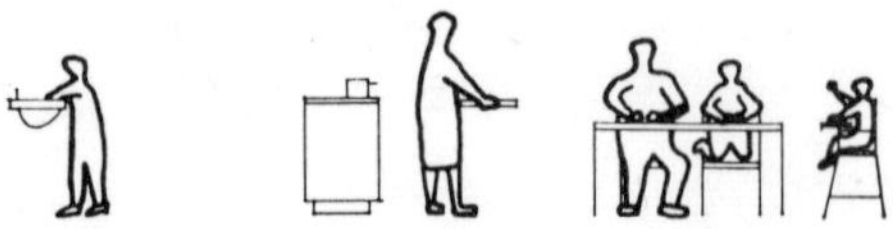

1430 The baby needs a place where it is quiet to sleep The toddler needs a place for play, where toys and other playthings can be concentrated, so the housewife does not have to be for ever tidying up.

1530   Space in the tidy area of the house is needed for adult visitors, while the children of both families play within sight but not too close to the teacups.

1700   Watching T.V. is a major family activity so the children come into the living room to watch.

1800   If people like watching T.V. while they are eating their evening meal, space for a low table is needed.

1830   People do not always want to watch T.V. when it is on, and need a place to sit away from it. The children need quiet when they are being settled down to sleep.

1900   When Father makes or repairs something, he needs to be out of Mother's way in the kitchen and where he will not disturb sleeping children.

2000   Sometimes visitors are being entertained while a child is watching his favourite T.V. programme.

2200   Mother may want to talk to visitors while she is preparing some snacks for them.

2330   The parents need to sleep near their young children, so that they can attend to them easily.

0300

Time and place of activities

Fig. 2. The older family
(Parents (mother working part-time) and boy aged 23, girl 20, boy 14)

0700 With 4 workers and a secondary school child wanting to wash before they leave home, a second W.C. and wash basin is needed. Hot water and warmth are again essential.

0730 There is a crush in and around the kitchen. Sandwiches are being cut, lunches packed up, breakfasts eaten, before all collect their things and leave home.

0830
1630 While the house is empty during the day, the bread, milk, parcels and perhaps laundry will have to be delivered and put in safe places, and the meter reader may call.

1630 When the wife gets back from work she wants to be able to warm the house, clear up and get a snack with as much speed and as little trouble as possible.

1830 The evening meal may be the only time during the week when the family sit down together. They may like to eat away from the kitchen area.

2000 In a practically adult family several individual activities may take place in an evening at home and room is needed for them.

2100 The family will sometimes split up into groups during an evening and the children may entertain their own friends separately. Room and privacy are needed for more than one group.

2230 Before going to bed, people at work often have to get things ready for the morning and meantime perhaps have a snack. Room is needed for several people to do their chores at once.

2330 Separate bedrooms are needed by each child when reaching adolescence, but they do not need to be near the parents.

Family development

Most households change in size over time, first expanding and then contracting. This has important implications for house design. It means that at each stage the needs to be met by the house are different, corresponding to changes in the size of family, to different demands made upon the available space, and to varying patterns of life. Unless people can move successively to houses which will give them the range of accommodation they need at different stages of family development – and only very few can manage this – adaptability to allow alternative uses of space in the one house is essential.

The diagrams in Figs. 3, 4 and 5 illustrate three typical family cycles. They show, for example, that a family which had three children might consist, over the whole family cycle, of two people for 9 years, of three people for 11 years, of four people for 9 years and of five people for 15 years. If such a family moved into a house after the birth of their first child and stayed until the last child left home, it would consist of its maximum of five people for less than half of its period of residence. Some of the

design implications of these facts are that for at least 9 years there will be a baby in the house, there will be at least one child under school age for about 13 years, and there will be for about 10 years four people having to get ready for work or school at the same time in the morning.

In addition to changes in the size of a family, ways of life in the home will also change during the family cycle. There will be phases when all the family prefer to be together, for instance when a couple just have one baby. When there are several young children they will need play areas under supervision and the parents will sometimes want to shut off part of the house from the children. As the children get older they will need more privacy, rooms of their own and places to entertain their own friends. Thus the disposition of both sleeping and living areas should be flexible. Children should be able either to share rooms or to have their own separate bedrooms. Living spaces are needed that can be kept open for use together or closed off into separate rooms. The extra space available before or after the family is at its maximum, needs to be suitable for use as living space as well as for occasional use as a bedroom.

Design considerations

The Family with Two Children

(The eldest child a girl, the youngest a boy)

There is a child under 3 for   6   years
        a child under 5 for   9½ years
        a teenager   for 11½ years
At least three go out to work or school for 14 years
The married couple are on their own for 12 years

Fig. 3

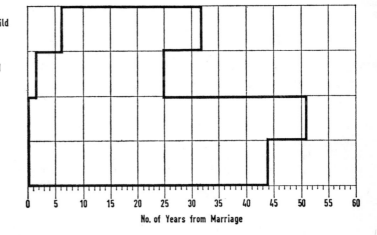

No. of Years from Marriage

The Family with Three Children

(The eldest child a girl, the two others boys)

There is a child under 3 for   9   years
        a child under 5 for 13 years
        a teenager   for 15½ years
At least four go out to work or school for 10 years
The married couple are on their own for 8 years

Fig. 4

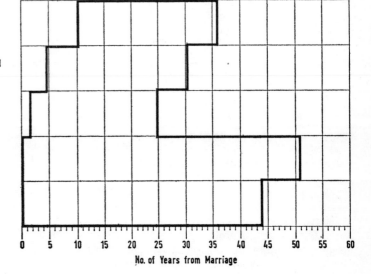

No. of Years from Marriage

The Family with Four Children

(The eldest and third children girls, the two others boys)

There is a child under 3 for 11 years
         a child under 5 for 16 years
         a teenager   for 17½ years
At least five go out to work or school for 8 years
The married couple are on their own for 6 years

Fig. 5

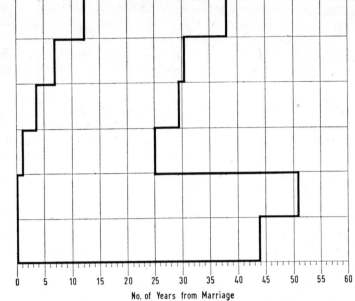

No. of Years from Marriage

Social and economic trends

In considering the detailed planning of the family house, the nature of the society in which its occupants will live should always be in mind. The problems of design should be tackled against the background of what is known about current social and economic change, and with an eye on likely trends in the future.

The principal changes in the post-war period are well known. Full employment has ensured a steady and secure income to almost all families and over a third of married women now work and add to the family income. Consumers' expenditure has risen by a third since the war, a development which is of enormous importance for the home and its design. The period of compulsory education has been extended, and many more children are voluntarily staying longer at school, a change which closely affects the type of accommodation a family needs. Occupational patterns are changing too and the proportion of non-manual jobs is increasing.

A large part of the increase in consumers' expenditure has been devoted to furnishings, decorations and equipment for the home. Over four families in five now have television, more than two in five a refrigerator, more than half a washing-machine and more than one in five a radiogram. Vacuum cleaners, floor polishers, spin driers, airing cabinets, tape recorders, cine-projectors, are other examples of things which already are or will soon become common enough. Ahead of us may be new arrivals such as dish-washing machines, deep-freezes and waste-disposal units. Another item which bulks large is of course the expansion of car-ownership. This is likely to go on rising and the family without a car may well become a rarity within the next decade. More equipment and more cars are factors which must be reckoned with when houses are designed. If they are neglected our homes are likely to fail to cope with current needs and will certainly not offer any elbow-room for future patterns of living.

The likely rise in the standard of living over the next twenty-five years will have a profound impact on housing standards. People will expect better accommodation, more effectively related to their needs. Aspirations now confined to the better-off will gradually become those of nearly the whole community. Working hours are likely to be reduced gradually, there will be more leisure, and people will want to use it in a variety of ways

for relaxation and recreation. There is some evidence that, with more free time, family-centred activities will increase, thus making fresh demands on the space in the home. Housework too will probably become more mechanised. Finally it is possible that many people will be prepared to spend a considerably higher proportion of their incomes on a home of a better standard.

Developments of this kind in the social and economic environment are an essential background to the study of family activities and housing needs. Awareness of them and of the users' reactions to their homes are a necessary part of the knowledge which the architect should bring to bear on the problems of design.

Home environment – internal and external

The designer has to consider the relation of the home to the spaces around it just as carefully as the problems associated with planning the internal arrangement of space. The preceding sections bear primarily on the interior of the home, and lead to the conclusion that the internal environment must be:

versatile to meet changing patterns of living of many different types of family

to suit the different stages of a family's life

to satisfy the varied needs of work, leisure and privacy at different times of the day

well-equipped to conform with rising expectations

easy to run to reduce the burden on the housewife

to give working wives a better chance of doing both jobs without too much strain.

Turning to the relation of the home to the world immediately outside, the most obvious fact to be taken into account is that people are constantly coming and going, both those living in the house and those who service it in one way or another. This elementary point makes an examination of access problems essential in connection with all designs and layouts, so that the designer can ensure that certain basic requirements are being met.

These stem from the movements of the members of the family, as well as of callers. The family will tend to fall into regular and frequent patterns of movement, such as children going to school or mother going shopping. Apart from relatives and friends visiting the family, callers will fall broadly into two categories, the regular and the intermittent. The milkman, the postman, the dustman, the meter reader and fuel delivery man come into the former group; the deliverer of garden materials or man coming to repair the roof for example fall into the latter group.

Clearly designs and layouts have to give most emphasis to the needs imposed by the first group, whilst seeking to ensure that those in the second are facilitated to the maximum extent possible within the limitations imposed by particular designs and sites.

Most people want to have their cars kept as near to the house as possible. But if the layout also provides for pedestrian segregation, which on grounds of safety is more likely in future terrace housing, then there must be access to both sides of the house. If this is allowed for, it can also help in solving the problem of how to provide access to the store, the garden, the dustbin and the fuel store without the need for anyone to enter the hall, living and kitchen areas of the house in order to reach them. These points are developed more fully in relation to houses with double access, in Part 3, Fig. 102.

The next part deals with the architect's 'tools' of dimensional design and sets out in detail space requirements related to activities. Finally, the last part is devoted to 'plan analysis' where an outline pattern is set out, enabling the quality of house plans to be assessed against the major requirements of performance standards.

Note on metric dimensions

The following principles have been applied in converting from the imperial units of the first edition to the metric system:

1. Linear dimensions are given in millimetres.

2. In cases where the source of data was metric, the original dimensions from the relevant publication have been adopted.

3. In general, dimensions have been rounded to the nearest multiple of 50 millimetres to the exact metric equivalent. However, in certain critical cases dimensions have been rounded to the nearest 50 millimetres above the exact metric equivalent.

Where dimensions shown are the subject of a British Standard, the metric equivalents given are intended as reasonable guides only, and will be superseded by the metric standards.

N.B.—In this bulletin a comma is used as the decimal marker. This decision has had to be taken in advance of the British Standards Institution decision on the practice to be adopted generally, and is therefore in no way to be taken as a precedent pending publication by the Institution of a firm recommendation.

Part 2 Space requirements related to activities

The diagrams in Figs. 6 to 99 show a large range of dimensional data which are useful in the design of homes and layouts. They are of value in evolving enclosures of space that will be suitable in size and shape for the living activities to be carried on in them: they can be useful too if the architect wishes to check his judgement when particular tight spots show up in the course of working up a plan.

The material is set out in three groups:

A Activities

B Furniture and equipment sizes

C Recommended schedule of furniture for assessing plans

ACTIVITIES

For convenience the diagrams in Figs. 6 to 41 are grouped under the following headings:

  i Food preparation

  ii Eating

  iii Refuse disposal

  iv Leisure

  v Sleeping

  vi Personal care

  vii Circulating

  viii Entering and leaving

The dimensions† throughout show space requirements of furniture and fittings, and the adjacent space reasonably required by the user. The furniture and equipment sizes in Figs. 6 to 41 are those shown separately in Figs. 42 to 99 which follow. Some of the examples illustrate the space needs of activities by a group of people: others show the space needs for individual activity. Sometimes the designer might choose to use smaller dimensions than some of those shown, in order to gain advantages elsewhere in the plan. On other occasions he may have to accept smaller dimensions for some activities because of overall limitations in size. The dimensions given throughout are intended as a starting point to design.

Four types of dimensions are included in the following diagrams:

1. Furniture sizes

2. Dimensions between furniture or people and adjoining walls or pieces of furniture higher than table top height

3. Dimensions between furniture or people and adjoining furniture of table top height or less – marked *

4. Dimensions between furniture or people and adjoining furniture of seat height or less – marked +

---

† The dimensions used in this section are based mainly on the results of research in Denmark and Holland. ('Møbleringsplaner', published by Staters Byggeforsknings-institut, Copenhagen, and 'Woningbouw' published by the Bouwcentrum, Rotterdam.) Original work on the same scale has not so far been carried out in this country. Although the dimensions given may show some divergence in matters of detail from our own conditions, they do nevertheless provide a useful basis for determining reasonable space requirements.

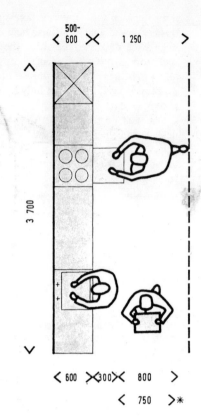

FOOD PREPARATION

**6 at the sink;
passing with a tray;
at the oven**

Note

Minimum dimensions and sequence of fittings in a straight run conforming with 'Homes for Today and Tomorrow'.

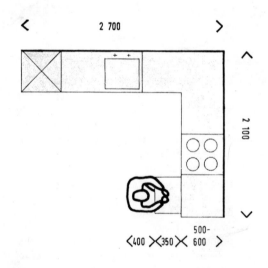

7 sitting at pull-out work top

Note

Minimum dimensions and sequence of fittings in an L shape conforming with 'Homes for Today and Tomorrow'.

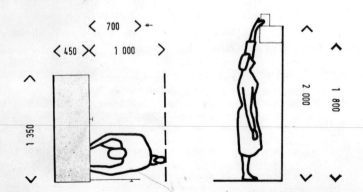

8 taking things from a sideboard or low cupboard

†9 maximum vertical reach and maximum shelf height for general use

†10   maximum vertical reach over work top

†11   comfortable vertical reach over work top

†12   shelf at eye level

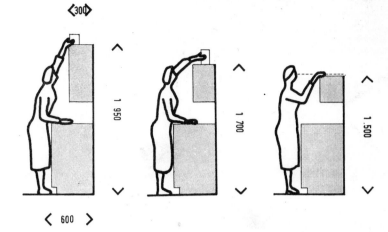

†13   comfortable height of work top for standing position and clearances for cupboards over. The larger dimension allows for the use of a mixer or similar appliance

†Assuming height of woman to be 1 630 mm

14   comfortable height of work top for seated position. Seat height 400 mm

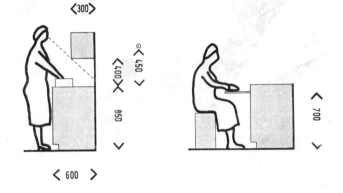

EATING

15   sitting at table and moving around

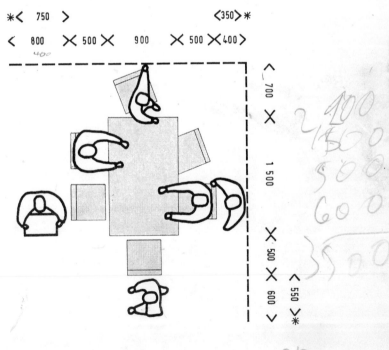

16   sitting at a work top with a person passing

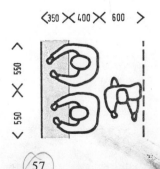

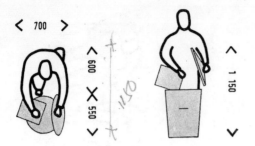

REFUSE DISPOSAL

17 using the dust bin – clearances on plan and section

LEISURE

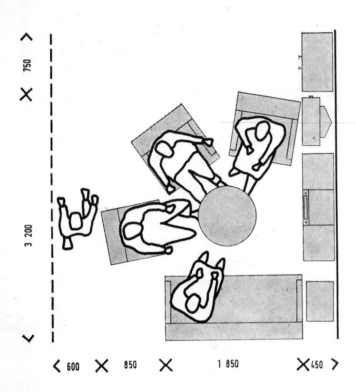

†18 eating at a coffee table

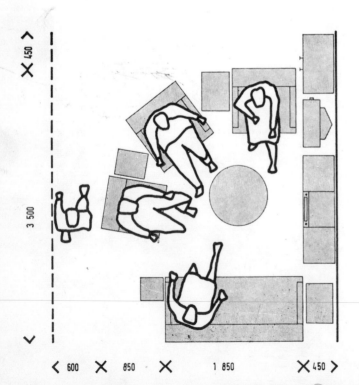

†19 talking and reading

†Note
These layouts show furnishing for a 5-person family

58

†20 looking at T.V.

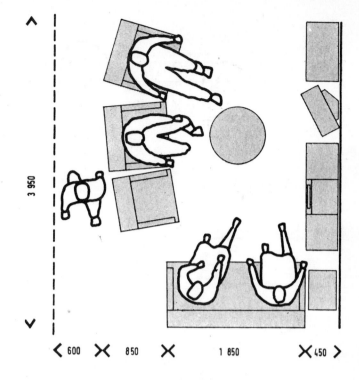

†21 sitting around fireplace whilst watching T.V.

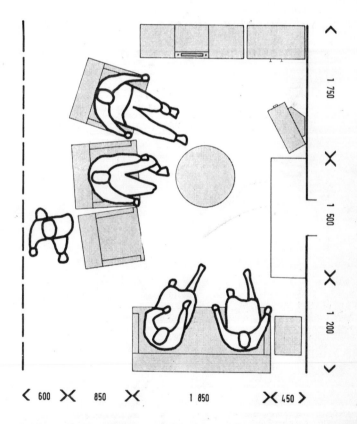

22 getting up from a table, desk, or writing bureau

†Note
These layouts show furnishing for a 5-person family

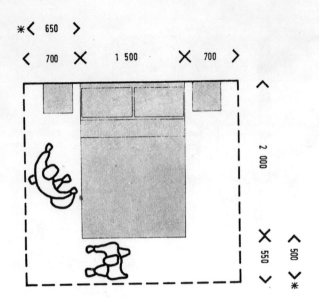

23   circulation around a double bed

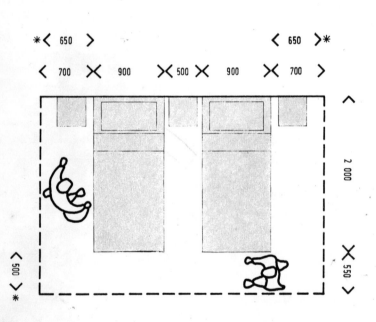

24   circulation around twin beds

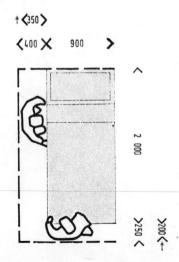

25   making a bed

60

PERSONAL CARE

26 face washing

27 at the dressing table

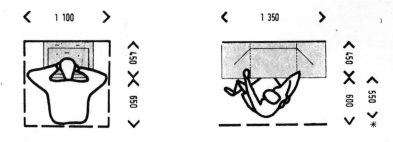

28 taking clothes from a wardrobe drawer

29 taking clothes from a chest of drawers

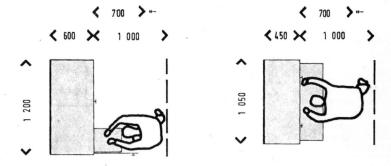

30 drying after a bath

31 drying a child after a bath

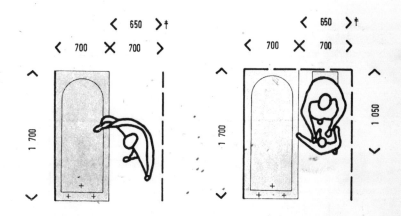

32 using the W.C.

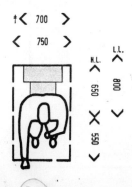

CIRCULATING

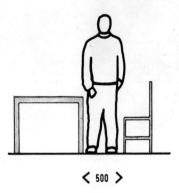

< 500 >

33 passing between two pieces of furniture at or lower than table height

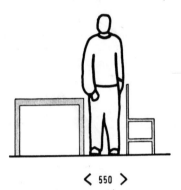

< 550 >

34 passing between a piece of furniture at or lower than table height, and a taller piece of furniture or wall

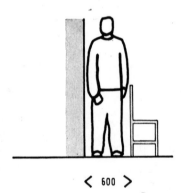

< 600 >

35 passing between a tall piece of furniture and a wall

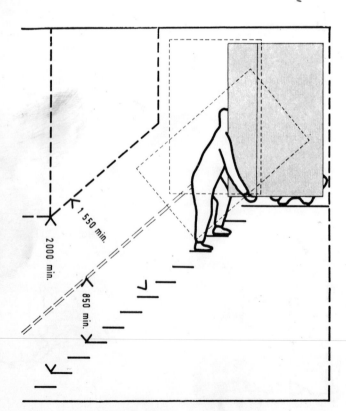

36 moving a double wardrobe up a staircase showing minimum headroom, handrail height, and a going and rise of 215 mm and 190 mm respectively

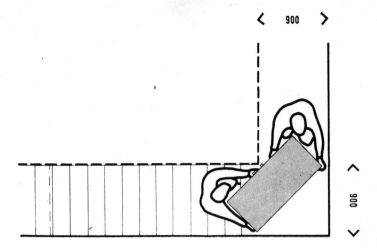

ENTERING AND LEAVING

37   getting in and out of a car

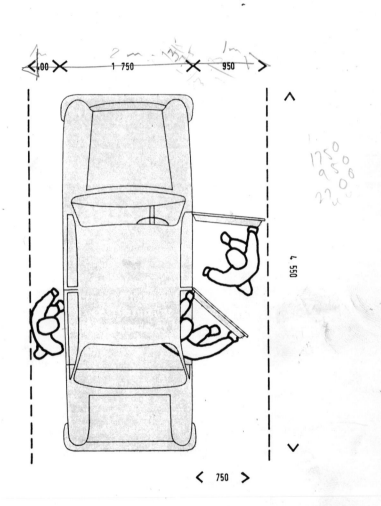

38   getting the pram ready

39   helping on with a coat

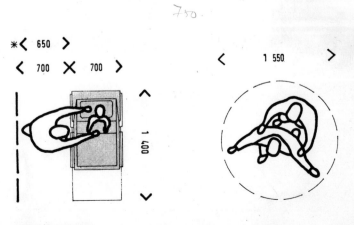

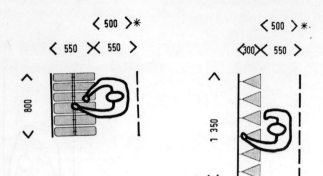

40   hanging coats on hangers

41   hanging coats on hooks

FURNITURE AND EQUIPMENT SIZES

Figures 42 to 99 show dimensional data for a wide range of furniture, fittings and equipment. The sizes given result from a quick assessment of leading manufacturers' current products.

Most of the sizes given can be taken as averages (although some are maximum) and should be a useful guide to designers when considering the dimensions of furniture etc. to fit in with their house plans.

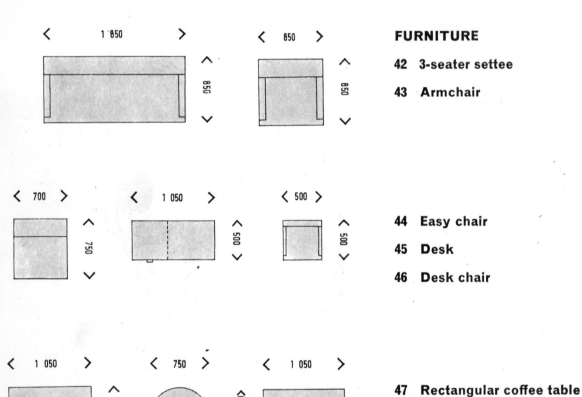

FURNITURE

42   3-seater settee

43   Armchair

44   Easy chair

45   Desk

46   Desk chair

47   Rectangular coffee table

48   Round coffee table

49   Bookcase

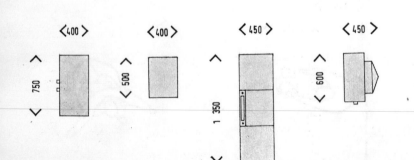

50   Record cabinet

51   Nesting tables

52   Radiogram

53   T.V.

54 Upright piano
55 Baby grand piano

56 Playpen
57 Card table

58 Table tennis table
59 Model railway

60 Dining table for 4
61 Dining table for 6

62 Dining chair
63 Sideboard

64 Trolley
65 Stool
66 High chair

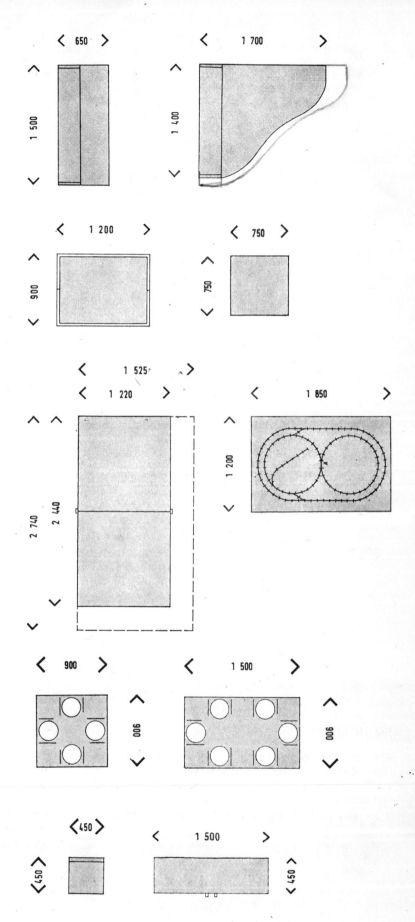

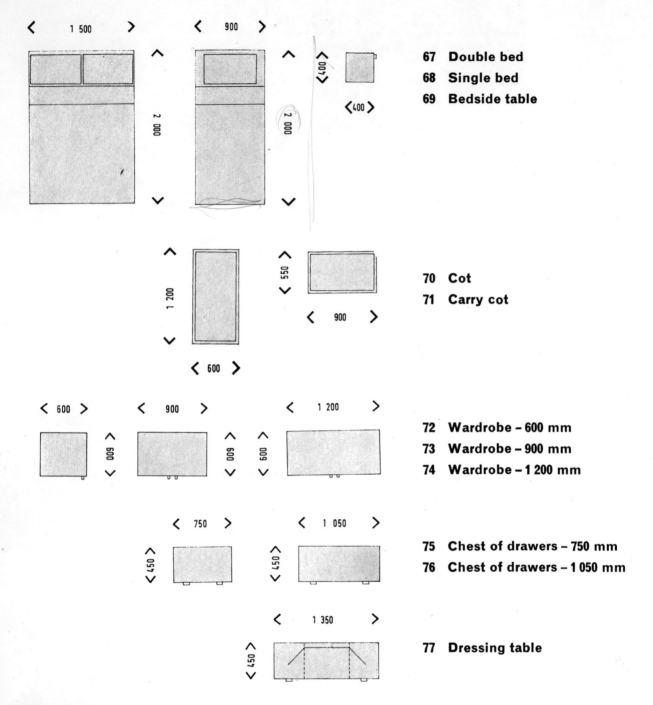

67 Double bed
68 Single bed
69 Bedside table

70 Cot
71 Carry cot

72 Wardrobe – 600 mm
73 Wardrobe – 900 mm
74 Wardrobe – 1 200 mm

75 Chest of drawers – 750 mm
76 Chest of drawers – 1 050 mm

77 Dressing table

EQUIPMENT

The dimensions given, in multiples of 50 mm, illustrate the range of current market sizes. Height, width and depth are shown with minimum dimensions marked O, average ⊙ and maximum ●.
The choice made by a designer will vary according to the particular items of equipment that are to be built-in and those that are left to be supplied by the occupier.
With smaller area houses particularly, the spaces left for occupiers' equipment will vary, but nearly always the designer will be faced with setting practical limits to the size of the spaces, and the size and number of items which the spaces can reasonably accommodate.

78 Cooker

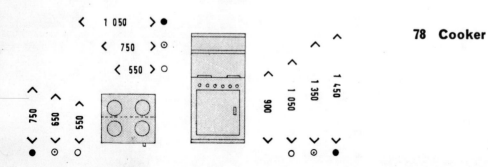

79 Refrigerator

< 1 050 > ●
< 600 > ⊙
< 550 > ○

750 600 550

● ⊙ ○

1 700
1 200
900

○ ⊙ ●

80 Washing machine

650 600 550

● ⊙ ○

900
850

○ ⊙
●

○ < 550 >
⊙ < 700 >
● < 750 >

81 Spin drier

⊙ 500 ○ 400

●

600 650 850

○ ⊙ ●

○ < 350 >
⊙ < 400 >
● < 450 >

82 Tumbler drier

600 550 450

● ⊙ ○

750 900 950

○ ⊙ ●

○ < 550 >
● ⊙ < 700 >

83 Ironing board
84 Broom
85 Dust-bin – 0,08 m³

< 400 >

< 500 >

1 350

1 350

700

550

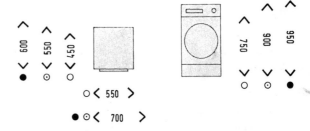

86 Pram – height to handle 1 050 mm
  height to body 950 mm

87 Push chair

< 1 400 >

700

< 950 >

500

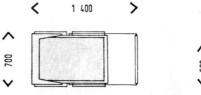
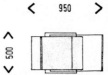

67

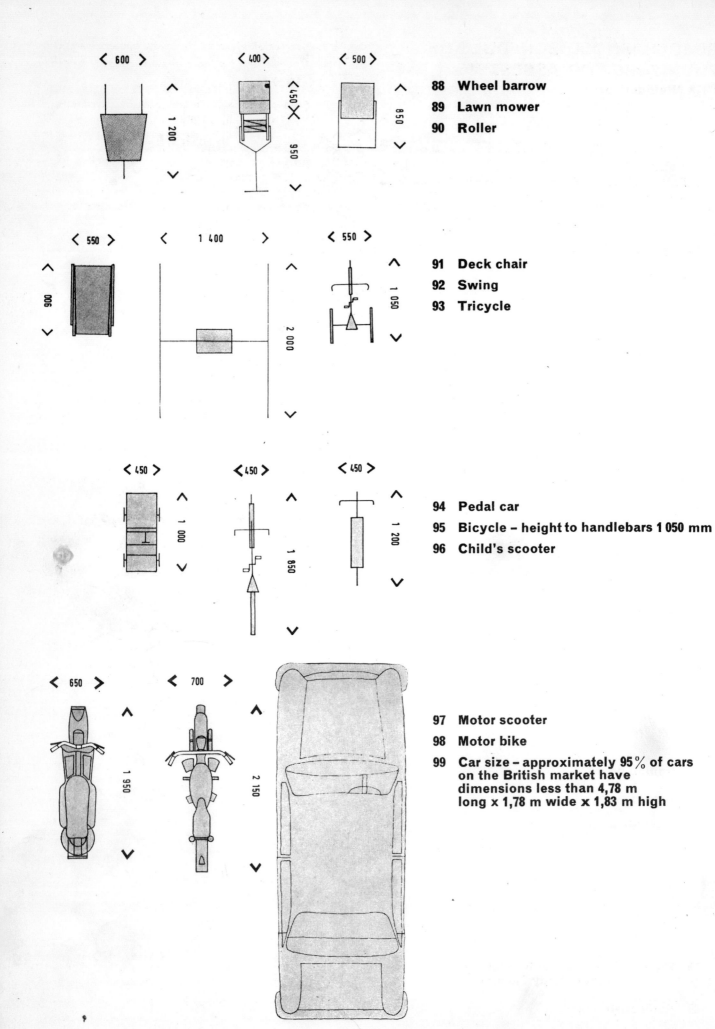

88 **Wheel barrow**
89 **Lawn mower**
90 **Roller**

91 **Deck chair**
92 **Swing**
93 **Tricycle**

94 **Pedal car**
95 **Bicycle** – height to handlebars 1 050 mm
96 **Child's scooter**

97 **Motor scooter**
98 **Motor bike**
99 **Car size** – approximately 95% of cars
on the British market have
dimensions less than 4,78 m
long x 1,78 m wide x 1,83 m high

RECOMMENDED SCHEDULE OF FURNITURE FOR ASSESSING PLANS

'Homes for Today and Tomorrow' points out that in order to ensure that a room is efficient and enjoyable to live in, the furniture must not only fit into the rooms in a sensible way, but must leave sufficient space to make the room convenient and comfortable to use. The report also includes the recommendation that, as an aid to understanding between laymen and architects, and as a means of showing that plans are workable, furniture should be shown on all plans for residential buildings; and that the Ministry should issue a guide to standard furniture sizes for design purposes.

The following list sets out the items of furniture referred to in that report; this, together with the furniture sizes given in Figs. 42 to 77, should enable the architect to meet the report's recommendations. It is to be noted that this list gives no more than what the Sub-Committee regarded as the essential minimum for the useful checking of plans. It is possible that the living space may need to take additional items such as an extra chair, a display cabinet or a sideboard. Similarly allowance may have to be made in both single and double bedrooms for one or two chairs.

Schedule of furniture to be assumed for assessing plans

1. Kitchen — A small table unless one is built in

Meals space — Dining table and chairs

Living space —
2 or 3 easy chairs
A settee
A T.V. set
Small tables

Reasonable quantity of other possessions such as
    sewing box
    toy box
    radiogram
    bookcase

2. Single Bedrooms —
Bed or divan
Bedside table
Clothes storage (a) built-in wardrobe
(b) chest of drawers
Storage for personal possessions

3. Study Bedrooms —
As (2) plus
    desk
    chair
    bookcase

4. Bedsitter Bedrooms — As (2) and (3) plus at least one easy chair

5. Main Bedrooms —
Double or two single beds
Bedside tables
Chest of drawers
Double wardrobe
Dressing table

6. Other Double Bedrooms — As (5) but with built-in double wardrobe instead of space for free-standing wardrobe

7. Cabin Single Bedrooms —
Bed or divan
Clothes storage
Chair
Small working surface

Part 3 Analysis of plans

To determine whether plans are satisfactory they need to be analysed in the broad as well as in detail. It is usually the basic allocation of space which determines whether a youngster can do his homework in peace, whether teenagers can have a room of their own, whether callers at the door can be seen without letting them see that the place is untidy or without letting all the heat escape, whether small children at play can be kept under observation, or whether looking after someone who is ill in bed is difficult or reasonably easy.

This Part first sets out general questions implying performance requirements, and then proceeds to amplify these in some detail by suggesting a number of points against which a particular plan can be checked in order to find out what it will do, and what it will not do. There then follows an example of plan analysis related to a design for a 5 person family house in a terrace with dual access. There will often be the difficulty of choosing between conflicting requirements and this is usually more acute with smaller overall areas. Obviously in houses with a larger floor area it is easier for the architect to satisfy the householder's needs in terms of performance with less overlapping in the uses of space.

The plan shown is no more than one example of an approach to design and analysis. In assessing quality and degree of satisfaction there is always the need to identify those things which are of especial importance for the particular households for whom they are intended.

The broad lines of such an analysis is outlined at right:

1. the extent to which the plan meets changing demands put upon it during weekdays and weekends, and by families at different stages of development;

2. the extent to which activities needing privacy and quiet can be provided for at the same time as noisy and companionable ones;

3. the extent to which spaces that are convenient to have near to each other are so in the plan;

4. the efficiency of the circulation system;

5. the convenience of entering and leaving, and the facilities for dealing with callers;

6. the relation of the house to other houses, to the garden and to the car; and

7. detailed performance of the various rooms and spaces.

These headings can then be sub-divided as in the following pages so that they yield a series of questions which permit a detailed check to be made whether performance requirements are being met.

QUESTIONS IMPLYING PERFORMANCE REQUIREMENTS

1 How far does the plan meet changing demands?

weekdays and weekends

can some meals be taken in the kitchen and others in a dining space?

will it perhaps be possible sometimes to use the dining space in conjunction with the kitchen, and sometimes with rest of the living area?

is there room for the family to gather together comfortably?

is there room to entertain a few relations or family friends?

is there somewhere to put a spare bed for a visitor staying for a night or two?

different stages of family development

is there anywhere for young children to play near mother while she is working in the kitchen?

can the parents and young children who might need attention at night sleep in rooms on the same floor?

will it be possible, by spreading out the sleeping arrangements over the house, for teenagers – or some of them – to have a room each?

when the house is not fully occupied, can it be used in such a way that the family still makes the most of it?

2 Is there somewhere for activities needing privacy and quiet?

are the bedrooms suitably designed for this?

can the dining space be used?

is there a downstairs bedroom that would be suitable?

if a teenager has a friend in the living room is there still room for the rest of the family elsewhere?

3 Are the right spaces near to each other?

is the dining space as close as possible to the kitchen?

70

does the kitchen overlook the place where small children are likely to play and where the baby will get an airing in its pram?

can the garden be used in summer as an extension to the living space?

4 Can you get from one part of the house to another without embarrassment or inconvenience?

can you get from each bedroom to the bathroom and W.C. without going through any other room?

is at least one living room not used as a passage?

if you come home in dirty working clothes can you get direct from the main door to a place where they can be kept and to a place where you can wash?

how far does the housewife have to carry the rubbish from the kitchen to the bin store, and can she manage without going through living areas?

is the fuel store near at hand?

5 Entering and leaving and dealing with callers

are there arrangements for storing bicycles and the pram without having to pass through entrance hall and living rooms or kitchen?

are the refuse bin store and fuel store arranged so that the collector or the delivery man does not have to enter the house, and at the same time are convenient to the household?

can the painter and the window cleaner get ladders to the other side of the house?

can the meters be read from the outside, and if not, can a reading be taken inside without causing inconvenience?

is there protection at the front door for casual callers in cold or rainy weather?

is there sufficient room at the entrance to receive visitors? is there room to pass?

can you shut the front door with three or four people in the hall?

is there adequate space for hats and coats?

6 House, garden, neighbours and car

can you get from the garden into the house without passing through the living room?

can large garden tools be shifted from where they are kept to where they are used without going through the house?

can you easily get from the kitchen to the washing line?

is there somewhere safe for children to play?

does the siting so far as possible avoid –

kitchen doors opposite each other with no barrier in between?

overlooking of the private garden by neighbours or passers-by?

people passing too close to windows?

nuisance and hazards from traffic?

is the car space or garage near to the house?

can refuse be collected and fuel delivered easily?

7 Detailed performance of the various rooms and spaces

does each have
   lighting
   aspect
   prospect
   heating arrangements
   ventilation arrangements
   sound insulation
satisfactory for its intended use?

can each space accommodate the required furniture in a sensible arrangement, leaving sufficient room to move about, open doors and windows and generally use the space efficiently and economically?

if the room could have alternative uses, for example at weekends, or at different stages in the family's development, will these different uses each be reasonably well accommodated?

are all windows easily accessible for cleaning?

safety in the home – does the plan take account of the points set out in 'Homes for Today and Tomorrow', Appendix 4, and the check list in Design Bulletin 13, 'Safety in the home'?

A HOUSE PLAN ANALYSED

The following pages illustrate a design for a 5 person terrace house with a net floor area of the minimum amount recommended in 'Homes for Today and Tomorrow'. The design is shown as an example illustrating the method of broad analysis just described, and its assessment can be undertaken by considering the extent to which it measures up to meeting the requirements implied by the various questions. Any plan can be studied and assessed in the same way, but the extent to which a plan can fulfil requirements is affected by the site, and by the size, cost and type of dwelling to be built, and by its relationship to other development. In this example it is assumed that a house is required which will not only suit a family with three young children but will by adaptation also suit the family at successive stages of development as the children grow up and the time comes when one of them has left the family home.

In the description of the illustrations which follows there is therefore a review of the house plan under the following conditions of occupancy:

A. With young children
B. With older children
C. When entertaining visitors
D. When one child has grown up and left the family home.

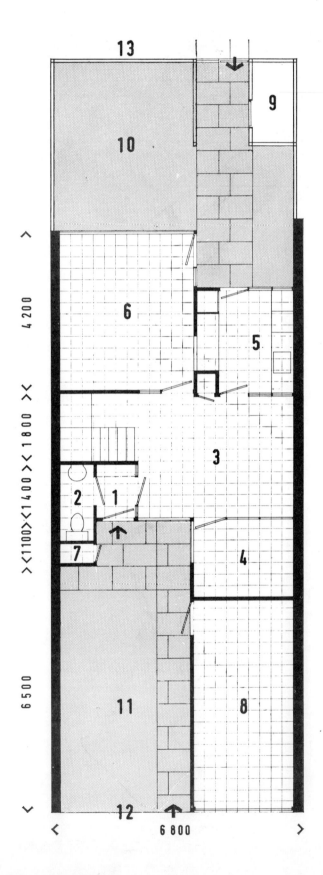

The house and layout

Figs. 100 and 101 show the ground and first floor plans. The house has been planned for a layout in which there is access to both sides of the house. A diagram layout of houses is shown in Fig. 102. An attached garage is shown although it could, at the cost of convenience, be detached and sited elsewhere without affecting the basic design of the house. There is vehicular access to one side of the house and pedestrian access only to the other side. The design assumes that the main space heating is by electric underfloor heating of the ground floor. The ground floor has a larger area than the first floor and this means that when three single bedrooms in addition to the double bedroom are needed, one has to be on the ground floor. While this bedroom may not be as quiet as the upstairs bedrooms the advantage of the larger ground floor means that the living area of the house can be increased when only two single bedrooms are needed.

72

Fig. 100. The ground floor arrangement is based on a dining-hall entered through a porch and an outer lobby off which there is access to a ground floor W.C. and wash basin. As vehicular access is only to the front and the kitchen is at the back, the dustbin is not in the most convenient position for the housewife, immediately accessible outside the kitchen door. Instead a refuse compartment containing the dustbin with a delivery hatch above it is placed alongside the entrance and is accessible under cover (*Fig. 100 at left*).

The dining-hall which has the staircase rising from it to the bedroom floor, gives access to the living room and the kitchen on the garden side of the house, and to an additional ground floor room on the road side. In this plan the dining-hall is part of the circulation area and it is not therefore suitable for activities needing privacy and quiet. There is a movable partition (the top section of which is glazed) between the additional room and the dining-hall. By combining or separating these areas the house can be adapted to the needs of particular families. Storage is provided on both sides of the house, on the road side within an extended garage and on the garden side in the form of an outside store. The way through the house from front to back is via the lobby, the dining-hall and the kitchen.

Fig. 101. On the first floor there are three bedrooms and a combined bathroom and W.C. The economy in circulation space should be noted (*Fig. 101 at right*).

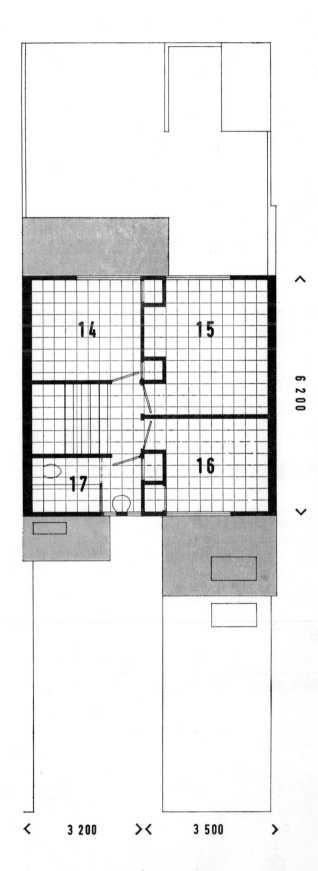

Key to Figs. 100 and 101

1	Lobby	
2	W.C.	
3	Dining-hall	13,59 m²
4	Bedroom 4	5,40 m²
5	Kitchen	7,02 m²
6	Living room	14,76 m²
7	Refuse/delivery compartment	
8	Garage/store	14,58 m²
9	Garden store	2,32 m²
10	Private garden	
11	Parking area	
12	Vehicular/pedestrian access	
13	Pedestrian access/common open space	
14	Bedroom 2	8,20 m²
15	Bedroom 1	10,71 m²
16	Bedroom 3	7,38 m²
17	Bathroom/W.C.	
	Total house area	
	87,21 m² + garage/store and garden store 16,9 m²	

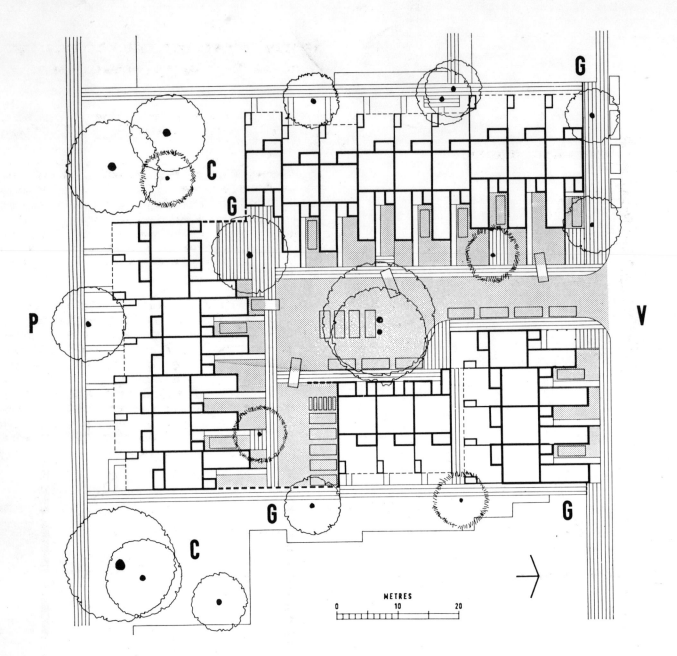

METRES
0   10   20

Fig. 102 shows a layout of houses and the facilities for access, with segregation of vehicular and pedestrian access.

The diagrammatic layout shown aims at both pedestrian safety and the maximum convenience for car users. It provides for 23 houses at a density of 42 houses, or 210 persons per hectare at maximum occupancy. In practice the density of such a layout would probably be less than shown here due to actual site conditions, and also to some degree of under-occupancy.

Vehicular access (**V**) is to one side of the houses, pedestrian access to the other. As well as the cars, most tradesmen and visitors, and the family itself, would usually approach the house from the road side: the pedestrian approach, linking to the private gardens, would be used mainly by children or adults when not using cars. The pedestrian approach gives safe access to children's play-spaces (**CP**) and, if connected up in a larger layout, to schools and shops as well. There is the advantage in this layout of a direct link between the private gardens and the children's play spaces which are sited somewhat apart from the dwellings to minimise nuisance from noise. The pedestrian way could be either open to the public as a whole or, in certain conditions of layout, it could be private to each group of houses with gates (**G**) provided to increase children's safety.

Storage for cars, bicycles, and motor-bikes is provided on the vehicular access side, and for garden equipment, toys and tricycles on the other side.

The provision for occupiers' cars is one space per dwelling. This comprises 18 garages attached to individual houses and 5 covered parking bays within 37 m. As the garages are attached to, and not incorporated in the dwellings, they can be erected as the demand for them arises. The provision of a proportion of communal car spaces gives flexibility in use to accommodate the two-car family along with those who do not have a car. In addition to the main car space provision for storing tenants' cars, the layout provides hardstandings for washing down of cars or for visitors' cars adjacent to each garage, and there are also additional car spaces for further visitors' and tradesmen's vehicles.

The ground surface treatment on the road side would need careful and imaginative detailing. On both sides of the houses the layout shows provision for the planting of forest trees, and for the screening of private gardens.

In Fig. 102 it is intended that the road leading to the cul-de-sac should itself be a minor loop or cul-de-sac, not a distributor road. Garages are set back 4,5 m from the front edge of the pavement, and each has a low barrier wall projecting to the back of the pavement. Continuous low kerbs are intended in front of garages and hardstandings.

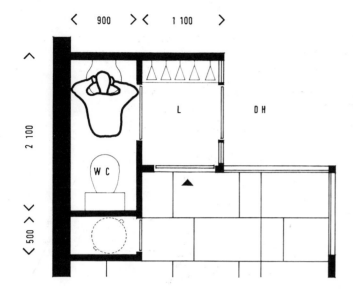

Spaces where the use remains the same during family development

Figs. 103-111 show those parts of the house where the use of spaces remains constant irrespective of the stage of family development.

Fig. 103 shows details of the covered porch, the dustbin compartment, the entrance lobby and the W.C. and wash basin. A cupboard for outdoor clothes, and a wash basin are shown in the lobby in positions where they could be screened by a curtain. Alternatively with a smaller lobby and the use of a sliding door the wash basin could be in a separate compartment. The W.C. is top lighted to minimise noise nuisance in the vicinity of the entrance.

Figs. 104-105 show the kitchen which in this plan is designed for food preparation, storage and laundry. It communicates with both the dining-hall and the garden. The arrangement of fittings and equipment is based on the recognised sequence (Figs. 6-7) and provides 2,65 m³ of storage. The storage is divided between 1,03 m³ at high level and 1,62 m³ at low level. There is floor space along two walls for household equipment of different types including a cooker, washing machine, spin drier, tumbler drier and a dishwasher. It is assumed that the larder unit might be removed or adapted when the householder wishes to install a refrigerator.

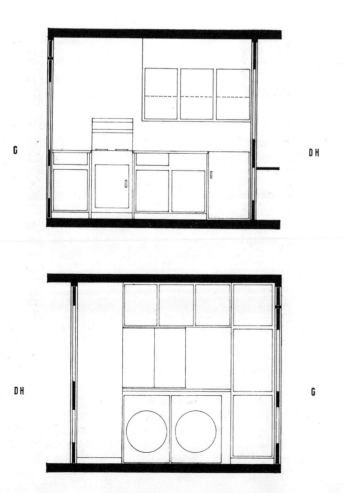

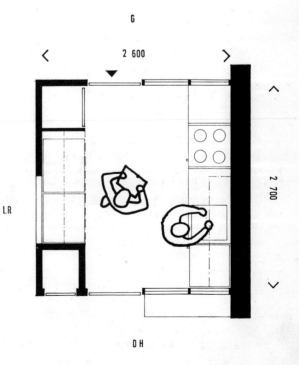

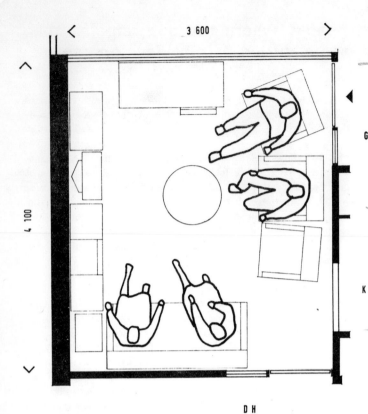

3 600

4 100

G

K

D H

Fig. 106 shows the living room which is generally suitable at all stages of family growth although at the earlier stages there might be fewer armchairs than the number shown. There is a door from the living room direct to a paved area in the garden. While this living room is not quite as large as many in a house for 5 people, especially when visitors are present (see Fig. 116) this has to be balanced against the advantage of having two or three living spaces downstairs in a house conforming to a minimum floor area (*Fig. 106 at left*).

Fig. 107 shows the bathroom. This is planned with a sliding door dividing the wash basin from the bath and W.C. The main window, with a centre panel to take a mirror, is over the basin and there is a high level window above the bath. If the compartment were not divided this high level window would not be necessary. The linen cupboard opens off the wash basin compartment.

Fig. 108 shows the parents' bedroom. This room is arranged to take either a double bed or two single beds. Two convenient positions are available for a double bed. It is assumed that the parents will have their own wardrobe but the recess could be fitted to provide built-in storage.

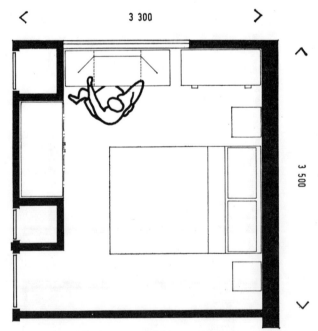

3 300

3 500

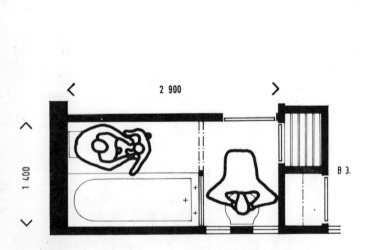

2 900

1 400

B 3.

76

Fig. 109 shows the third bedroom, which is suitable at all stages of family development, as a study bedroom. It is fitted with a wardrobe cupboard. The bed can be placed at right angles to the window or parallel to it as shown.

Fig. 110 shows the garage. The garage is longer than usual and the space at the back is part of the storage provision. There is room for a work bench and the shape of the garage allows for the storage of bicycles or mopeds as well as the car. If the householder has a small car there would be space for a motor-bike as well, or the work bench area would be enlarged. There is a parking space by the side of the garage for a visitor's car and for car washing.

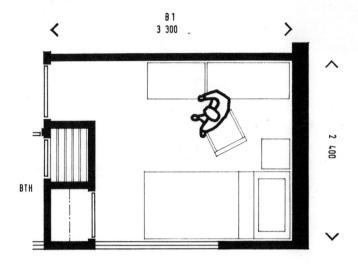

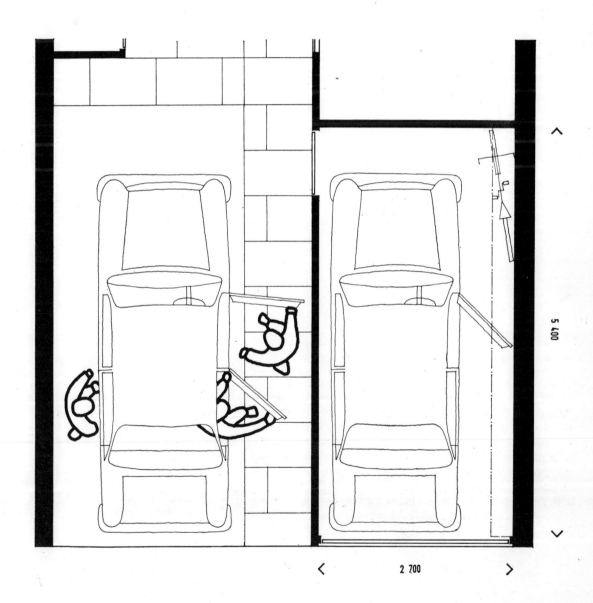

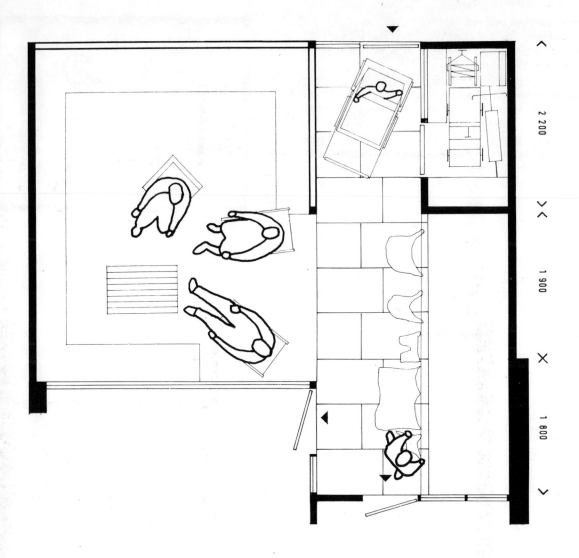

Fig. 111 shows the private garden. The garden plan is diagrammatic only as the length of the garden will vary with different layouts. The layout shows a paved area from the kitchen to the rear gate giving access to the drying line position, the store and living room, as well as providing a sitting out area. The activities in the garden will vary at different stages of family development and the store will be used for different things at different times. In this plan the store is shown in use for toys as well as garden equipment. A gate gives access to the public footpath on this side of the house which would lead to a safe play space for older children. The boundary of the garden facing the living room might be an enclosing wall or it could be open and connect to a communal garden on this side of the house. The degree of privacy obtained in the garden depends very much on the layout in relation to other houses but due to the shape of the rear wall of the house there is a screened area immediately outside the kitchen window and the position of the store gives additional privacy from adjacent gardens.

Spaces where the use changes during family development

The next two groups of diagrams show the other spaces in the house at particular stages in the family development. The spaces concerned are the dining-hall, the additional downstairs room and the second bedroom on the first floor.

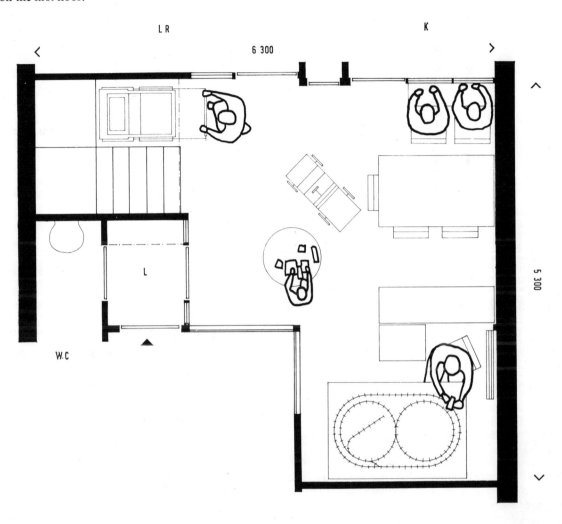

A. WHEN THE CHILDREN ARE YOUNG

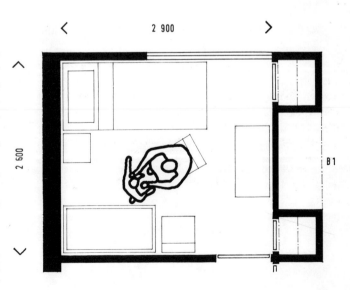

Fig. 112 shows the dining-hall and the additional ground floor room. The arrangement shown assumes that the two younger children sleep in the second bedroom. Here the combined space is shown in use as a dayroom with the additional room used as a play area. Alternatively this space could be separated off by a folding partition and used for play, study or hobbies or sewing, and it might also be used for a visitor sleeping overnight. The pram is shown in its place under the stairs.

This arrangement provides for a high degree of flexibility in the use of space as it can be quickly sub-divided to change its use: the partition can close off the additional room and a curtain could be used to screen the meals table from the rest of the hall.

Fig. 113 shows the second bedroom in use for two young children. A single bed and a cot are shown with a minimum of additional furniture. The use of bunk beds would of course free more floor space and make room for additional pieces of furniture.

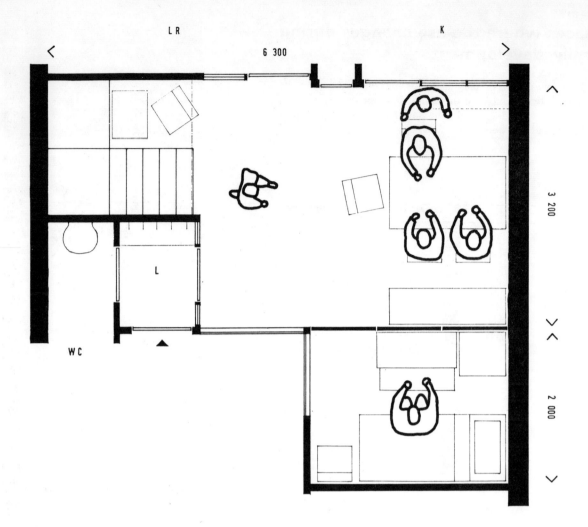

B. WHEN THE CHILDREN ARE OLDER

Fig. 114 shows the dining-hall with the additional ground floor room in use as a child's bedroom. At this stage of family development each child has his own bedroom. If a visitor is accommodated overnight this can be provided for by the child temporarily vacating the ground floor room and doubling up in the second bedroom upstairs.

Fig. 115 shows the second bedroom in use as a single study bedroom for one of the children.

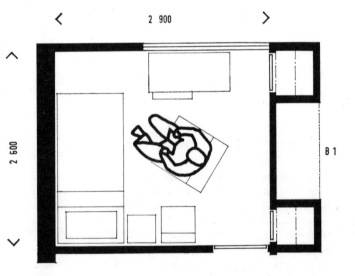

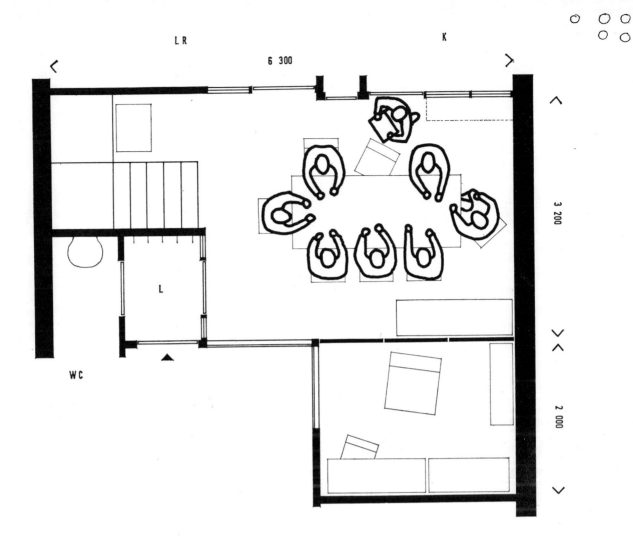

C. ENTERTAINING VISITORS

When visitors are entertained to meals, or for a party, the living and dining spaces have to accommodate them as well as the family and these spaces are temporarily subjected to stress. Figs. 116 and 117 show these spaces on the assumption that the family are entertaining three visitors. The dining-hall is large enough to seat eight people at a meal, and the living room seats eight people by bringing in additional chairs.

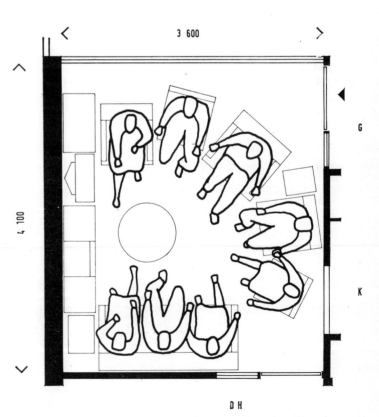

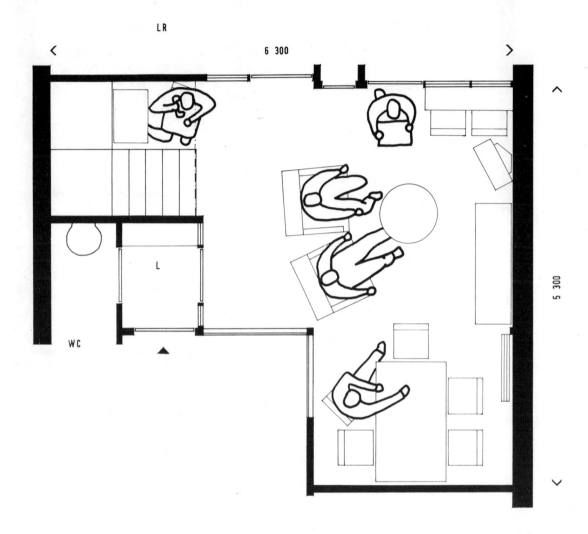

D. WHEN ONE OR MORE OF THE CHILDREN HAVE LEFT HOME

If the family stays in the house when one or more of the children have grown up, and left home, the remaining children can have a bedroom of their own on the first floor. The downstairs room on the road side can then become part of the living area, as when the children were young. It could be still kept separate from the dining-hall and used as a study, or it could be combined with the dining-hall into a family living room with T.V., while the living room on the garden side is kept for separate activities such as courting, reading and record playing. The latter arrangement is shown in Fig. 118.

When some of the children have left home the room on the road side could also be used when required for an aged relative.

Appendix

Selection of some of the more important minimum standards
recommended in 'Homes for Today and Tomorrow'

A. SPACE

i Dwelling space   (Table following para. 158)

A home to be built in the future for occupation by:

6 people	5 people	4 people	3 people	2 people	1 person

should be designed with a net floor area of at least:

m²

	6	5	4	3	2	1
3 storey house*	98	94	—	—	—	—
2 storey centre terrace	92,5	85	74,5	—	—	—
2 storey semi or end		82	72	—	—	—
Maisonette				—	—	—
Flat	86,5	79	70†	57	44,5	30
Single storey house	84	75,5	66	57	44,5	30

*These figures will require modification if a garage is built in
†67 if balcony access

Definition

Net floor area is the area on one or more floors enclosed by the
walls of a dwelling and is measured to the opposing unfinished
faces. It includes the area occupied by partitions, the area taken
up on each floor by any staircase, the area of any chimney breast
or flue, and the area of any external W.C. It excludes the floor
area of any general store, dustbin store, fuel store, garage or
balcony; any area in rooms with sloping ceilings to the extent
that the height of the ceiling does not exceed 1 500 mm; and any
lobby open to the air.

ii General storage space   (Table following para. 158)

6 people	5 people	4 people	3 people	2 people	1 person

m²

	6	5	4	3	2	1
Houses*	4,5	4,5	4,5	4	4	3
Flats and maisonettes;						
Inside the dwelling	2	2	2	1,5	1,5	1
Outside the dwelling	1,5	1,5	1,5	1,5	1,5	1,5

*Some of this may be on an upper floor; but at least 2,5 m² should
be at ground level.

Definition

General storage area is measured to exclude floor area occupied
by any dustbin store, fuel store, or pram space, and any space
required inside terrace houses as access from one side of the
house to the other – taken as 700 mm wide.

Where there is a garage integral with or adjoining the house
any area in excess of 12 m² may count towards the general storage
provision. (para. 99)

Where there is a garage integral with a flat or adjacent to the
block any excess area may count towards general storage provision only if it is 1,5 m² or more. (para. 99)

iii Fuel storage

1,5 m² min. where there is only one appliance
2,0 m² min. where there are two appliances or in rural areas
1,0 m² min. in flats if there is no auxiliary storage. (para. 109)
(But see M.O.H.L.G. Circular No. 50/62 for increased fuel
storage provision in Smoke Control Areas.)

B. FITTINGS AND EQUIPMENT

i W.C. and wash-basin provision.   (Table following
para. 158) W.Cs. should be provided as follows:

A. In 1, 2 and 3 person dwellings, 1 W.C. is required, and may
be in the bathroom.

B. In 4 person 1, 2 or 3 storey houses and two-level maisonettes,
and in 5 person flats and single storey houses, 1 W.C. is required,
in a separate compartment.

C. In 2 or 3 storey houses and two-level maisonettes at or
above the minimum floor area for 5 persons, and in flats and
single storey houses at or above the minimum floor area for 6
persons, 2 W.Cs. are required, one of which may be in the bathroom.

D. Where a separate W.C. does not adjoin a bathroom, it must
contain a wash-basin.

ii Kitchen fitments

In 4 and 5 person dwellings provide minimum of 2,3 m³ of installed
storage in connection with:
i preparation and serving of food and washing up;
ii cleaning, washing, ironing and decorating; and
iii food. (para. 87)
In smaller dwellings nearly as much is required. (para. 87)
Using standard units of 600 mm width the recommended arrangement of fittings to suit the requirements of the 'kitchen sequence'
requires either a straight line arrangement with uninterrupted wall
space 3 700 mm in length, or an L. shape with lengths of uninterrupted wall space of 2 100 mm and 2 700 mm. (para. 81)

iii Bedroom cupboard

Except in main bedroom built-in cupboards should be provided
at the rate of 600 mm of rail per occupier.
Clear depth internally to be not less than 550 mm. (para. 103)

iv Socket outlets (para. 115)

The following scale can be used for dwellings for other sizes of household as well:

Part of dwelling	Desirable provision	Minimum provision
Working area of kitchen	4	4
Dining area	2	1
Living area	5	3
1st (or only) double B.R.	3	2
Other double B.R's	2	2
Single B.R's	2	2
Hall or landing	1	1
Store/Workshop/Garage	1	—
	20	15
Single study B.R's	2	2
Single bedsitting rooms in family dwellings	3	3
Single bedsitting rooms in self contained bedsitting room dwellings	5	5

C. HEATING

The minimum standard should be an installation capable of heating the kitchen and the areas used for circulation to 13°C, and the living and dining areas to 18°C when the outside temperature is −1°C. (para. 69)

(Note) Minimum Thermal Insulation standards to be those of The Building Regulations 1965 (Part F).

3

SAFETY IN THE HOME

Introduction

1. The steady rise in the accident rate has been described as 'the modern epidemic plague'*. The diseases which caused the epidemics in the past are one by one being brought under control: but nobody yet has found a way of controlling the modern epidemic of accidents. Everybody who reads a newspaper knows about the appalling number of people killed on the roads every year. The shocking fact remains that even more people die from accidents in their own homes – roughly 7,000 to 8,000 in England and Wales each year, with probably ten times as many seriously injured. Why?

2. In a Building Research Station survey† the causes of domestic accidents have been analysed as follows: 67%, personal factors; 25%, faulty maintenance; 8%, faulty design.

At first sight the proportion of accidents put down to personal factors and faulty maintenance – 92% together – seems overwhelmingly large. But the human or personal factors referred to suggest that accidents are more apt to have a multiple than a clear-cut cause. They include:

(a) **Mental Causes**
  (i) In children; curiosity, disobedience, temper, ignorance.
  (ii) In adults; worry, temper, haste, fatigue, muddle, carelessness, depression.

(b) **Physical Causes**
  (i) Failing sight and hearing, impaired sense of smell, lack of sensation especially in feet.
  (ii) Physical disease or disablement, dizziness, faintness.

3. Many of these factors can be exacerbated and brought to accident point by bad design. For example, a woman in a bad temper may fail to see the single dangerous step or an inquisitive child may pull over a hot saucepan in a crowded, badly-planned kitchen. It is difficult to analyse the real cause of such an accident. Personal factors are aggravated by badly designed environment: faulty maintenance has personal factors behind it: a house with shoddy finishes invites faulty maintenance. Where does one begin and the other end?

4. We cannot wait to find out before taking action – the situation is too urgent. All we can say for certain is that, as far as the 8% of accidents due to faulty design is concerned, a great deal could be done, even in existing property, to identify and rectify faults; and in new homes it should be possible to avoid them altogether. It is also probable that a far larger proportion than we realise of the accidents attributed to personal factors and faulty maintenance could be prevented by good design.

5. Worst hit are the under-fives, the over sixty-fives and the disabled. 70% of fatal home accidents happen to the elderly, and these are mostly falls. A similar accident may be a minor mishap for an active housewife, but fatal for an old person. In the field of education, experiment with backward children has led to a better understanding of teaching methods in ordinary school work. In the same way, research which has recently been made into the special needs of the old‡ and the disabled§ can be shown to have an important bearing on designing for ordinary families by drawing attention to hazards which might not otherwise be obvious.

6. This bulletin sets out to show how, by taking safety into account as a permanent factor of design, architects and everybody concerned with building can make a real contribution towards bringing the modern epidemic plague of accidents under control. *It deals with safety in the home and the area immediately around it. It does not deal with means of escape from fire.*

The new approach to design

7. The starting point in designing a new home is to consider the people who are going to live in it. If there is a family, how will they change at different stages of life? What are their activities likely to be? What furniture and equipment will they need? How can the space be arranged so that the activities can take place easily?

8. By answering these questions in order, the arrangement of rooms and their relationship to one another is built up. This is the approach to design adopted in *Homes for today and tomorrow*¶ where minimum overall areas are given related to the number of people to live in them. It is further amplified in *Space in the home*‖ which illustrates some of the main family and personal activities for which the design of a house has to cater, and sets out suggested space and furniture requirements related to these activities. It is opposite to the old method of fixing numbers and minimum sizes of rooms. This fundamental change has a direct bearing on home safety.

9. *The aim of designing for safety is not merely to prevent accidents by the use of elaborate precautions and gadgets. It is to prevent the strain which leads to accidents long before they happen, by providing an environment really in tune with human beings and their activities.* cool!

Arrangement of the bulletin

10. The material is set out in two groups:

Activities (i) Food preparation, eating and refuse disposal
  (ii) Laundering
  (iii) Housework
  (iv) Leisure
  (v) Sleeping and personal care
  (vi) Circulating
  (vii) Entering and leaving
Elements (i) Service installations
  (ii) Heating
  (iii) Windows
  (iv) Floors

The Check List at the end is a condensed version of the same material and serves as an index to the rest of the bulletin.

Dimensions based on heights and reaches relate to the majority of people; they are not specific. Where it can be done it should be made possible for occupiers to adjust heights of fittings.

* ROYAL COLLEGE OF SURGEONS *Report of the convention on accident prevention and life saving*. The College, 1963, page 9.
† Building Research Station Digest 43 (second series), *Safety in domestic buildings* – 1. HMSO, 1966, page 1.
‡ MINISTRY OF HOUSING AND LOCAL GOVERNMENT. Design Bulletin 1, *Some aspects of designing for old people* (metric edition). HMSO, 1968.
§ SELWYN GOLDSMITH. *Designing for the disabled* (2nd edition). Royal Institute of British Architects, 1967.
¶ MINISTRY OF HOUSING AND LOCAL GOVERNMENT. *Homes for today and tomorrow* ('The Parker Morris Report'). HMSO, 1961.
‖ MINISTRY OF HOUSING AND LOCAL GOVERNMENT. Design Bulletin 6, *Space in the home* (metric edition). HMSO, 1968.

ACTIVITIES

Food preparation, eating and refuse disposal

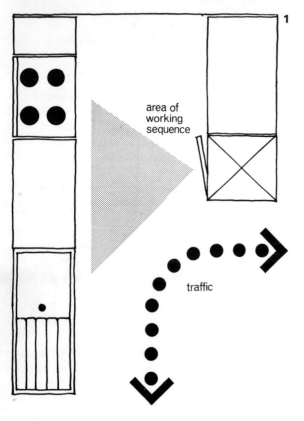

11. Food preparation is more complicated and potentially dangerous than any other activity which goes on at home. The most frequent home accidents are falls, burns and scalds and 40% of such accidents happen while meals are being prepared, served or eaten*. They are mostly in connection with the cooker, the electrical installation, or out-of-reach storage.

12. An increasing amount of equipment is involved. As well as the sink, cooker, cupboards and worktop which are part of every kitchen, a family may possess a refrigerator, electric kettle, mixer, toaster, or percolator. In the future the list may grow to include a dish-washing machine and waste disposal unit as standard items. This equipment has to be carefully arranged if the sequence of work is to flow smoothly. Food has to be taken in, unpacked, stored in the right place for its special needs, taken out and measured, cut up, chopped, scraped, washed or mixed, cooked in one of a number of different ways, dished up at the right time and put where the family are going to eat. After the meal the crockery and utensils must come back to the sink to be washed, dried and stored, and the rubbish must be got rid of.

13. The housewife may be doing all this under great pressure. Several complicated cooking processes may be going on at once while members of the family come in and out of the kitchen. Children may be around distracting attention, and getting themselves into trouble. In an activity so much concerned with heat, it is easy for an unexpected interruption to cause an accident. Safety in the kitchen can be helped by providing ample space and designing the best possible layout for the work process itself. This includes getting the food on to the table and bringing the dishes back to be washed (Figures 1 and 2).

Kitchen layout

Work sequence

14. The work sequence recommended in *Homes for today and tomorrow* of work surface/cooker/work surface/sink/work surface uninterrupted by access door or larder, reduces the risk of collisions, falls and spillages of hot liquid (Figure 3).

Position of cooker

15. Because the cooker in this sequence has a work surface on each side of it, the risk of projecting saucepan handles and of children climbing up is lessened (Figure 4). A cooker should never be put in a corner or too far from the sink. If the cooker is placed too near doors or windows, draughts can blow out a low flame and cause an explosion, or curtains can blow across the cooker and catch fire. A cooker too near a door is also dangerous in other ways (Figure 5).

Doors

16. If doors are placed so that people constantly go through the kitchen the housewife's attention will often be distracted, with consequent risk of accident, quite apart from probable collisions. The amount of traffic will determine the hazard, and a cul-de-sac kitchen layout will minimise interruption.

17. All the door swings in a kitchen, including cupboard doors, need careful consideration. Side-hung cupboard doors above or adjoining work surfaces may be left open and cause head injuries (Figure 6). Sliding doors should be considered.

* Building Research Station Digest 43 (second series), *Safety in domestic buildings* – 1. HMSO, 1966, page 1.

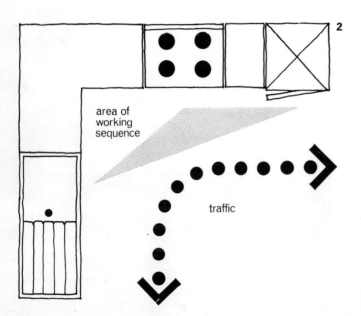

3 Individual hob units are becoming more easily available: these are best arranged in line to enable pan handles to be put out of reach and provide a working surface for transferring foods from pan to plates, etc.

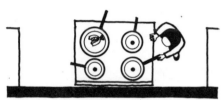

bad

bad

good

4 A working surface on each side of cooker lessens the risk of projecting saucepan handles

5 A door next to a cooker is dangerous

6 Side-hung cupboard doors above work surfaces may be left open and cause head injuries

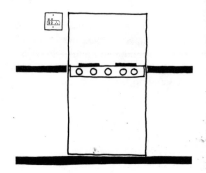

7 Surfaces either side of the cooker should be at the same height

9 Play spaces should be provided in and out of doors within sight of the kitchen

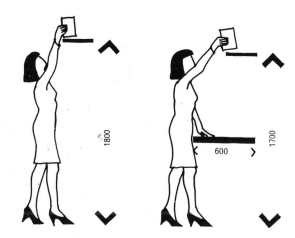

8 Comfortable vertical reach for placing and removing articles

10 Space in the kitchen for a casual meal

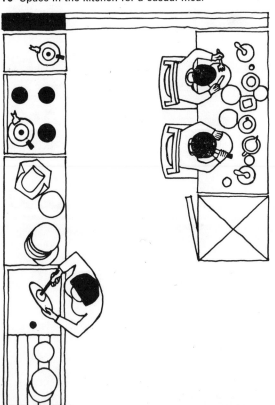

Worktop height

18. Scalds to adults are often caused by lifting pans of hot liquid from one place to another. To avoid this, the surfaces at each side of the cooker should be the same height as the boiling plates or rings (Figure 7). The worktops need not necessarily run at the same height throughout.

Fittings above cooker

19. If a ceiling-mounted airer or a cupboard is fixed directly over a cooker or boiler, clothes may fall down on to it and catch fire, or accidents may be caused by reaching over.

Lighting

20. Burning and wounding accidents are more likely if a housewife is working in her own light. The position of windows and lighting points should be considered in relation to this.

Storage

21. Falls caused by reaching up or balancing on furniture are less likely if there is enough storage space at normal height of reach for everything in daily use (Figure 8). If storage space is inadequate, things will be put on the floor and people may fall over them.

Space outside the kitchen

Children's play space

22. If young children play in the kitchen they may get burned or scalded. On the other hand, if they are too far away their mother may be even more distracted wondering if they are all right. Play space should be provided in and out of doors within sight of the kitchen (Figure 9).

Dining space

23. Even if separate dining space is provided, people will sometimes want to eat in the kitchen. There should be enough table or counter space for a casual meal to be eaten without clearing away the cooking things first (Figure 10).

24. If the dining space is separate, the route to the table has to be carefully considered. A person carrying a tray or pushing a trolley full of dishes may have an accident if there is any change of level or awkward corner to be negotiated.

Laundering

25. A good many burning and scalding accidents happen in connection with clothes washing and drying. As with food preparation, the amount of equipment involved is growing and may include a spin dryer, tumbler dryer or drying cabinet and ironer, as well as the usual washing machine and electric iron.

26. Washing and ironing often have to be done against time, subject to much interruption, and fitted in with other household jobs.

27. If they also have to be done in cramped conditions and a steamy atmosphere, with a floor surface easily made slippery by water, accidents will be much more likely. These may include scalds and electric shock or crush injuries from washing equipment, as well as falls. There must be enough room for equipment, enough room to move about and enough work surfaces for sorting, folding and laying out clothes.

28. It is important that household traffic does not interfere with the laundering and that small children are kept out of danger by providing somewhere in sight where they can play safely.

29. On the other hand, if the housewife is too far away from the centre of activity while she is washing and ironing, hurried rushes to and fro may result in falls.

Heating

30. If efficient methods of heating both water and space are provided, there will be less temptation to heat water by kettle or to bring in portable heaters – especially dangerous in a steamy atmosphere.

Ventilation

31. If there is not enough easily adjustable high level ventilation, the hot, steamy atmosphere of laundry work may lead to accidents from over-fatigue. More air changes than usual are needed.

Floor finish

32. The floor is bound to get wet. It is especially important to specify a non-slip floor in an area which will often be wet. Recommendations are made on page 108.

Lighting

33. In washing and ironing, as in other forms of housework, poor lighting will increase hazards.

Drying and airing

34. If proper provision is not made for drying or airing, clothes are likely to be put around or on top of heating appliances.

Electrical equipment

35. A laundering area is similar to a bathroom as regards electrical risks, and similar precautions should be taken. Apart from switches built into washing machines, spin dryers, etc., switches should, if possible, be out of reach of persons standing at sinks and washing machines. All switches, lamp holders, etc., should be of the type constructed of insulated material, to the appropriate British Standard. Ceiling-mounted pull-cord switches may be used with advantage.

Clothes line

36. Falls while hanging out the washing are common. The path to the clothes line should be as free from hazard as possible.

Housework

Leisure

37. The housewife of today, with an increasing independence and range of activities, does not want to spend any longer over housework than she has to, especially if she is out at work for some of the day. She wants to use as much mechanical equipment as possible to make the work lighter, and other members of the family less expert than herself are expected to take a share in the work. Common accidents relate to out-of-reach storage, open fires and window cleaning.

Storage

38. Storage space out of reach presents a hazard because people may fall whilst climbing to get at it. This applies particularly at spring cleaning time, when people go to cupboards which they do not often use. Some ordinary household cleaning fluids and polishes are poisonous and need a lockable cupboard to keep them out of children's reach.

39. Going up into the roof space to inspect water tanks or to get at stored goods may be dangerous unless there is a light with a switch handy to the trap door access (Figure 11). Cold water tanks in the roof space should be securely covered.

Fuel store and dustbin

40. The journey to and from the fuel store and dustbin will be made carrying a heavy load of coal or hot ashes, sometimes at night. If it can be made under cover all the way, with plenty of light, there will be less danger of falling.

41. Leisure at home holds different hazards for people of different ages. The very young and the very old – the two most accident-prone groups – are also those with the most time to spare at home. Young children are at leisure while grown ups are busy; their energy and curiosity lead them into danger before they are old enough to learn caution: common accidents are falls, burns, scalds, suffocation, poisoning and electric shock. Older children and adults have leisure mostly in the evenings and at weekends. Space is needed for different leisure activities away from the living centre, and plenty of space to store equipment.

42. If storage is not provided for possessions such as bicycles, prams, toys and tools, they will be left about in halls and passages for people to fall over.

Workshops

43. Home workshop equipment may include power tools so potentially dangerous that in a factory they would be heavily guarded. Sharp tools also are a danger, particularly to young children. Workshops and garden sheds should have lockable doors.

Children's play space

44. Small children need somewhere out of doors where they can play safely on their own. It should be possible to shut them into such a play space with reasonable security.

Water

45. Even a shallow pond can be a danger to young children, particularly if it is situated far away from supervision. Every year a number of children are drowned. Water tanks and butts should be fitted with secure lids.

11 Light in the roof space with an easily reached switch. The ladder top forms a handhold

Sleeping and personal care

12 Tablets and medicines are a danger to small children if they are not kept in a safe place

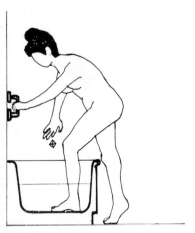

13 Bath with a flat bottom and a grab rail

46. Accidents often happen when people get up in the night They may not be properly awake. Old people, especially, suffer from a loss of sense of direction or giddiness when they first wake up. If there is no light switch at hand they may fall in the darkness as they get out of bed. It is important to be able to see on the journey between bedroom and w.c. and to avoid changes of level.

47. The commonest accidents to do with bathing and washing are falls from slipping in the bath. There are also the dangers from electric shock.

Light switches
48. Socket outlets should be positioned so that bedside lights can be placed conveniently for alternative bed positions. Switches should be placed in convenient positions for the way ahead to be lit whether going out on to a dark landing or into a dark bedroom or bathroom. Pull switches in bathrooms and w.cs. should be low enough for a child to reach. On landings and in passages, illuminated switches will prevent the need for groping in the dark.

Electrical installations in bathrooms
49. Electrical appliances are particularly dangerous when the body is wet. This is why socket outlets (except shaver points) in bathrooms are prohibited* and why there are special requirements in the I.E.E. Regulations for ordinary switches and lighting points. People may be tempted, however, to connect various portable appliances, such as hair dryers, electric razors and heaters to the light fitting if it is not an enclosed type.

50. If the bathroom is warmed by some safe method, there will be less temptation to bring in an electric fire. Possible methods are central heating, a heated towel rail fixed above the height of a small child's head (750 mm) from the floor or an overhead heater well away from the bath.

Medicine cupboard
51. Tablets and medicines are a danger to small children if they are not kept in a safe place, such as a lockable cupboard in the bathroom (Figure 12).†

Baths
52. A normal bath has a slippery surface and high sides. Elderly people find it very hard to get in or out, especially out. They may fall, perhaps slipping further on the wet floor. A non-slip floor finish is absolutely necessary in a place which is bound to get wet. Recommendations are made on page 108. A grab rail or other device for steadying the balance, a flat bottom to the bath and a grip handle will be safer not only for elderly people but for everybody else (Figure 13).

W.c. and bathroom doors
53. Locking devices on w.c. and bathroom doors should be openable from outside in an emergency.‡ If the stops are to be removable so that the door can swing outwards, two-way hinges are necessary also.

*INSTITUTION OF ELECTRICAL ENGINEERS *Regulations for the electrical equipment of buildings*, 14th edition 1966. Reprinted in metric units incorporating Amendments 1970. The Institution, 1970; Regulations D 15–19, pages 75–76.

†BRITISH STANDARDS INSTITUTION BS 3922: 1967, *Domestic medicine cabinets*.

‡ Building Research Station Digest 44 (second series), *Safety in domestic buildings – 2*. HMSO, 1966, page 3, and MINISTRY OF HOUSING AND LOCAL GOVERNMENT Circular 82/69 (Welsh Office 84/69) *Housing standards and costs: accommodation specially designed for old people*, HMSO 1969, Sections H and I page 6.

Circulating

54. Circulating means moving around. People moving around are often in a hurry or thinking about something else. In the places where people move around the most, it is important to plan properly so that they are not impeded or caught unawares. Problems of circulation include the surface of the floor, the layout of the kitchen, the turning space outside the garage, and the way to the dustbin, as well as the more obvious problems of stairs, landings, doorways and sharp projections which might be a danger to children.

Private stairs

55. The whole family uses the staircase, often more than one person at a time. They may be carrying a load which blocks their view or impairs their balance. It is important that the staircase and its landing places should be big enough, well lit and designed so that going up and down can be a smooth automatic operation with no awkward changes of direction or pitch. Stair riser and tread sizes should comply with those laid down in the Building Regulations.*

Handrail

56. A handrail is used automatically for balance and support. If it terminates abruptly or changes in level or pitch, it may cause loss of balance and a fall. There should be a strongly fixed continuous handrail on at least one side of the staircase, of a shape and size which can be comfortably gripped by a small hand (Figure 14).

57. If there is any gap wider than a child's head between railings there is a danger that the head may be trapped, or a small child may be able to climb through. A maximum gap of 90 mm between railings is suggested.

Single steps

58. If a single step is isolated from any other change of level or occurs in an unexpected place, it is likely to cause a fall (Figure 15). Where a change of level is expected, at thresholds or entrances to buildings, it is not dangerous. A single step which already exists can be made safer by a definite change of colour and a good light. An adjacent handrail may be provided to indicate change in level.

Shallow steps

59. Shallow steps less than 75 mm in height are likely to make people trip.

Winders and spiral stairs

60. Winders and spiral stairs are likely to cause falls if the going provided by the tapered step is not enough for a firm foothold (Figure 16)†. If possible they should be avoided.

*These dimensions are the metric equivalents of those in Parker Morris Report and are presently under review.
†The present metric dimensions are rounded equivalents of imperial values and may be revised in the metric edition of the Building Regulations.

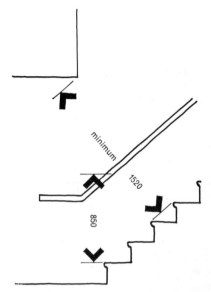

14 Stairs with minimum headroom and height of handrail. The handrail is continued beyond the lowest riser, where most falls occur

15 A single step in an unexpected place is dangerous

16 Winders are likely to cause falls

Top and bottom steps

61. If top or bottom steps of a flight encroach upon the landing space people may fall down the stairs or trip over a projecting step (Figure 17).

Open risers

62. A staircase with open risers has special hazards. Small children may climb or fall through. Somebody slipping may catch a leg between the treads. Older people may feel a sense of insecurity from being able to see through the open spaces.

Lighting

63. It is important to be able to see ahead, especially going down the stairs. If the staircase is lit from the top anyone going down will be in his own light. Light should shine towards the stairs. Two-way switches should be put at top and bottom of the flight. Lighting fittings and windows on staircases should be within normal reach; otherwise changing the bulb or cleaning the window may be a dangerous job.

Doors in circulation spaces

64. If a door opens outwards into a landing or hall, or swings so as to obstruct the top and bottom of the stairs, there is risk of collision with people passing. This also applies to cupboard doors.

Thresholds

65. With the increase of factory-made building components, thresholds to internal doors are likely to become more general. If fitted carpet is used each side of them they are not dangerous, but otherwise, unless they are carefully tapered off, they are likely to make people trip. A threshold associated with a change of level is not so dangerous because it is obvious and expected (Figure 18).

Pivot and swing doors

66. Off-centre pivot doors need special detailing to avoid the risk of trapped fingers, especially to small children (Figure 19). Swing doors should be glazed sufficiently for anyone approaching on the other side to be seen (Figure 20).

Glazed doors

67. If a door is glazed to the floor people may try to walk through it. Obscured glass or a guard rail will help to make the door obvious. Glass in doors has to be strong enough to withstand slamming. Glazed doors should never be put at the bottom of stairs.

Floor finish

68. A non-slip floor finish is important in circulation areas, where people are in a hurry, especially when they are going from one level to another and making sudden turns of direction. Floors near entrance doors may get wet from people's shoes. Recommendations are made on page 108.

Mat wells

69. Mat wells are needed at entrance doors to keep doormats flush with the floor.

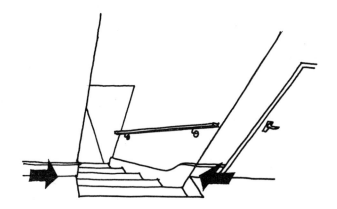

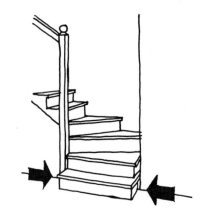

17 The top step of a flight encroaching on to a landing space is a hazard

A projecting step at the bottom of a flight may also cause a fall

bad

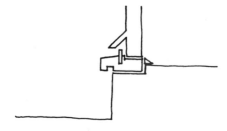

good

18 A threshold forming the nosing of the step is safer than one set back

Bad: door opens outwards
Good: door opens inwards

19 Off-centre pivot doors need special detailing to avoid risk of trapped fingers, i.e. they should **not** be double-swing

20 A swing door glazed enough for anyone approaching on the other side to be seen — and with a guard rail

Entering and leaving

70. Many activities at home involve going in and out of doors. Putting rubbish in the dustbin, hanging out the washing, fetching fuel and putting the baby to sleep in the pram are all part of the household routine. There is a growing tendency for indoor and outdoor living to overlap and for any suitable space out of doors to be used as an extension of the living area. This means that circulation has to be considered in relation to everything that happens in the immediate neighbourhood of the house.

71. A good deal of circulation also goes on between home and the outside world. Both pedestrian and vehicular traffic must be considered, and safe access is needed between vehicles and buildings for people and goods. More than a quarter of all domestic accidents happen in the area immediately surrounding the home. Falls predominate*.

72. The design of circulation areas out of doors needs especially careful consideration. The surface underfoot is exposed to the weather and always liable to be slippery. Also, the fact of being in the open probably encourages people to move more freely and with less caution than they would indoors. Any unexpected change of level, blind corner or obstacle, such as a door or window opening on to a traffic route, is therefore especially likely to cause an accident. The fact that some of the people entering and leaving the house may be strangers who are not familiar with their surroundings makes it particularly important to ensure that there are as few hazards as possible. The value of adequate artificial lighting is emphasised for every outside space likely to be used at night.

Layout
73. Layouts which separate vehicles and pedestrians† greatly reduce the risk of accidents. Parking and turning space should be carefully thought out in relation to the owner's car, visiting cars, refuse collecting vehicles, fire engines and removal vans, and clearly indicated so that there is no likelihood of vehicles endangering passers-by. Children's play areas should be shut off completely from traffic and parking places, with fences and gates if necessary.

Thresholds
74. A change of level is normally expected at an entrance doorway, and the change of surface involved makes it even more obvious. A threshold forming the nosing of the step is safer than one set back.

External steps and ramps
Dimensions
75. External steps need to be on a more generous scale than they would be indoors, with easier going. A step too shallow to be noticed, however, makes people trip.

Single steps
76. Out of doors a single step, isolated from any other change

of level, is even more dangerous than it would be indoors because it may be more unexpected. People are likely to walk faster than they would indoors and to have their eyes and attention focused at a longer range. If a single step cannot be avoided it should be marked by some feature that can be seen well ahead, such as a very marked change of surface or colour, or both.

Ramps and slopes
77. An unexpected ramp is even more dangerous than a single step because it is more difficult to see. Risk will be reduced if attention is called to it by the use of a handrail (Figure 21). Any ramp may become a slide in frosty weather and a rough surface will reduce the risk.

Access stairs and balconies in blocks of flats
78. Access staircases which are open to the weather are also liable to become dangerously slippery in winter conditions.

Open stair well
79. Children invariably use access stairs for play. Open stair wells are a potential danger, especially from falling objects (Figure 22), and should be avoided if possible. If they are essential, high unclimbable balustrades should be provided.

Lifts
80. It is more convenient, and safer, when the route from lift to flat entrance door has no changes of level.

Balconies
81. Children climb up on balconies if they want to look over, and thus risk falling. Railings or a fine wire mesh* which they can see through are safer for this reason. The top must be bulky enough to give reassurance but should not provide a flat surface wide enough to sit or balance on. There should be no toe-holds or space for a small child's head between vertical bars in any balustrade on access stairs or on public or private balconies. Possible footholds for climbing near a balustrade, such as a drainpipe, add to the danger. Because vertigo in adults is an additional hazard, balconies should not only be safe but feel safe (Figure 23).

Paving
82. People's movement out of doors can be directed to a large extent by layout and the choice of paving materials. Kerbs, bollards, or a change of surface can make the turning and parking spaces for vehicles obviously distinct from pedestrian areas. Flower beds, loose gravel, cobbles, or other surfaces uncomfortable for walking on can be used to keep people away from hazard.

83. Paved surfaces out of doors need to be non-slippery when they are wet, and in garages and car parks when they are oily as well. Drainage of paved areas needs careful consideration in order to avoid unnecessarily slippery conditions.

---

* BRITISH MEDICAL ASSOCIATION *Accidents in the home*. The Association, 1964, pages 40–41.
† A study of pedestrian and vehicle separation is given in MINISTRY OF HOUSING AND LOCAL GOVERNMENT Design Bulletin 10 *Cars in housing – 1*, HMSO, 1966.

* 'The balcony should be so designed that it is possible for an occupier to fit a protective net screen easily' (*Homes for today and tomorrow*, Appendix 4).

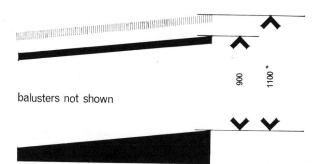

balusters not shown

21 Height of handrails to ramps
* Height of additional safety rail, necessary
where there is a considerable drop

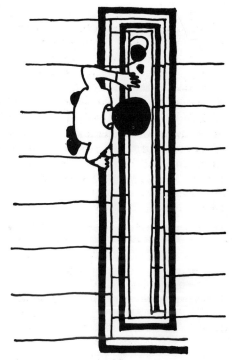

22 Open stair wells are a potential danger
from falling objects

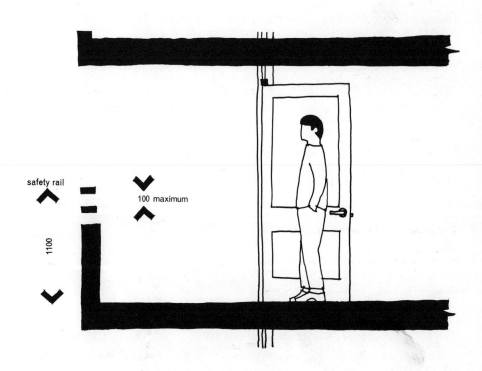

safety rail

100 maximum

1100

23 Suggested ways to avoid vertigo:

a solid balcony
safety rail to balcony

Paths

84. There are various risks if footpaths are designed close up to a building. People approaching the blind corner from opposite directions may collide, and the path is likely to be obstructed by outward-opening doors and windows. Manhole covers and upstands round gulley gratings may also cause obstructions. For these reasons it is safer to separate the path from the wall by a strip of earth, or loose gravel, or cobbles. Because people are likely to be walking faster, an unexpected change of level, pitch or direction, or obstruction at ground level, is more dangerous in a path outdoors than it would be indoors. A hazard should be made obvious in some way which can be seen well ahead. Paths which are used at night (such as the way between garage and house) must have artificial light, so arranged that the way ahead can be seen.

Fences and gates

85. Fences and gates should be so designed that small children find them difficult to climb or unfasten (Figures 24 and 25).

86. Very low fences can cause accidents from tripping, unless they are designed to be clearly visible.

24 Easy to climb

Hard to climb

25 Easy to climb – potentially dangerous

ELEMENTS

Service installations

Electrical

87. A modern electrical installation need not be a source of danger. The installation should comply with the Regulations.* Contractors who are on the roll of the National Inspection Council for Electrical Installation Contracting (NIC) are bound to work to these Regulations and to carry out the tests on the installation as contained in the Regulations. It is also the practice of Area Electricity Boards to test installations before connection to the mains supply; the extent of the test will depend on whether certificates for the installation have been issued by a NIC contractor. The Boards, the British Standards Institution and consumers' organisations, as well as reputable manufacturers, pay particular attention to the electrical safety aspect in the design and construction of electrical equipment.

88. The designer's responsibility in this connection is to provide an adequate layout. Enough socket outlets in convenient positions should be provided for present and future needs so that the risks from overloading and from trailing flexes are minimised. The scale of socket outlets recommended in *Homes for today and tomorrow* is set out below. Socket outlets fitted with switches are to be preferred.

Part of dwelling	Desirable Provision	Minimum Provision
Working area of kitchen	4	4
Dining area	2	1
Living area	5	3
First (or only) double bedroom	3	2
Other double bedrooms	2	2
Single bedrooms	2	2
Hall or landing	1	1
Store/Workshop/Garage	1	–
	20	15
Single study-bedrooms	2	2
Single bed-sitting rooms in family dwellings	3	3
Single bed-sitting rooms in self-contained bed-sitting room dwellings	5	5

89. The lighting installation in every part of the home must be planned with consideration for the different activities taking place. Adequate lighting is especially important in circulation spaces, areas immediately outside the house, and work spaces, such as the kitchen, where complicated activities may take place.

Meters

90. Meters, main switches and fuse boxes fixed too high for normal reach are a potential cause of falls. Switches should preferably be near the entrance, and should be readily available so that they can be turned off in case of fire. They should, however, be high enough to be out of reach of small children (Figure 26).

Electrical equipment in the kitchen

91. It is particularly important to provide enough socket outlets in the kitchen because of the number of activities carried on there, and also because of the likelihood of wet. Moreover, if there are not enough outlets, flexes may trail across the cooker or sink. The cooker control unit should be located to the side of the cooker.

Electrical equipment for housework

92. Trailing flexes of vacuum cleaners and electric polishers may cause falls if enough socket outlets in easy reach are not provided. Places where these appliances are likely to be used include hall, stairs, landing.

Gas

93. Gas installations should comply with the British Standard Codes of Practice which are prepared in conjunction with the Institution of Gas Engineers with safety as the main consideration. Obsolete equipment is the main source of risk.

26 The gas meter should be out of reach of small children

* See INSTITUTION OF ELECTRICAL ENGINEERS. *Regulations for the electrical equipment of buildings*, 14th edition 1966. Reprinted in metric units incorporating Amendments 1970. The Institution, 1970.

Heating

94. Most people nowadays refuse to accept a cold home. They want to be warm. Because today's families demand freedom of choice to spend their leisure either together or separately, warmth is needed all over the home and not simply round the living room fire and in the kitchen.

95. *Homes for today and tomorrow* suggest a minimum standard* of warmth of 13°C for kitchen and circulation areas and 18°C for living areas. In a home equipped for this standard, heating in bedrooms can be topped up at little extra expense if they are to be used as studies or bed-sitting rooms. This is the standard which will soon be expected as a matter of course by most people moving into a new home. If it is not provided by a properly designed and safe installation, they will achieve it for themselves in ways which may or may not be safe. Portable oil and electric heaters with their greater risks are examples of the sort of apparatus likely to be used if the built-in form of heating is not acceptable because it is inadequate, inflexible, too expensive or difficult to control. A heavy burden of responsibility for safety is therefore laid on the designer.

96. Allowance should be made for an adequate fresh air supply to combustion type heating appliances, and in all cases permanent openings should be provided for the intake and transfer of fresh air. In no circumstances should gaps under doors etc. be relied upon for fresh air supply. In the case of warm air heating systems proper consideration should be given to the circulation of smoke and fumes by the system should a fire occur within the dwelling.

97. The open fire has a traditional and obvious attraction but it is a serious potential hazard for children and the elderly, unless it is carefully guarded. Openable or closed stoves are much better. The modern housewife, with her wider scope of activities, is likely to be out for part of the day. When she returns in the evening she needs to find the home already warm – or at least to be able to heat it up quickly and easily. An open fire does not meet this need.

Position of appliances
98. There is a risk of fire if furniture (including open cupboard doors) comes within 900 mm of a radiant heating appliance. It is highly dangerous to provide fixed radiant fires in small spaces such as bedrooms unless they are at high level. Although gas and electric heating appliances must by law be adequately guarded, this is not complete protection for children or old people. Additional precautions are required.

Solid fuel
99. When an open fire is necessary a correctly attached fixed fire or spark guard will minimise hazard. Failing a fireguard,

fixing points can be installed to enable a guard of standard design† to be fitted later. A raised edge to the hearth is an advantage.

Mantelshelf
100. Any horizontal surface such as a mantelshelf, or any mirror above an open fireplace is a hazard, because somebody trying to reach it may get burned.

---

* Standards in both public and private sectors have now been established. For the public sector the standards are given in MHLG and Welsh Office Circular 1/68 *Metrication of housebuilding*, HMSO 1968 Appendix 1 Section D Space heating, page 9; and Circular 82/69 (Welsh Office 84/69) *Housing standards and costs: accommodation specially designed for old people* HMSO 1969 Appendix 1 Section F page 5. For houses built under the aegis of the National Housebuilders Registration Council the standards are given in NHBRC *Registered housebuilders handbook* Part II Section Hv Paragraph Hv. 8 *Central heating*.
† See BRITISH STANDARDS INSTITUTION BS 2788: 1956 *Fireguards for solid fuel fires*.

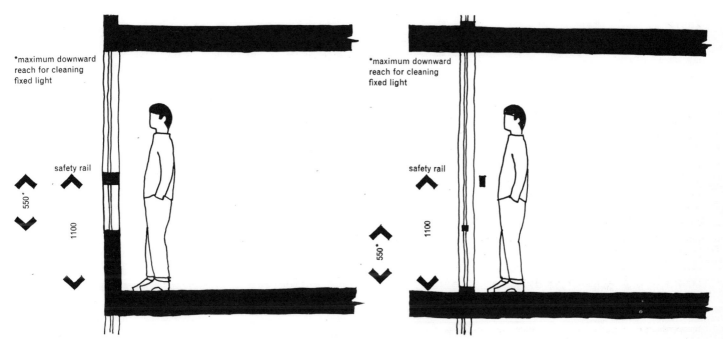

*maximum downward
reach for cleaning
fixed light

safety rail

550*

1100

*maximum downward
reach for cleaning
fixed light

safety rail

550*

1100

27 Suggested ways to avoid vertigo: a
substantial safety rail as part of window
design

28 Suggested ways to avoid vertigo: a
projected floor slab

30 Danger of collision from projecting
windows

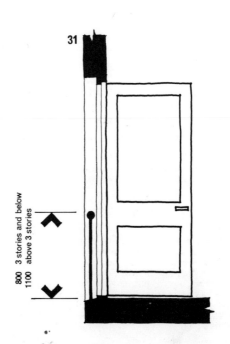

31

800 3 stories and below
1100 above 3 stories

Windows

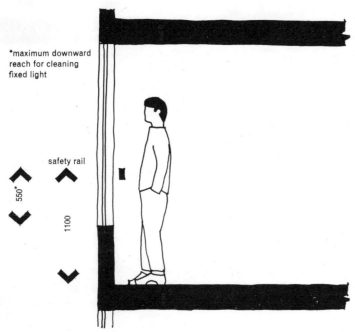

*maximum downward reach for cleaning fixed light

safety rail

550*

1100

29 Suggested ways to avoid vertigo: a solid upstand under the window

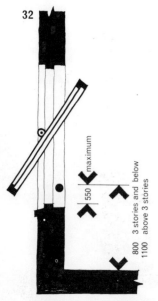

32

maximum

550

800 3 stories and below
1100 above 3 stories

31, 32 Suggested ways of providing a safety rail at recommended height

101. The chief risk with windows is, of course, someone falling out of them. Victims are mostly young children and people who have to clean their windows from inside. The feeling of vertigo produced by looking down a sheer wall face also has to be considered. Because anxiety increases in proportion to the height of the building, it is necessary to increase the safety precautions accordingly (Figures 27–29). Apart from the risk of falling out, falls indoors while trying to clean or open out-of-reach windows are common.

Windows on staircases

102. A fall while trying to reach an awkward window is especially dangerous on a staircase. Staircase windows should be within normal reach for cleaning and opening.

Glazing

103. Glass which is too thin may break under pressure or blow out with the wind. Glass weight should always be specified in accordance with the current Code of Practice.*

Projection

104. There is danger of collision with windows or window furniture which project beyond the thickness of the wall, either inside or outside. At ground level people can be kept away from the wall by a strip of loose gravel or a flower bed, but in balconies and public areas of flats where this is not possible, projection must be avoided (Figure 30).

Windows above ground floor level

105. If opening lights are lower than 800 mm from the inside floor some additional protection is necessary. Possible examples include inward-opening french windows with a balcony rail immediately outside (Figure 31) and pivoted or side-hung casement windows protected with a guard rail (Figure 32).

Windows above third storey height

106. A window cleaner's ladder will only reach to three storeys. Above this height (and below this height where access for ladders is not convenient) windows should be designed so that they can be cleaned and reglazed (though not necessarily repainted) from inside, unless there are balconies.

107. 550 mm is the maximum reach through or across an adjacent opening for cleaning windows. Even this is impossible without standing on steps or furniture, if there is fixed equipment below the window (Figures 33–38).

108. Side-hung casements should have easy-clean hinges with a clearance of at least 95 mm. Unless the window is within a few inches of the wall face, the window surround should be smooth to avoid people's arms being scratched as they reach through to clean. Horizontal and vertical pivot windows should be reversible through 180° so as to be cleaned from inside. Sliding aluminium windows can be cleaned from inside, if both leaves slide or if they can be taken out of their frames.

* See BRITISH STANDARDS INSTITUTION CP 152: 1966 *Glazing and fixing of glass for buildings*.

33 Maximum reach for cleaning windows

34 Fixed equipment below a window restricts the reach for cleaning

35 Difficulty of cleaning a fixed light next to a horizontal pivot window

37 Difficulty of cleaning an extending window if it is too deep

38 Difficulty of cleaning a horizontally pivoting window if it it is not reversible through 180°

39 The easiest way of cleaning vertical sash windows — by sitting on the cill — has obvious risks

40 Louvre windows with controls readily accessible over the sink

36 Difficulty of cleaning a fixed light above a pivot window

Staircase windows in blocks of flats

109. Staircase windows in flats are often cleaned by contract. This needs to be taken into account at design stage, so that special means of access can be provided if necessary. Opening lights should be fitted with budget locks and should not be lower than 1140 mm from the floor. It is better to have some visual indication as to whether the lock is open or shut.

Extra precautions for high buildings with sheer wall faces

110. Above three floors the safe internal cill height for opening lights increases from 800 to 1100 mm. Below this it is necessary to give the additional protection already suggested. Any fixed light below this level must not extend more than 550 mm because of cleaning difficulties.

111. All other windows should be reversible through approximately 180° so that they can be cleaned entirely from inside. This includes high level vents, if these are glazed. Alternatively, some form of adjustable vents can be used.

Vertical sliding sash windows

112. Vertical sliding sash windows are so traditional that they are usually assumed to be safe from the point of view of cleaning: however, although it is actually possible to clean the outer face of both sashes from inside, it is so difficult that the easier way of cleaning from the outside by sitting on the cill is usually resorted to with obvious risk (Figure 39).

Window controls

113. The maximum height to which most women can reach to operate simple controls is 2000 mm and something less than this is desirable. The height to which they can reach is in any case considerably reduced if there are fixed obstructions such as a sink or a bath below the windows, and in such circumstances it may be necessary to consider special controls (Figures 40 and 41). Fastenings to casement and pivot windows above ground level should limit the initial opening to 100 mm and provide continuous control of the window's movement. This will prevent gusts of wind from snatching casements suddenly out of reach and guard against the risk of a person leaning against a window and finding that it opens to its full extent.

114. Windows which are reversible for cleaning should have locking bolts to fix them in the fully reversed position. Independent fastening at each side of such windows, far enough apart to be beyond a child's reach, may help to prevent accidents.

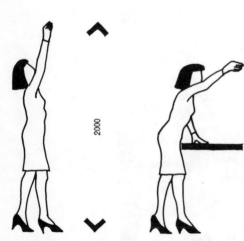

Maximum vertical reach further than is desirable

Comfortable vertical reach over a 600 mm wide worktop

41 Height of window controls

Floors

115. Uneven or slippery floors make every activity potentially dangerous.

116. Durability and non-slip performance – the chief safety factors – have to be considered in relation to the particular use to which the floor will be subjected; for example, rubber flooring, which has good non-slip qualities when dry, is very slippery when wet and therefore quite unsuitable for washing or cooking areas.

117. Durability is affected by the care and skill with which the floor is laid and the behaviour of the sub-floor. Failure to provide adequate damp proofing* and ventilation, or a proper screed† can lead to serious deterioration in finish, such as buckling of wood block floors or loss of adhesion in tiled finishes.

118. Non-slip performance, however, is also bound up with maintenance, an aspect which it is impossible for the architect to control. Any floor can be made dangerously slippery by polishing, and unfortunately a high degree of polish is associated with cleanliness in the minds of many housewives.

119. Certain sealers and polishes made from natural or synthetic resins are, if used properly, less slippery than those made from wax, and are greatly to be preferred in the interests of safety.

* Recommendations in Building Research Station Digest 54 (second series) *Damp-proofing solid floors* HMSO 1968.
† Recommendations in Building Research Station Digest 104 *Floor screeds* HMSO 1969.

Table of floor finishes and coverings, external and internal

Material	Slip resistance	Notes on use
Carpet	VG	Where carpet adjoins a different floor finish at doorways a dividing strip or threshold should be provided.
Clay tiles	G – F	Poor when polished. Exceptionally poor when polished and wet.
Clay tiles – textured finish	VG	Suitable for external stairs or steps. Panelled finish easier to clean than ribbed. Tiles are also available with a carborundum finish.
Concrete	G	Slippery when wet unless a textured finish is applied or non-slip aggregate used.
Concrete paving slabs	G	'Ripple Finish' is non-slip even when wet. Slabs available with carborundum or other non-slip finish.
Cork carpet	VG	Susceptible to damp. Threshold or dividing strip necessary where cork carpet adjoins a different floor finish.
Cork tiles	VG	Susceptible to damp.
Flexible PVC	VG – G	Slippery when wet, unless textured. Susceptible to damp. Sheets liable to come up at edges, making a tripping edge if not fixed to base. Threshold or dividing strip necessary as for carpet.
Felt-backed flexible PVC	V G – G	Susceptible to damp; slippery when wet unless textured.
Flexible PVC incorporating non-slip granules	VG	Non-slip even when wet. Hessian-backed types are susceptible to damp.
Granolithic	G	Poor when wet. On external steps a carborundum finish should be specified.
Linoleum	G	Susceptible to damp. Sheets liable to come up at edges, making a tripping edge if not fixed to base. Threshold or dividing strip necessary as for carpet.
Mastic asphalt	G – F	
Rubber – sheet or tiles	VG (VP when wet)	Unsuitable for areas connected with cooking, washing or laundering or in spaces near entrance doors.
Terrazzo	G (VP when polished)	Exceptionally slippery when polished. Polish should be avoided on surfaces adjacent to terrazzo as it can be transferred by treading. On stairs non-slip nosing is necessary.
Thermoplastic tiles	G	Slip-resistance fair when wet. Although not completely grease-resistant, suitable for domestic kitchens except under cooker.
Timber – softwood boards or blocks	G	Poor if wax-polished.
Timber – hardwood boards or blocks	F	Very poor if wax-polished. On stairtreads a non-slip nosing is necessary.
Vinyl asbestos tiles	G – VG	Slip-resistance fair when wet. Have rather better abrasion-resistance than thermoplastic tiles, good grease- and oil-resistance and suitable for domestic kitchens.

CHECK LIST

Food preparation, eating and refuse disposal

Work sequence

1 Arrangement of working area should provide an uninterrupted sequence of work surface/cooker/work surface/sink/work surface, closely related to storage and eating areas (Para. 14).

Position of cooker

2 The cooker should not be immediately next to a window or door (Para. 15).

Doors

3 Doors to the kitchen should be placed to minimise through traffic (Para. 16).

4 The swings of all doors and cupboard doors in the kitchen should be planned to avoid collision (Para. 17).

Worktop height

5 Worktops on each side of the cooker should be the same height as the boiling plate or rings (Para. 18).

Fittings above cooker

6 A ceiling-mounted airer or a cupboard should not be fixed directly over the cooker or boiler (Para. 19).

Lighting

7 Lighting of working areas should be arranged to avoid shadow (Para. 20).

Storage

8 Storage space within normal reach should be provided for all articles in daily use (Para. 21).

Play space

9 Play space for children should be planned within sight of kitchen (Para. 22).

Dining space

10 There should be enough table or counter space in the kitchen for a casual meal to be eaten (Para. 23).

Laundering

Heating

11 Efficient means of heating both water and space should be provided (Para. 30).

Ventilation

12 Ventilation to laundering space should be adjustable and adequate (Para. 31).

Floor finish

13 Floors should be non-slip under wet conditions (Para. 32).

Lighting

14 Light should avoid shadow on work areas (Para. 33).

Drying and airing

15 Proper provision should be made for drying and airing (Para. 34).

Electrical equipment

16 Switches and socket outlets should be specially considered for safety (Para. 35).

Clothes line

17 The route to the clothes line should be direct and free from unnecessary changes of level (Para. 36).

Housework

Storage

18 Enough storage space should be provided within normal reach for articles in frequent use (Para. 38).

19 The roof space should be provided with artificial light switched at the access (Para. 39).

Fuel store and dustbin

20 Routes to the fuel store and dustbin should be under cover and well lit (Para. 40).

Leisure

Storage

21 Storage space should be provided for a reasonable amount of leisure equipment (Para. 42).

Workshops

22 Workshops and garden sheds should have lockable doors (Para. 43).

Children's play space

23 A play space for children out of doors should be provided into which they can be shut with reasonable security (Para. 44).

Water

24 Water tanks and butts should be fitted with secure covers (Para. 45).

Sleeping and personal care

Light switches

25 A light should be provided by each bed (Para. 48).

26 Light switches between bedroom and w.c. should be placed so that the way ahead can be lit from either direction. Pull switches in bathrooms and w.cs. should be low enough for a child to reach (Para. 48).

27 Illuminated switches in circulation areas are desirable (Para. 48).

Electrical installations in bathrooms

28 I.E.E. Regulations for bathrooms should be carefully followed (Para. 49).

29 Some space heating for the bathroom should be provided (Para. 50).

Medicine cupboard

30 A lockable cupboard should be provided for medicines, out of small children's reach (Para. 51).

Baths

31 A bath with flat bottom and grab rail or other device for steadying the balance should be provided (Para. 52).

Floor finish

32 The bathroom floor should be non-slippery in wet conditions (Para. 52).

W.c. and bathroom doors

33 Locks on w.c. and bathroom doors should be openable from outside in an emergency (Para. 53).

Circulating

Handrails

34 Fixed handrail should be continuous on at least one side of staircase (Para. 56).

35 Gaps of more than 90 mm between balustrades or railings should be avoided (Para. 57).

Single steps

36 Single steps should be avoided; if inevitable they should be differentiated by change of colour (Para. 58).

Shallow steps

37 Steps less than 75 mm in height should be avoided (Para. 59).

Winders and spiral stairs

38 Tapered steps must not provide too small a going (Para. 60).

39 Winders are better avoided (Para. 60).

Top and bottom steps

40 Top and bottom steps of a flight should not encroach on to circulation areas (Para. 61).

Open risers

41 A staircase with open risers has special hazards (Para. 62).

Lighting

42 Artificial lighting should shine towards stairs to obviate shadow (Para. 63).

43 Windows and lighting fittings on staircases should be within normal reach (Para. 63).

Doors in circulation spaces

44 Doors or cupboard doors obstructing circulation spaces should be avoided (Para. 64).

Thresholds

45 Thresholds to internal doors should be detailed to minimise tripping (Para. 65).

Pivot and swing doors

46 Off-centre pivot doors need special detailing to avoid trapped fingers. Swing doors should be glazed sufficiently for people approaching from the other side to be seen (Para. 66).

Glazed doors

47 Doors and panels glazed to the floor should be made obvious by the use of obscured glass or a guard rail (Para. 67).

48 Glazing in doors must be strong enough to withstand slamming (Para. 67).

Floor finishes

49 Floor finishes in circulation areas should be non-slip. Near entrances they should be non-slip in wet conditions (Para. 68).

Mat wells

50 Mat wells should be provided at entrance doors (Para. 69).

Entering and leaving

Layout

51 Layout should separate pedestrian and vehicle traffic. Parking and turning space must be adequate for the traffic expected (Para. 73).

Thresholds

52 Thresholds should be designed to form the nosings of steps (Para. 74).

External steps and ramps

53 The dimensions of external steps should be designed to give easy going, but shallow steps less than 75 mm should be avoided (Para. 75).

54 Single external steps and unexpected ramps should be avoided; if inevitable they should be conspicuously marked by a change of colour or material or a handrail (Paras. 76, 77).

55 Measures should be taken to prevent ramps and open access stairways becoming slippery in winter conditions (Paras. 77, 78).

Open stair wells

56 Open stair wells should be avoided. If they are inevitable the balustrade should be unclimbable (Para. 79).

Lifts

57 In blocks of flats there should be no change of level between lift and flat entrance door (Para. 80).

Balconies

58 Balcony railings should be unclimbable and bulky enough to give reassurance. There should be no room for a small child's head or toes between the members of balustrades (Para. 81).

Paving

59 Paved external surfaces need to be non-slippery when wet and in garages and car-parking areas when wet and greasy. Drainage of paved areas needs careful consideration (Paras. 82, 83).

Paths

60 Paths should be kept away from buildings by a separating strip which is uncomfortable for walking on (Para. 84).

61 Paths used at night should be lighted (Para. 84).

Fences and gates

62 Fences and gates should be so designed that small children find them difficult to climb or open (Para. 85).

63 Very low fences must be designed to be clearly visible (Para. 86).

Service installations

Electricity

64 I.E.E. *Regulations* should be carefully followed (Para. 87).

Electrical layout

65 The layout must be adequate for the different activities involved, with particular reference to the kitchen, circulation spaces, and areas immediately outside the house. Provision should never be less than the minimum recommended in *Homes for today and tomorrow* (Paras. 88, 89).

Meters

66 Meters, main switches and fuse boxes should be fixed at a height within normal reach. Switches should be readily accessible, preferably near the entrance (Para. 90).

Gas

67 British Standard Codes of Practice for gas installations should be strictly followed (Para. 93).

Heating

Standards

68 Homes should be equipped with some form of heating installation capable of giving 13°C in kitchen and circulation areas, and 18°C in living areas (Para. 95).

Position of appliances

69 Fixed radiant fires should be avoided in small rooms unless they are at high level (Para. 98).

Solid fuel

70 If an open fire is provided there should be a permanent fixing to enable a guard of standard design to be installed. The edge of the hearth should be raised. Mantelshelves and mirrors above an open fireplace must be avoided (Paras. 99, 100).

Windows

Windows on staircases

71 Staircase windows should be within normal reach for cleaning and opening (Para. 102).

Glazing

72 Glass weight should be specified in accordance with the current British Standard Code of Practice (Para. 103).

Projection

73 Projection over paths and circulation areas must be avoided (Para. 104).

Windows above ground floor

74 If opening lights in any windows above ground floor level are lower than 800 mm from the inside floor additional protection is needed. Above third storey height, the minimum internal height should be increased to 1100 mm. Above third storey height (and also below this height where access for ladders is not convenient) windows should be designed so that they can be cleaned and reglazed (though not necessarily repainted) from inside, unless there are balconies. 550 mm is the maximum reach for cleaning windows through or across an adjacent opening (Paras. 105–107).
Side-hung casements should have easy-clean hinges with a clearance of 95 mm minimum (Para. 108).

Staircase windows in blocks of flats

75 Staircase windows which are cleaned by contract should have no opening lights lower than 1140 mm from the floor and should be fitted with budget locks, preferably with a visual indication whether the lock is open or shut (Para. 109).

76 Windows should be reversible through approximately 180° so that they can be cleaned entirely from inside. This includes high level vents if these are glazed. A fixed light below the safety level of 1100 mm (Para. 110) must not extend beyond 550 mm because of cleaning difficulties (Paras. 110, 111).

Window controls

77 2000 mm is the absolute maximum height for hand-operated controls. This should be reduced if there are fixed obstructions below the window. Fastenings to casement and pivot windows above ground level should limit the initial opening to 100 mm and provide continuous control of the window's movement (Para. 113).

78 Windows which are reversible for cleaning should have locking bolts to fix them in the fully reversed position. Independent fastenings at each side of such windows, far enough apart to be beyond a child's reach, should be considered (Para. 114).

Floors

79 The non-slip performance of floors must be considered in relation to the particular use to which the floor will be subject (Para. 116). A table of finishes is appended (Page 108).

References

Acknowledgment

This short list gives reference to a number of publications and articles which contain some further information and statistics: no attempt has been made to compile a comprehensive bibliography.

The help given by officers of the Greater London Council in preparing this design bulletin is gratefully acknowledged.

ACLAND (Anne S.)
Home safety check list.
Architects' Journal, 23 October 1963, pages 839–840.

BRITISH MEDICAL ASSOCIATION
Accidents in the home.
The Association, 1964.

CARGILL (D.)
Accidents in the home.
Hamish Hamilton, 1967.

GRAY (Barbara)
Home accidents among older people.
Royal Society for the Prevention of Accidents, 1966.

MACQUEEN (I. A. G.)
A study of home accidents in Aberdeen.
Livingstone, 1966.

REPATH (Elizabeth)
Planners should give lead in home safety.
Municipal Journal, 16 May 1969, page 1253.

ROYAL SOCIETY FOR THE PREVENTION OF ACCIDENTS
Home safety Conference proceedings.
The Society, 1966.

TUSER (P. A.)
Survey of accidents in and around the home.
College of General Practitioners' Journal, November 1962, pages 575–589.

UNIVERSITY OF ILLINOIS
Small Homes Council *Kitchen planning guide* (R. Wanslow).
Illinois: The University, 1965.

WORLD HEALTH ORGANISATION
Public Health Papers No. 26 *Domestic accidents* (E. M. Backett).
Geneva: The Organisation, 1965. (Obtainable through HMSO.)

4

CHILDREN AT PLAY

Introduction

The importance of play

1. A century or so ago the full importance of play was not appreciated and even for the children of the wealthier classes it was frowned upon as frivolous, unnecessary and a manifestation of idleness. But it is now widely accepted that children have a deep and urgent need for play.

2. One of the first people to bring about this change of heart was the educationist Froebel. It is nearly 150 years ago since he stated that 'Play is the highest expression of human development in childhood'.*[1] He was convinced that play was essential to a child's full development. Since his teachings, there have been many theories of play which have been well documented[2,3,4,5], the most comprehensive of which was expounded by Piaget[6]. He saw play as part of the child's response to his environment – a crucial process in reaching conceptual proficiency and intellectual development. He focussed attention on the need to provide the right type of environment and situation at each stage of development so that a child's potential could be fully realised. What all theories of play hold in common is that the child is father of the man; that play is not an end in itself, but has a purpose; and that therefore the child's opportunity – or lack of opportunity – for play determines to some considerable extent the sort of adult that he will become.

3. Play is generally believed to be one of the principal ways in which a child learns how to give as well as take, and in so doing he learns how to adapt to adult society as he grows up. Between birth and maturity, the child comes to terms with the world around him, and comes to accept that he has to take his fellows into account. The extent to which a child successfully learns how to live in and not outside society depends on a wide range of factors. These include not only his genetic inheritance, the social and physical background of his family, educational facilities, and relationships with his parents, but also the opportunity for play.

4. The realisation that play is essential to development has slowly but surely permeated our educational system and cultural heritage. Pre-school play groups, nursery schools, educational toys, youth clubs, and school playgrounds have all come into being at different times, from a belief that the child is rather different from a miniature adult, and that at each stage of his development he needs and enjoys these provisions.

5. The child who has not had the opportunity to meet his fellows, take part in their games, or explore his environment is deprived and therefore at a disadvantage. So at the very least we should ensure that opportunities for play suitable for each stage of development are available as far as possible to all children.

Aims and scope of this bulletin

6. It is the aim of this bulletin to deal with the facilities, layout and building form of the immediate housing area which will ensure the best possible opportunities for play. In doing this, we have enveloped in the word play all the activities of young children near their homes. The bulletin is mainly concerned with those under 11, as the research showed that older children spend less of their time near to their homes. Because the leisure needs of the over-11s are more sophisticated, it is unlikely that they can all be fulfilled within the immediate housing area, but only in the wider neighbourhood. Nor have we explored the play habits and requirements of children inside the home. They both clearly deserve further investigation.

7. This bulletin is therefore no more than an attempt to guide designers and managers to plan for the play needs of children at the design stage of new housing schemes. It also tries to provide practical guidance, and where possible, solutions for making good the deficiencies of play opportunities in existing housing areas, where space may be at a premium. Although the study was carried out almost entirely on estates of local authority housing the conclusions would seem to be generally applicable to all housing schemes whatever their tenure and wherever they are built.

8. Though the main emphasis of the bulletin is on attaining the best physical environment for play, we know that for many children their social environment is crucial. Therefore the chapter on play supervision discusses some of the social problems which reduce opportunities for play, and possible solutions.

The research

9. The evidence of where children played when they were out of doors, how many of them were outside, and what they were doing, has been based on over 50,000 observations of children's outdoor activities on 15 modern housing estates, one older area scheduled for redevelopment, one adventure playground, and on a recreation ground before, during and after a supervised play scheme came into operation. Design recommendations which follow from the conclusions of the research are on page 122. The observation method and characteristics of the areas in which observations took place are described in more detail in paragraphs 12–16. The observation data were subjected to tests of significance. Therefore throughout the text the word 'significant' refers to a statistically meaningful correlation.

10. On nearly all the estates on which observations were carried out and on a further 50 local authority estates surveyed subsequent to the play studies, housewives, both those with and those without children, were asked questions about problems associated with play and for their opinions of existing facilities. In addition, in Oldham and Paddington, interviews were carried out with a random sample of children between seven and 11 living on or near new estates. They talked about where they played, what they did with their spare time and their play preferences.

11. All the estates where observations took place were subjected to detailed cost analyses by the Department of the Environment's quantity surveyors. This has enabled the relative popularity of various play areas to be related to their overall cost.†

---

*A numerical list of bibliographical references is given on page 195.

†The quantity surveyors' estimates included the cost of: construction; play equipment; seats, litter bins and lighting; surrounding walls, fencing and balustrading; planting; paving; grassing and turfing; drainage and general excavation.

1 Estate characteristics (photographs appear on pages 118 - 121)

Estate	Date completed	Number of dwellings	Bed-spaces per acre	Building forms
Low rise				
GLOUCESTER STREET, Sheffield	1964	39	80	27 2-storey houses, 12 patio houses
WOODHOUSE, Sheffield	1964	162	70	2-storey houses
WOODWAY LANE, Coventry	1965	132	75	2-storey houses, old people's bungalows
FLEURY ROAD, Sheffield	1962	148	51	2-storey houses
Medium rise				
ST MARY'S, Oldham	1967	520	110	182 2-storey houses, 3, 4 and 5-storey deck-access blocks
THE BONAMY, Southwark, London	1966	342	173	3 and 4-storey balcony and deck-access blocks (39% flats, 61% maisonettes)
CURNOCK STREET, Camden, London	1966	283	161	4-storey balcony-access blocks – maisonettes, 1 6-storey block – flats. 9 3-storey houses
ROYAL COLLEGE STREET, Camden, London	1967	317	145	4 and 5-storey balcony-access blocks
EDITH AVENUE, Washington, Durham	1968	673	135	3, 4 and 5-storey deck-access blocks (50% flats, 50% maisonettes)
ACORN PLACE, Southwark, London	1963	534	136	7-storey balcony-access block, 2 and 3-storey houses, staircase access flats at second floor level over maisonettes
Mixed rise				
PARK HILL, Sheffield	1961	995	200	4 to 14-storey linked deck-access blocks
SCEAUX GARDENS, Southwark, London	1960	403	136	2 16-storey internal corridor slab blocks – maisonettes, 6-storey balcony-access slab blocks – flats and maisonettes, terraces of bungalows
CANADA, Southwark, London	1964	253	161	2 21-storey point blocks, 5 3 and 4-storey balcony-access cluster blocks, flats and maisonettes
WINSTANLEY ROAD, Wandsworth, London	1966	530	154	1 22-storey internal corridor slab block, 3 11-storey point blocks, 4 and 5-storey linked balcony-access slab blocks
WARWICK, Westminster, London	1962	1,099	137	21 and 22-storey tower blocks, 3, 4 and 5-storey maisonette blocks, renovated Victorian terrace houses

% mothers satisfied with dwelling	Play facilities	% mothers satisfied with estate
95%	None	89%
100%	None	64%
100%	6 areas with brick structures	97%
98%	1 unequipped area	98%
92%	1 area with moving, static conventional, architectural equipment and paddling pool. 1 area with swings. 4 areas concrete structures	87%
87%	1 area, conventional static equipment, empty sand-pit	54%
94%	4 areas each with moving and conventional static equipment and concrete structures	74%
86%	None	77%
90%	3 ball-games areas, 6 sand-pits. 3 empty paddling pools	62%
62%	1 ball-games area, 2 conventional areas with static and moving equipment	38%
83%	3 equipped areas with conventional static equipment and concrete structures, each with sand-pit, 2 ball-games areas, bowling alley	72%
84%	1 climbing frame	54%
59%	3 areas each with concrete structures. Park adjacent to estate with conventional moving and static equipment, and ball-games area	40%
89%	1 area moving and static conventional equipment. 6 areas static and concrete structures. 1 ball-games area	80%
not known	8 areas with static or concrete structures. Adventure playground (run by voluntary organisation) with hut for indoor activities	not known

Observation method

12. In order to study the outdoor activities and locations of children at play, an observation sampling method was employed similar to the one used in earlier play studies by the Building Research Station[7,8] (now part of the Building Research Establishment). This consisted of observers making set walkrounds, devised so that every part of the area being studied came under surveillance. The rounds were made at fixed intervals during the day, the observer noting on specially devised schedules all children seen during a round, their sex and estimated age and what they were doing. The position of each child was recorded on a site plan and a record of the weather conditions was kept. On some of the estates, additional information was collected about the size and composition of groups of children, and the number of children accompanied by adults. The observer also noted what the children were doing. An attempt was made to categorise these activities in some detail but it soon became apparent that to interpret accurately the full range of play activities was impossible. The broadest of categories were therefore adopted. These, with the location codings, are shown in Appendix I.

13. The observations were carried out generally for 12 hours a day during the summer school holidays when outdoor play is assumed to be at its peak. Each estate was observed for four days – two weekdays, a Saturday and a Sunday.

Characteristics of observation areas

14. The 15 housing estates on which observations took place were local authority estates in Coventry, London, Oldham, Sheffield and Washington New Town, built since 1960. They are described in detail in Appendix II. All except four were in the central areas of these towns surrounded by busy streets and built-up areas with few open spaces nearby. The four exceptions, Fleury Road and Woodhouse in Sheffield, Woodway Lane in Coventry and Edith Avenue in Washington New Town, were situated on the outskirts and near open country; in fact Woodway Lane and Woodhouse had fields actually adjoining the estates. Warwick, in Paddington, had an adventure playground which was included in the observation area.

15. All the estates were selected to give a comprehensive range of building forms at a variety of densities (Figure 1). They varied in size from 39 to 1,099 dwellings and in density from 51 to 200 bedspaces per acre. Schemes of houses below 70 bspa have been defined as low-density, schemes between 70 and 120 bspa as medium-density, and schemes built at more than 120 bspa as high-density. The low-rise estates consisted of two-storey houses and bungalows. The medium-rise estates contained houses, flats and maisonettes up to five storeys high.† The mixed-rise estates were a mixture of storey heights and all had at least one block over 13-storeys high.

16. The other housing area in which observations took place was in Oldham adjoining the St Mary's Estate, and was scheduled for redevelopment. The remaining observation area was the Emslie Horniman Pleasance Recreation Ground in Kensal Town.

---

†The only exceptions were Curnock Street, which had one six-storey block of flats and Acorn Place, which had one seven-storey block of flats and maisonettes. As no children lived above the fifth floors and as they were similar in other respects to medium-rise estates, they were included in the medium-rise category.

2 GLOUCESTER STREET, Sheffield

4 WOODWAY LANE, Coventry

3 WOODHOUSE, Sheffield

5 FLEURY ROAD, Sheffield

6 ST MARY'S, Oldham

9 ROYAL COLLEGE STREET, Camden, London

7 THE BONAMY, Southwark, London

10 EDITH AVENUE, Washington, Durham

8 CURNOCK STREET, Camden, London

11 ACORN PLACE, Southwark, London

12 PARK HILL, Sheffield

13 SCEAUX GARDENS, Southwark, London

14 CANADA ESTATE, Southwark, London

15 WINSTANLEY ROAD, Wandsworth, London

17 THE OLDER AREA, Oldham

18 THE EMSLIE HORNIMAN PLEASANCE RECREATION GROUND,
Kensington and Chelsea, London

16 WARWICK ESTATE, Westminster, London

Design recommendations

Dwellings for families with young children

17. Wherever possible families with young children should be allocated houses. If density or other design factors make this impossible, only the dwellings on the ground or first floor of a multi-storey building should be considered. It was found that the under-11s played outside more if they lived in dwellings with ground or first-floor access, and it was clear that if they lived in houses mothers found their children's play less of a problem. This may mean at high densities that households without children will have to be housed off the ground or first floor. However, they are the people least adversely affected by this solution, and in many cases prefer the privacy, views and quiet it gives them.

Play areas

18. The number of children who used play areas was significantly influenced by the amount of play space per child and by the type of equipment available. Play areas on housing estates should therefore conform to the standards recently laid down in one of the Department's circulars.[9] On all schemes containing ten or more bedspaces, play space should be provided on the basis of 3m² (32.3 sq ft) per child bedspace. (The number of child bedspaces in a scheme is calculated by subtracting from the total number of bedspaces in the scheme all the bedspaces in old people's dwellings, all bedspaces in one and two-person dwellings, and two bedspaces in family dwellings.) Play space should also be equipped from the list in Appendix I of the circular; this equipment was selected because it was well-used and liked by children. This does not prevent a council from providing extra, different, pieces of equipment, in addition to those on the list, if it considers this appropriate.

19. The standards require play space to be provided at all densities. In those high-density schemes where children have to live off the ground and therefore play outdoors less, it is hoped that play space will attract them outside. At low densities, where children play more on roads and pavements than in gardens, well-equipped play areas can succeed in attracting them away from roads.

20. Neighbourhood play provision should not be regarded as a substitute for play space within housing areas.

21. Play areas should where practicable be sited close to family dwellings and away from dwellings designed for elderly and adult households.

22. Play areas are used by children of all ages, though they are less popular with the over-11s. Out of school hours young children are often informally supervised by older brothers and sisters, and so play areas may be used less if they are segregated by age groups.

23. Accidents may occur wherever children play; to minimise the possibility of them, however, play equipment should be checked regularly for wear, damage, and the need for replacement.

24. Play equipment should be cleaned and maintained like any other communal property on estates. Although sand-pits and paddling pools are very popular with children, they should only be provided if daily attention is possible.

25. Play areas should be carefully landscaped and sheltered from extreme weather conditions and wind tunnels from high flats. Natural features and planting should be retained wherever possible and a variety of hardwearing surfaces considered.

Supervised play facilities

26. All authorities should consider whether they have made sufficient provision for supervised play, over and above the facilities for unsupervised outdoor play on housing estates. Supervision can extend the range of play activities, help to compensate physically and socially deprived children, and for some pre-school children provide opportunities for acquiring language and social skills. Supervision also makes possible the use of indoor accommodation, so necessary in this climate. Skilled play-leaders can enable the resources of built-up inner areas to be used to better and fuller effect by the children.

27. As wide a range as possible of all types of supervised play facilities should be considered not only by the educational and social services but by the housing managers, planners and designers. It is they who will make the decisions about the scale and type of community provision in the planning of new schemes and who can allocate for play purposes existing premises on housing estates to organizations, many of whom will be voluntary. Very often tenants' halls and clubs for old people can be used by young children.

The estate

28. By no means all of a child's time is spent in play areas, however well designed and equipped. Therefore the whole estate should be planned with the children's needs in mind. Attention should be given to each of the following areas:

(a) *Roads*. Roads and all spaces adjacent to them should be designed to reduce as many known hazards as possible. Children will play on or near roads if they are the areas nearest to home; they are significantly more popular for play than gardens.

(b) *Gardens*. Gardens attached to family dwellings should be adjacent to either the kitchen or the living area used during the day. They should also be as close as possible to the main comings and goings of the estate. Adequate fencing should be provided to prevent young children getting out. If this is done, gardens, though by no means the main place for play, should be more popular.

(c) *Paths*. Paths suitable for play should be sited away from old people's dwellings. Where the play is not likely to create a disturbance, paths can be linked to make tricycle-riding – and other play with wheeled toys – easier, perhaps by the use of ramps rather than steps.

(d) *Access areas*. If councils have to house children above the ground, the provision of wide, well-balustraded access decks will go some way towards overcoming the disadvantages. Dwellings for families with children and for childless households should not be situated on the same decks, so that childless households are not disturbed by children's noise.

(e) *Grassed areas.* Where they are intended for children, they should be as large as possible, to reduce intensity of use. Several points of access will also help to avoid excessive wear and tear. If grassed areas are largely decorative then they should be carefully landscaped to discourage children's play.

(f) *Planted areas.* Similarly, planted areas which are part of the landscaping need protecting from children. They are less likely to be used for incidental play if they are raised above the path level and contain prickly plants. Planted areas require regular care if the plants and shrubs are to flourish, and need to be renewed when necessary.

(g) *Walls, railings, garage roofs, trees etc.* These should all be either strong enough to withstand a certain amount of use by children, or protected.

(h) *Open country.* In planning children's play needs, open country, unless an integral part of the estate, should not be taken into account.

Play in older areas

29. The most urgent need is to create spaces for play where none exists, and to make better use of existing space. Clearing waste and derelict land, and making better use of school premises, parks and recreation grounds, are some of the ways of achieving this.

30. As so much of children's play is spontaneous, and takes place near to home, improvements for play should be looked at street by street.

33. Although the recommended play equipment has been used throughout the country for many years, accidents do occur while the children are using it. Research is needed to investigate causes and possible solutions.

34. The following suggestions relate to supervised play:

(a) though the importance of supervised play has been recognised, little design research has been done on the indoor accommodation most appropriate to different types and ages of children, and the costs involved. We should try and get away from the view that any hut is good enough for children's play needs. Housing authorities, particularly, should consider the possibility of making tenants' halls and old people's clubs suitable for play;

(b) one of the major drawbacks to making supervised play facilities more widespread is the expense of staff salaries. There is some evidence to show that supervision can reduce vandalism. Further study should probe whether the cost of supervision is more than offset by a reduction in vandalism;

(c) more work needs to be done to find ways of improving the working conditions and staff ratios of playleaders. This should encourage them to stay longer which will give the children a feeling of continuity.

Suggestions for further research

31. Less than one in ten of the under-11s were seen with adults. As so many of the children played on or near roads, we need to know far more about why so few adults accompanied them, even in situations which the parents themselves would admit were subject to traffic dangers. With this knowledge it would be easier to know how to make parents more aware of the physical limitations of young children's capabilities to deal with traffic hazards.

32. Although mothers considered their children's play needs to be less of a problem when they lived in houses, over half of those were still worried about this question. The provision of play facilities and safety from traffic did little to alleviate these worries. It could be that mothers were reflecting more than play problems in their answers, that is, more general difficulties of bringing up young children. Far more should be done to probe these difficulties.

a – Play on Local Authority Housing Estates

1 The children outdoors

35. Never more than a fifth of the resident children were seen outdoors on the average observation walkround,* but this proportion varied from one age group to another. Approximately 17% of the under-fives, 30% of the five-to-tens and 13% of the over-tens were seen outside. It is perhaps not surprising that the five-to-tens were the age group most frequently observed. Though still too young for most of them to be allowed to wander far from home (and therefore beyond the scope of the observations) they were old enough for most parents to let them play near their own homes, especially with friends. Three-quarters were seen in groups and the majority of these were groups with at least one five-to-ten in them.

36. It is perhaps equally to be expected that the children of secondary school age were the least often seen on the estates. At this age most children are allowed to come and go very much as they please, and few parents feel it necessary to keep them continually in sight. It is unlikely that the average housing estate can provide a sufficient range of facilities to meet all their needs. Certainly the ball-games areas were little used. Two ball-games areas at Park Hill, including a large area of 12,740 sq ft, attracted in all no more than a tenth of the observed boys over ten, and this was considerably more than on any other estate or for any other age group of either sex. Even the existence of an adventure playground on Warwick Estate did not increase the numbers of older children seen out. In fact a census taken at the playground for two days during the summer holidays of 1969 showed that of the 186 children using the playground only a quarter were between 11 and 15.

37. However, for the under-11s,† it seemed that the physical characteristics of the housing areas studied *did* affect the extent they played outdoors.‡ A higher proportion of under-11s were observed outdoors on the medium and low-density estates than on the high-density ones (Figure 19), and more were out on the low-rise estates than on either the mixed or medium-rise ones (Figure 20). Once the estates of houses were excluded from the analysis, the numbers seen out were not affected simply by either the size, or rise or density of the estates but only by the proportion of under-11s living on the ground or very close to it. It is

---

*This was calculated by taking the number of children seen out during each walkround as a percentage of the resident child population. This method is by no means foolproof and the results should be interpreted with caution. It is for this reason that detailed age breakdowns have not been attempted.

†It is regrettable that it was not possible to separate the pre-school children from the five-to-tens as their needs are often different from those of school age. One can only hypothesize that, as pre-school children are even more likely to play near their homes than the older ones, the tendency for building form to affect the proportion of outdoor play would have been even more pronounced with a larger sample of pre-school children.

‡We were not able to correlate the social characteristics of the children or their families with the extent to which they were seen outdoors. The subsequent discussion of significant relationships should therefore be interpreted with caution as there may have been influential social factors which were not distributed randomly throughout all of the estates.

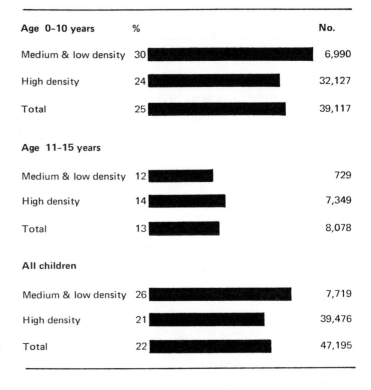

19 Percentage of resident children seen outdoors; by density of estate

Age 0–10 years	%		No.
Medium & low density	30		6,990
High density	24		32,127
Total	25		39,117

Age 11–15 years			
Medium & low density	12		729
High density	14		7,349
Total	13		8,078

All children			
Medium & low density	26		7,719
High density	21		39,476
Total	22		47,195

20 Percentage of resident children seen outdoors; by 'rise' of estate

Age 0–10 years	%		No.
Low rise	30		6,990
Medium rise	24		17,854
Mixed rise	24		14,273
Total	25		39,117

Age 11–15 years			
Low rise	12		729
Medium rise	12		3,351
Mixed rise	15		3,998
Total	13		8,078

All children			
Low rise	26		7,719
Medium rise	21		21,205
Mixed rise	21		18,271
Total	22		47,195

highly likely, therefore, that the most important contributing factor to the extent children played outdoors was whether they lived in a dwelling with ground-floor access. Ready and easy access to the outdoors was clearly important. On multi-storey estates where a high proportion of children lived in ground-floor or first-floor flats, more of them played out than where they lived further from the ground. Moreover, there was no significant difference between the numbers of under-11s seen out on the estates of houses and on estates where a high proportion lived in ground or first-floor flats.

38. There would therefore seem to be no intrinsic superiority* in houses over any other ground or first-floor dwelling in the effect they have on the extent children play outside. Even though more of the houses had gardens, these could not have been the prime reason for allowing the children out, as children spent less than a fifth of their time in gardens (paragraphs 64–67). For mother and child to be in sight and sound of each other is probably what counts, whether the outdoor spaces are private or communal. From our evidence it appeared that once the child lived off the ground or above the first floor, increasing height above the ground was immaterial to the extent he played out. Thus the mother living on the second or third floor was no more likely to let her child out to play than the one living on the tenth or twentieth floor.

39. The only other research which throws further light on this question has been carried out in Denmark[10] and Sweden[11] and reveals broadly similar findings although the methodology was slightly different. The main difference was that it included second-floor dwellings in the definition of 'near to the ground' and these made a significant difference to the extent young children played outside. This research also showed that the children who lived near to the ground were more likely to play out alone, came out to play a greater number of times, and stayed out for longer each time, than those who lived on the higher floors. It would seem that proximity to the ground means that the mother and young child are less likely to treat the outside as a special outing but rather as part and parcel of normal home life and a continuation of the home environment.

40. The patterns of play where children lived in multi-storey blocks with wide access decks were similar to those found at ground and first-floor level. At Park Hill, for instance, a similar proportion of under-11s were seen out as at Woodway Lane, an estate of houses, and half of these played in access areas irrespective of the height above the ground. Apart from Edith Avenue, where two-thirds of the young children lived on or near the ground, Park Hill was the only estate studied where *all* the above-ground dwellings were served by a wide deck. It is therefore impossible to say whether the Park Hill pattern is generally applicable. Certainly it would seem that the type of access is one of the important factors affecting the extent children play out. Judged solely on this criterion, a Park Hill type of solution would seem preferable to point blocks, or blocks with narrow access balconies or internal access arrangements.

41. Wherever possible then families with young children should be housed no higher than the first floor and preferably at ground level. The children's mothers are at any rate more contented if they do not have to cope with prams, children and shopping baskets in lifts or upstairs.[12] Families with young children dislike using stairs more than any other type of household.[13]

42. At low densities (under about 70 bspa) it is possible to provide all the family dwellings at ground level. At higher densities, however, designers and housing managers need to work closely together to ensure that many if not all the families with young children live at ground or first-floor level. Within our sample, density on its own was not the main determinant of how many children were housed on ground and first-floor levels (Figure 21). At Park Hill, with a very high density of 200 bspa, more children lived at these levels than on four other estates with lower densities. It is probably true to say that certain types of scheme made the task of allocation easier. In all the medium-rise schemes we studied, significantly more young children lived on the ground or first floor than in the mixed-rise high-density schemes (Figure 22). However, it is not only the type of scheme which determines how much freedom the housing manager has to allocate the right kind of dwelling to young families, but design decisions made at the drawing board stage about the distribution in the scheme of various dwelling types. At Royal College Street mainly small flats unsuitable for families were on the ground. At Sceaux Gardens old people were housed in bungalows, and most family dwellings were off the ground. It is also fairly common practice to utilise the ground floor in blocks of flats for stores, laundries and other common services.

21 Percentage of children aged 0–10 living on the ground and first floor on each estate

Estate	Density in bed-spaces per acre	%		No.
Fleury	51	100		74
Woodhouse	70	100		318
Woodway	75	100		232
St Mary's	110	90		249
Edith	135	66		458
Acorn	136	78		345
Sceaux	136	22		138
Warwick	137	33		500
Royal College	145	51		175
Winstanley	154	18		402
Canada	161	23		235
Curnock	161	55		175
The Bonamy	173	54		273
Park Hill	200	31		407

*Here we are only discussing the houses in respect of the influence they had on the extent children played out. This is not to say that the merits or otherwise of certain types of dwelling may not appear in quite a different light when related to other issues.

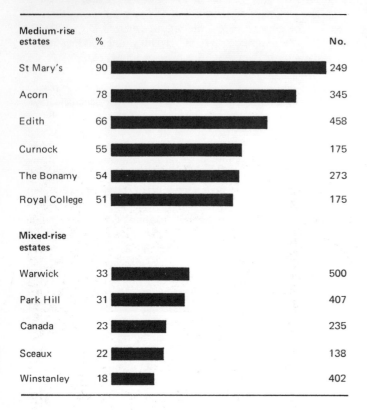

22 Percentage of children aged 0–10 living on the ground and first floor on medium and mixed-rise estates

Medium-rise estates	%		No.
St Mary's	90		249
Acorn	78		345
Edith	66		458
Curnock	55		175
The Bonamy	54		273
Royal College	51		175
Mixed-rise estates			
Warwick	33		500
Park Hill	31		407
Canada	23		235
Sceaux	22		138
Winstanley	18		402

46. In an ideal world mothers would have the time and inclination to see that these demands were met irrespective of their physical surroundings. One might imagine, for instance, that if they were in any way worried about their young children playing outside they would accompany them. In our study no more than a third of the under-fives were seen with adults and it was usually considerably less (Figure 23). One alternative to allowing children out with adults is letting them play with older siblings and friends. Half the pre-school children observed were with children from older age groups. Many mothers either have other children to consider, or work part or all of the time, or simply do not appreciate the value of outdoor play. For them, the only alternative to allowing the child out alone or with other young children, which many will understandably be reluctant to do, will be to keep the child indoors. But this, as we have seen, imposes limitations on physical activities and social interactions.

23 Percentage of children aged 0–4 seen with adults

Estate	%		No.
Edith	30		1,042
Warwick	19		565
Royal College	18		351
The Bonamy	15		526
Curnock	15		610
Fleury	7		217
Winstanley	6		919
Acorn	5		677
Canada	5		551
Park Hill	4		962
Sceaux	3		319

Note – At Gloucester Street, Woodhouse, Woodway Lane and St Mary's, observations were not taken of adults accompanying children.

43. Here it should be recognised that adult and elderly households do not share the other families' needs to be on or near the ground. Research has shown that most childless households are not only happy to live off the ground, but in certain circumstances actually prefer it.[13,14,15,16] Thus at high densities opting for a solution where *all* old people are housed on the ground may result in pleasing no one: it may fail to give them reasonable privacy, views and quiet; reduce the children's opportunities for ground-floor dwellings, and their ability to play without incurring the displeasure of neighbours. At higher densities, many childless households may be better off in schemes without families, or in multi-storey dwellings. At Curnock Street, for example, all the small dwellings occupied by adult and mainly elderly households were in one six-storey block. The people living there were well pleased with their accommodation and with the estate.[16] Over half of the young children on that estate lived at ground level even though the density was 161 bspa.

44. The question remains, however, whether outdoor play is sufficiently important to warrant strong recommendation that designers and planners should aim at producing schemes at densities and in design terms that do not inhibit it. It is widely held to be so.[17]

45. When the Newsoms wrote 'the average four-year-old in England today is healthy and well-nourished; in consequence he has an abundance of physical energy'[18], they were describing a condition characteristic of most young children. The healthy unrepressed child has tremendous physical energy which cannot find sufficient outlet indoors. To expend this energy is an essential part of growing up. The child needs outdoor space to develop basic physical skills, such as running, jumping, balancing; and also to meet his friends. 'The degree to which he (the child) learns to direct his own body and co-ordinate his movements is partly dependent upon the kinds of stimulation which his environment provides'.[18]

126

2 Where the children played

47. Most outside play took place near dwellings. Irrespective of density and building form, at least three-quarters of the children, whatever their age, but particularly the under-fives, were observed playing near to home. The differences found in where children played were caused by the types of spaces available adjacent to dwellings at the different densities and building forms. Though we do not know for certain whether children were playing near their own homes, it seems likely that this was so. Not only do mothers like to keep an eye on what they are doing, but the children themselves prefer to play in the orbit of their mothers. This tendency for children to play in the direct vicinity of the dwelling – 'doorstep play' – in spite of suitable alternative places, has been confirmed by other studies, not only in this country[7,8] but in Denmark[10], Sweden[11] and Holland[19].

Doorstep play
Most outside play took place near to home

24 CANADA

25 ST MARY'S

27 PARK HILL – access deck

26 ACORN PLACE

	Access areas	Paved areas	Roads & pavements	Gardens	Play areas	Grassed areas	Wild areas	Unorth-odox areas	Planted areas	Other areas	Number
LOW-RISE ESTATES											
0– 4 yrs	No 'Access areas'	25%	38%	21%	2%	10%	3%	3%	1%	No 'Other areas'	4,332
5–10 yrs		24%	38%	17%	5%	11%	6%	4%	1%		5,257
11–15 yrs		22%	42%	13%	4%	8%	9%	8%	1%		1,217
Total		24%	39%	18%	4%	10%	5%	4%	1%		10,806
MEDIUM-RISE ESTATES											
0– 4 yrs	27%	41%	10%	3%	9%	6%	2%	3%	2%	2%	4,695
5–10 yrs	22%	41%	10%	2%	12%	7%	1%	4%	3%	2%	13,160
11–15 yrs	21%	40%	14%	2%	12%	6%	1%	4%	2%	3%	3,351
Total	23%	41%	11%	2%	11%	7%	1%	4%	3%	2%	21,206
MIXED-RISE ESTATES											
0– 4 yrs	48%	20%	7%	1%	13%	5%	16%	2%		4%	2,751
5–10 yrs	40%	23%	8%	—	13%	8%	12%	2%	No 'Planted areas'	6%	8,071
11–15 yrs	33%	27%	11%	—	11%	11%	10%	2%		6%	2,676
Total	40%	23%	9%	1%	13%	8%	12%	2%		6%	13,498

These percentages were adjusted to exclude the numbers of children observed on-the estates which did not have locations in a particular category. Therefore totals exceed 100%.

Roads and pavements

48. On the estates of houses, two-fifths of the children were seen at play on roads (including garage courts) or adjoining pavements,* and this was significantly more than played in gardens, play areas or paved areas (Figure 28).

49. This was because children mainly play near to their homes as discussed above. On the more conventional estates of houses, home is more likely to be near roads and pavements than on the mixed or medium-rise estates. On these latter estates of mainly flats and maisonettes, roads tend to be segregated from dwellings and there is a choice of other hard-surfaced spaces such as paved or access areas closer to the dwellings. Fleury Road was the only low-rise estate that did not fit into this pattern; just under a fifth of the observed play took place on or near roads, the reason being that roads were located away from dwellings, thus making paved areas adjacent to the dwellings the most popular play location.

50. The finding that so many children played on or near roads cannot be ignored. An average of less than a tenth of the under-11s were seen with adults, even though on most of the estates where we interviewed mothers about this almost half of them considered their children to be safe from traffic. Indeed a survey carried out by the Office of Population Censuses and Surveys for the former Road Research Laboratory[20] showed that 26% (averaged) of the two-year-olds in their sample, and 77% of the five-year-olds, were considered by their mothers to be able to cross the road outside their homes by themselves.

51. In 1971, 37,926 child pedestrians under 15 were killed or injured on the roads† and it was established that pedestrians under 15 were three times as likely to suffer from a road accident as adults over 15 and under 60. The child's physiological limitations for coping with traffic are only just becoming realised. A Swedish child psychologist[21] has shown that, because of the immaturity before the eleventh or twelfth year of various important mechanisms, such as sight, hearing and the ability to differentiate right from left, fast and slow, near and far, children are especially vulnerable in traffic situations. For such reasons, the Danish and Swedish Building Institutes recommend traffic-segregated layouts.

52. In this country too, a study in Stevenage[22] has shown traffic-segregated layouts to have 'positive advantages ... in terms of safety for children', and the differences in accidents between two neighbourhood units, one traffic-segregated and one not, were statistically significant.

30 ST MARY'S

Play on roads and pavements
These locations were popular on estates where dwellings were near to them

29 WOODHOUSE

---

*We did not separate out the observations for roads and their adjacent pavements as we considered that there was a potential traffic danger from playing near the roads. At the pilot stage it became obvious that many activities took place on roads and pavements concurrently (Figure 31).

†The Transport and Road Research Laboratory which collects national accident statistics does not divide the type of road beyond category c, which covers most roads in housing developments whether they are segregated or not.

31 GLOUCESTER STREET

53. Some would argue that children will only learn to cope with traffic if they are introduced to it at an early age and that a segregated layout does not give them this opportunity. There is also the question of whether the traffic which is diverted away from one particular area is building up and creating traffic hazards in another. An interesting study carried out by the Building Research Station on the location of primary schools in St Albans and Stevenage[23] showed that an accident to a child on a major road was more than twice as likely to be serious in Stevenage than St Albans. One reason put forward was that, because of the segregated areas in Stevenage, traffic was firmly channelled into distributor roads and built up speed, whereas at St Albans residential roads could be used as short cuts, thereby cutting down the traffic flow on the major roads.

54. Until research, at present being undertaken by the Department, can demonstrate more conclusively the effect of segregation on accidents one can only suggest that designers and traffic engineers opt for a compromise solution. This would recognise that where roads are near to dwellings they will be used extensively for play even where gardens and safe play areas are provided. Attempts must be made to make roads as safe as possible for the children by reducing the hazards conducive to accidents, rather than by deciding that complete segregation is the answer at this moment. The Stevenage study[22] showed that a new area which was not segregated from traffic had a lower accident rate than an older non-traffic-segregated area, indicating that it is possible to decrease accidents in non-traffic-segregated areas with careful design.

Paved and access areas

55. Paved areas were a popular play location when situated close to the dwellings. Their popularity seemed to depend on the comparative accessibility and attraction of roads and access areas. On estates like Fleury Road, which were traffic-segregated and had no communal access areas, paved spaces were by far the most popular location, and two-fifths of all play activities took place on them (Figure 32). At Gloucester Street, Woodhouse and Woodway Lane less than a quarter of the children played on paving. Here the bustle and activities of the estates were centred more on the roads and garage courts than the pedestrian walkways. Children were therefore attracted away from the safer paved areas onto the roads and into garage courts which were large enough for many of the more popular activities (Figure 33).

56. On the mixed and medium-rise estates, paved areas were situated more conveniently to the dwellings than were the roads, as all these estates tended towards complete traffic segregation, and significantly more children played on them than on roads

32 Percentage of children observed in doorstep locations on each estate

ESTATES	Access areas %	Paved areas %	Roads & pavements %	Gardens %	Other areas[†] %	No.
LOW RISE						
Gloucester	*	21	47	18	14	3,087
Woodhouse	*	24	34	24	19	3,524
Woodway	*	23	43	13	21	3,215
Fleury	*	41	18	13	28	980
MEDIUM RISE						
St. Mary's	4	43	17	3	32	5,169
The Bonamy	27	42	10	*	21	3,163
Curnock	25	42	6	*	28	2,846
Royal College	42	36	18	*	4	1,435
Edith	31	41	5	*	23	4,861
Acorn	26	39	11	1	22	3,732
MIXED RISE						
Park Hill	48	16	4	*	33	4,424
Sceaux	29	40	8	0	24	1,732
Canada	31	26	10	1	33	3,780
Winstanley	46	22	14	0	18	3,562
Warwick	25	18	30	0	28	4,773

* No locations in this category on this estate.

† Play areas, grassed areas, wild areas, unorthodox areas, planted areas, other areas.

33 WOODWAY LANE
On the estates of houses many children played in the garage courts which were closer to the activity of the estate than the paved areas

Play on paved areas

34 WOODWAY LANE

(Figure 28). Warwick was an exception to this; though a mixed-rise estate it was not traffic-segregated and in its layout more like the low-rise estates of houses.

57. On the mixed and medium-rise estates paved and access areas were nearly always the two areas closest to the dwellings, and thus the two most popular places for play. On the mixed-rise estates a quarter of the play took place on paving and two-fifths in access areas. On the medium-rise estates this pattern was completely reversed and two-fifths of the play took place on paving and only a quarter in access areas. The most likely reason for this clear difference between the two types of estate is the differing proportions of children living at ground level. On the medium-rise estates, except for Royal College Street where the play patterns were similar to those on a mixed-rise estate, significantly more children lived at ground level than on the mixed-rise estates. More of them were able to make use of the paving at ground level for doorstep play. For the greater numbers of children living off the ground on the mixed-rise estates, the deck and access balconies fulfilled the same functions for doorstep play, particularly for the under-fives.

58. Paved areas were the most popular location for active pursuits, particularly for riding tricycles and wheeled toys. Though a path system has to be provided for access, with a little care and at little extra cost it can be an interesting and stimulating environment for children. While a series of unconnected paths and paved areas may meet the needs of adults, they are not so suitable for play unless they are connected together to form a linked system through which the child can circulate and use wheeled toys and ride tricycles (Figure 36). Preferably such a path system should be sited on the more active parts of the estate near shops, schools, play areas and dwellings where children live. Pathways with few outlets should be placed near the dwellings of elderly residents and other families without children, to reduce the possibilities of disturbance from the noise of children's play (Figure 37).

59. Steps often prevent children from using paths as freely as they may wish. The steps at Fleury Road led children to create their own cycle paths in the grassed slopes alongside the steps, which

35 ST MARY'S

resulted in worn grass (Figure 38). Ramps, which were used at Curnock Street and Gloucester Street, can help to overcome this problem (Figure 39). However, the use of steps may help to keep children away from old people's dwellings or any other part of the estate where quietness is required.

60. Part of the popularity of access areas, apart from the fact that they were close to dwellings and were focal areas for the comings and goings of the estate, may well have been that they provided a sheltered play environment. Their suitability and safety can perhaps be questioned and were largely dependent on the design and type of the access. Dark areas under stairs or by refuse chutes, and the internal landings and corridors lit by artificial lights, were very bleak and unsatisfactory play areas; other access areas were positively unsafe (Figures 42 and 43). In contrast, the wide decks at Park Hill (Figure 44), which were very popular, provided safe covered areas open to light and fresh air, where the children could play away from traffic and without hindering pedestrians.

Play on paved areas

36   WINSTANLEY ROAD
An interesting and well-used route suitable for bicycles and wheeled toys

37   WOODWAY LANE
The children's activities extended onto the paths outside the old people's dwellings

38   FLEURY ROAD
Steps made bicycle riding down the paths difficult, resulting in worn grassed areas alongside

39   CURNOCK STREET
Ramps made the use of bicycles easier

133

Play in access areas

40 EDITH AVENUE

41 WINSTANLEY ROAD

42 WINSTANLEY ROAD
An unsuitable area for play

43 WINSTANLEY ROAD
A potentially dangerous deck

44 PARK HILL
  The wide decks were popular play areas

61. It is interesting to note that at Park Hill, for the children at least, the designer's aspiration of creating 'streets in the air' seems to have been realised (Figure 44). Half of the under-11s observed at Park Hill were on the decks, similar to the proportion playing in roads and on pavements on the estates of houses we studied. Much of this popularity was due to the width of the decks. Significantly more children played on the decks on Park Hill and Winstanley Road estates where the decks were 10ft and 5ft (with 10ft 6ins indentations by some of the front doors) respectively, than on other estates with much narrower decks or balconies* (Figures 44 and 45). As well as being close to home, the access areas on these estates allowed the children to circulate freely about the buildings without going outside.

62. Access areas had the further advantage of being covered spaces which provided areas for play even in wet weather. Some were large enough for active play in any weather. At Winstanley Road and Park Hill the popular wide decks were used almost as much in dry weather as wet. But at Acorn and Canada, where the balconies were narrow, their use rose by about a quarter and a third respectively in wet weather.

63. In qualitative terms concrete decks are obviously not ideal play places. However, if councils have to house children above the ground, the provision of wide, well balustraded access decks will go some way towards overcoming the disadvantages by providing play spaces near the dwellings without greatly interfering with pedestrian traffic through them. With ingenuity these play spaces could be made interesting, e.g. by the use of indentations as at Winstanley Road. Dwellings for families with children and for childless households should not be sited on the same decks, so that childless households are not disturbed by children's noise.

*At Edith Avenue where the decks were 8ft wide, insufficient children lived at deck level to draw conclusions about the popularity of these decks for play.

45 ACORN PLACE
  The narrow balconies were little used for play

46 Play locations on estates where most children had access to gardens

	Gloucester Street %	Woodhouse %	Woodway Lane %	Fleury Road %	St. Mary's %
Roads & pavements	47	33	43	18	18
Paved areas	21	24	23	41	43
Gardens	18	24	13	13	3
Grassed areas	7	12	7	23	9
Play areas	*	*	5	0	18
Wild areas	*	4	7	*	2
Unorthodox areas	6	3	2	5	3
Access areas	*	*	*	*	4
Planted areas	1	*	*	*	0
Total	100	100	100	100	100
Number	3,087	3,524	3,215	980	5,169

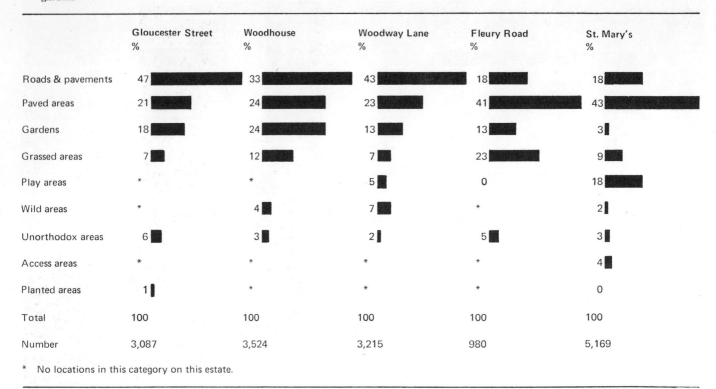

* No locations in this category on this estate.

Gardens

64. All the dwellings on the estates of houses studied had gardens, most of which could be easily observed. Apart from St Mary's and Edith Avenue, few of the dwellings on the mixed-rise and medium-rise estates had gardens, and on those that did it was difficult to observe children at play in them. This means that there was a great difference between low-rise, medium and mixed-rise estates in the number of children playing in gardens. Yet though considerably more children both had the chance to play in gardens and actually played in them on the estates of houses, gardens were by no means the main place for play even for the under-fives (Figure 28). This is contrary to the popular belief that the chief benefit of allocating families to dwellings with gardens is that the garden provides young children with a safe play space. Significantly fewer children of all ages played in gardens than on roads or paved areas, even on the estates where they had equal opportunities to play in either location – Gloucester Street, Woodhouse, Woodway Lane, Fleury Road and St Mary's, (Figure 46). Only in relation to the less popular 'second league' places not immediately adjacent to the dwelling – such as wild and 'unorthodox areas' – were gardens used significantly more for play.

65. The popularity of gardens for play did not depend on their size. For instance the front gardens at Woodhouse measured only 166 sq ft and were the most intensively used of any of the estates and far more popular than the back gardens of 300 sq ft. Similarly at Fleury Road, gardens which averaged 645 sq ft were largely ignored in favour of the smaller paved yards at the back of the houses which were mostly 112 sq ft. The reason seems to be that the preferred areas were closest to the main footpaths and thus to the comings and goings of the estate, providing an interesting and changing environment in which the child could play. Only 3% of all children observed at St. Mary's, were playing in gardens. Though this is probably an underestimate, as not all the gardens could be observed, and can partly be explained by the popularity of the play areas, the gardens were adjacent to little-used pedestrian alleys, and many were screened from any activity going on there by a high fence. The front gardens at Woodhouse, the back yards at Fleury Road and the back gardens at Woodway Lane were also in direct view of the kitchens so that the mothers could keep an eye on their children who could go from garden to dwelling without passing through the best living room (Figure 47).

66. The popular gardens in the above schemes gave a suggestion of intimacy and security by being enclosed on three sides by fencing even though, except at Woodway Lane, the fencing was very low. As gardens are popular for inactive play a sheltered area is appreciated by the children. The anxiety of mothers with very young children is also decreased if adequate fencing is provided. The low railed fence in the back gardens of Woodhouse was considered most inadequate by many mothers (Figure 48). One mother told how her baby had crawled through the fence and onto the road. She and others had filled in the gap and increased the height of the fence by using wire netting. Adequate fencing should obviously be provided to ensure that young children cannot get out.

67. If the under-fives at least are to be encouraged to play in gardens, where they will be safe from traffic and least likely to disturb other households, designers should try to see the garden as one part of the child's play pattern and to relate it to the kitchen or adjacent living area and to the main circulation routes of the estate. Although the size of gardens did not affect the amount they were used for play, it may be that gardens which are both large and meet the above criteria will be additionally attractive to children. Designers should consider providing larger gardens, at densities where this is possible.

47 WOODWAY LANE
The garden's direct access to the kitchen enabled mothers to keep an eye on their children

48 WOODHOUSE
Mothers complained that the type of fencing provided was not toddler-proof

Planted areas

68. The remainder of the observed play took place in planted, wild, 'unorthodox' and grassed areas. Together these accounted for between a fifth and a third of the observations (Figure 28). Differences in their popularity were not related to building form or density but to characteristics of particular estates.

69. At Acorn Place there were several planted areas consisting of paved squares alternating with shrubs and planted squares in a chequer-board fashion. Many of them were in the courtyards of houses where a predominant amount of play took place on the paved areas. Because the planted areas were not raised above the paving the children counted the paved and planted areas as one, to the detriment of the shrubs and plants (Figures 49 and 50).

70. On all other estates, areas planted with traditional flowerbeds and shrubberies held little attraction for the children. Despite this, the use of these areas by even a few children sometimes created problems, such as plants being destroyed and loose earth scattered on paths. At Gloucester Street, the children had turned the steep banks into slides with disastrous results to the planting (Figure 51). This was remedied by the Council's Parks Department planting thick and prickly shrubs which have now been given a chance to flourish (Figure 52), to the satisfaction of the residents. We know from other studies[13,14,16] that residents particularly appreciate attractive planting as part of the general appearance of their estates.

71. Planted areas should in some way be protected from children. They are less likely to be used for incidental play if they are raised above the path level and contain prickly plants (Figure 53). Management must be aware that these areas will require regular maintenance. If necessary, plants, shrubs, trees and earth should be replaced. With these precautions planted areas should flourish.

49

50

49 and **50**   ACORN PLACE
To the detriment of shrubs and plants children counted
the paved and planted areas as one

51

52

51 and **52**   GLOUCESTER STREET
The steep banks were used for climbing and sliding by
the children. To remedy the resulting damage the Council
replanted the slopes with thick planting

53 If prickly plants are used for landscaping as in this play area at Basildon New Town, they are less likely to be damaged

Wild areas

72. Having countryside close at hand did not necessarily mean that children played there frequently. Both Woodhouse and Woodway Lane estates were surrounded by open country. Yet only 4% and 7% of children were seen there. At Sceaux Gardens, built on the site of a hospital, the mature gardens had become overgrown. They were an integral part of the estate and more used, accounting for 12% of the observations; the children could play there and still be close to their homes. For the under-fives and five-to-tens these wild areas were the most popular location after paved and access areas.

54 WOODHOUSE
Open country adjacent to the estate–little used for play

73. Open country should not be regarded as playspace for children under 11 unless it is an integral part of the estate. At Woodway Lane significantly more over-11s than under-11s were seen in the wild areas. For these older children, the wild areas presented an attractive alternative area for play and were the third most popular location. The more active pursuits in these areas included digging.

74. It cannot be assumed that mothers in low-density suburban and rural areas any more than their urban counterparts are going to be willing to let their children, particularly those under 11, out of their sight into the adjacent wild areas. Their worries are the same if for different reasons. Holme and Massie,[3] in comparing the attitudes and habits of mothers and children in Southwark and Stevenage, found that a fifth of the mothers in both areas

were worried about the dangers of their children being molested by strangers. In Southwark they were concerned about people like meths drinkers, and in Stevenage that 'sex maniacs' might be lurking in the nearby bushes and fields. At Woodhouse, some of the mothers complained that the stream on the edge of the estate, which one might have thought an ideal play place, was dirty and unhealthy, and some forbade their children to play there.

55 SCEAUX GARDENS
Wild areas were an integral part of the estate–well used for play

75. It is important when estates are built adjacent to wild areas that designers appreciate that they must provide for children's play both in the design of the whole estate and also in the provision of specific play facilities, just as when they are designing an urban estate. However where wild areas are within the confines of sites they should be retained in their natural state if possible. Where a stream runs through a site it should be seen as a valuable asset and kept clean and maintained.

'Unorthodox areas'

76. 'Unorthodox areas' included tops of walls and railings, garage roofs, trees etc. in fact, any place children were not supposed to be. Only 3% of children were seen in these areas pursuing their 'unorthodox' activities. The only estate on which a disproportionate number of children were seen in 'unorthodox areas' was Gloucester Street. Here a high stone wall bounded the estate; it belonged to the University of Sheffield's Genetics Department and playing 'on the genetics' was very popular with the 11 to 15-year-old boys, a fifth of whose outdoor activities took place there. At Edith Avenue, a popular activity with some of the children, which was coded as 'unorthodox', consisted of making swings from the thick wires supporting saplings.

77. It seems clear that any feature of the site that offers children the opportunity to climb or pursue other activities will be put to use. For example, where garages had flat roofs children climbed on them. It is probably not possible to prevent this, so such roofs should be strong enough to cope with it, and the waterproofing designed to withstand a certain amount of use. It is probable that features of the site will be used by children and designers must consider the effect on the feature or structure itself, on the surrounding spaces, and on people living close by. Where a structure or feature could be used by children without causing any major difficulties it should be designed with their needs in mind.

56 Woodhouse

'Unorthodox areas'

Any feature of the site which enables children to climb or pursue other activities should be strong enough to withstand them

57 Gloucester Street

Grassed areas

78. On average, slightly less than one-tenth of the children were observed playing on grass. This is probably because, unlike hard surfaces such as roads and pavements, grass is suitable for only a small range of activities, particularly after rain. Children are also discouraged from playing on grass if residents feel that this detracts from its appearance. This was certainly so at Gloucester Street, where, on a small estate of 39 houses, the only grassed area was a large communal one in the centre measuring over 5,000 sq ft. Residents without children complained that children damaged the area and spoilt its appearance, and they wanted it fenced in with more shrubs, flowers and seats. Pressure had resulted in the Housing Department putting up a notice forbidding the playing of ball games (Figure 58).

79. On several of the estates there was a definite rule that children were not allowed to play on grass, though whether or not the rule was kept depended largely on the attitude of individual caretakers, who were often prepared to turn a blind eye to children playing on grass. On one estate where this rule applied, a tenth of children were observed on grass. At another, where older children were officially not allowed to play on grassed areas, a fifth of 11–15s' play took place there.

80. As with the planted and wild areas, it was the character of the grassed areas rather than the density or rise of the estate which affected the amount and type of play that took place there. They varied considerably between the different estates. On those where the grass was reasonably flat and large enough for games of football they were popular for play; but less so on those with the same amount of grass but where it was broken down into small areas, or dotted with shrubs and trees or was sloping. For instance at Park Hill, Canada and Warwick there were large areas of uninterrupted grass which were extremely popular for ball games, particularly with boys from 11 to 15. At Park Hill, where almost half of the space was taken up by large grassed areas, almost half of all ball games were played on them, perhaps because the spacing of trees provided suitable goal posts (Figure 59), although there were two hard-surfaced pitches of 5,220 sq ft and 12,740 sq ft on the estate. Consequently the grass became very worn. In contrast, at Woodway Lane, the grassed areas were split up by pedestrian footpaths and so unsuitable for organized ball games. Though the total amount of grass was similar at both Woodway Lane and Canada estates – just over a quarter – only 3% of the 11–15s at Woodway Lane played on it compared with 13% at Canada. However the grassed areas on both estates attracted a tenth of the under-fives, the reason being probably that at Woodway Lane the grass was close to the dwellings and so was included in small children's doorstep play.

81. The highest proportion of play on grass – almost a quarter – was at Fleury Road. As at Woodway Lane, children could play on the grass and still be near home although the paving, also close to home, was more popular.

82. Some estates like Acorn Place and Curnock Street had very little grass and on others the grass was carefully landscaped to prevent excessive use. At Winstanley Road the areas of grass were fairly small, heavily contoured and raised above the level of the walkways within retaining walls (Figure 61). Also, few of the grassed spaces provided through routes, as they were surrounded by dwellings and caretakers discouraged their use.

83. The designer, when considering a grassed area, must decide whether its purpose is for appearance or for children's use. If it is to be largely decorative, friction between tenants is less likely, and management problems will be fewer, if grassed areas are designed and placed so that children will not be inclined to use them. Where it is intended that children should use them they should be large enough to reduce intensity of use, and there should be several points of access to avoid excessive wear and tear in some parts. As they will undoubtedly be used for ball games and other active pursuits they should be sited away from dwellings in order to reduce noise and the possibility of broken windows.

Play on grassed areas

58   GLOUCESTER STREET
The Housing Department put up a notice forbidding ball games following complaints by residents without children who valued the communal grassed area for its appearance only

59   PARK HILL
Grass was well worn particularly where the spacing of trees provided suitable goal posts

60 CANADA
Low railings did not prevent children from playing on the grass

61 WINSTANLEY ROAD
A rolling grassed area, raised above the level of the paving, is less likely to be used for play

3 What the children were doing

84. The way the children used their time outside is shown in Figure 62. But it should be remembered that only broad activity classifications were used. Because it was not possible to define the precise nature of the activities, conclusions about the quality of the children's play have not been attempted.

85. *Where* children played was greatly affected by the layout, density and rise of the estate; *what* they were doing was not (Figure 63). Certainly from interviewing some of them (Chapter III) the limitations they mentioned did not concern the layout of the estates, but those imposed by adult management, like not being able to play ball on the grass at Warwick. The exceptions to this were that on the estates of houses more children were seen running and walking and on bicycles and playing with wheeled toys than on medium and mixed-rise estates. Here, the roads and paths formed a large network linking all parts of the estate, and were thus suitable for those activities. On these estates and at Sceaux Gardens, where a fifth of children were seen with bicycles and wheeled toys (Figure 65), there were better facilities on the ground for storing bicycles and cumbersome wheeled toys. More observations of 'physically inactive' play were recorded on the higher than on the lower-density estates. This was partly due to the prevalence of access areas on these estates. A third of all children sitting, standing or lying down were seen in these areas,

which were not only near to the dwellings, but sheltered from all weathers, providing intimate nooks and crannies suitable for quiet play.

63   What the children were doing, by types of estate

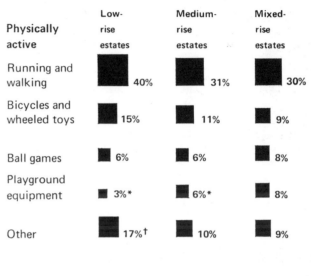

Physically active	Low-rise estates	Medium-rise estates	Mixed-rise estates
Running and walking	40%	31%	30%
Bicycles and wheeled toys	15%	11%	9%
Ball games	6%	6%	8%
Playground equipment	3%*	6%*	8%
Other	17%†	10%	9%

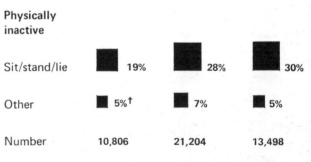

Physically inactive			
Sit/stand/lie	19%	28%	30%
Other	5%†	7%	5%
Number	10,806	21,204	13,498

* Percentages were adjusted to exclude the numbers of children observed on those estates which did not have play equipment.

† Percentages were adjusted to exclude the numbers of children observed on those estates where the activity category was not divided into physically active and inactive.

Therefore totals exceed 100%.

62   What the children were doing

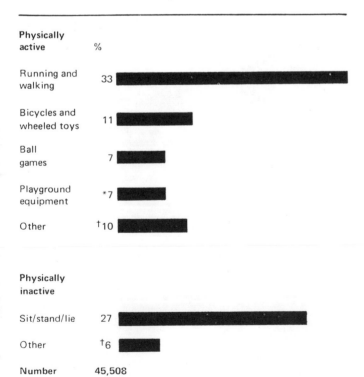

Physically active	%
Running and walking	33
Bicycles and wheeled toys	11
Ball games	7
Playground equipment	*7
Other	†10

Physically inactive	
Sit/stand/lie	27
Other	†6
Number	45,508

* This percentage was adjusted to exclude the numbers of children observed on the estates which did not have play equipment.

† These percentages were adjusted to exclude the numbers of children observed on the estates where the activity categories were not divided into physically active and inactive.

Therefore totals exceed 100%.

86. Most groups of children seen out were of various ages and both sexes, showing that in housing estates the design of play spaces and other areas specifically for one age group may be unwise. Further, children of all ages and both sexes seemed to enjoy the same things with a few differences (Figure 68). Play with wheeled vehicles and toys was enjoyed by small children of both sexes: for the over-11s it was mainly a male pursuit. Few small children of either sex were seen playing ball; as with play with wheeled vehicles, by the time secondary school age had been reached, this was predominantly a male activity. A seventh of the boys but only a twentieth of the girls in this age group were observed playing ball games. Girls of all ages were seen walking

and wandering more than boys, reaching a peak with adolescent girls, where a third of the observations were in this category. Girls spend more time than boys on household chores and possibly many of the girls, in particular 11 to 15-year-olds seen walking, were on errands for their mothers.

87. Many mothers see the main advantage of outdoor play as a release from the restrictions of being indoors. Outside, the children can benefit from fresh air, take part in boisterous games and generally use their immense physical energy in freedom. Two-thirds of the observed activities were classified as 'physically active' and the remaining third as 'physically inactive' or 'quiet' (Figure 62). The peak ages for active play for both sexes were from five to ten, and rather more boys of all ages were 'physically active' than girls. However, by no means all outdoor play was boisterous. A third of the observed activities were classified as 'physically inactive'. These included imaginative games such as playing shops, hospitals, dressing up and playing with their own toys and books.

88. Most of the quiet play was accounted for by children seen sitting, standing or lying down. Such largely unspecific activity is not necessarily aimless and wasteful. No doubt many of the children observed sitting or standing around the estate were resting. It is generally recognised that children especially younger ones often pursue any one activity for a relatively short period and then look around for something else to do. They may also have been quietly watching the life of the estate and learning from the many adult activities going on around them. It is interesting to note that even at the Warwick Estate Adventure Playground, where a wide range of activities was provided, a quarter of the children were observed standing or wandering around, not noticeably engaged in any purposeful pursuit.

89. Designers should therefore remember that not all a child's time out of doors is spent in boisterous play. Children need opportunities for quiet. The provision of sheltered enclosed areas near to home as discussed above, and benches, seats and low walls, can go a long way towards ensuring that the spaces outside the home are sociable meeting places for children.

90. No doubt some of the children were bored and under-stimulated at times. The immediate housing environment cannot meet the total needs of the child and it can reasonably be expected that only good supervised play facilities can provide a sufficient variety of creative activities to supplement the experiences of un-supervised outdoor play. (This is discussed in more detail in paragraphs 182–208.)

65 SCEAUX GARDENS
Bicycles were also popular on this mixed-rise estate where there were good facilities for storing them at ground level

66 Acorn Place

64 GLOUCESTER STREET
Bicycles and wheeled toys were popular on the estates of houses

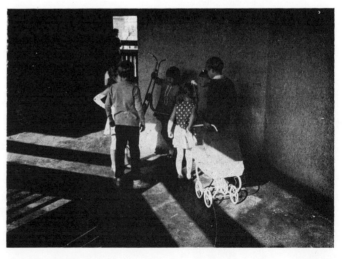

67 Park Hill

66 and **67** Access areas were popular places for quiet play

144

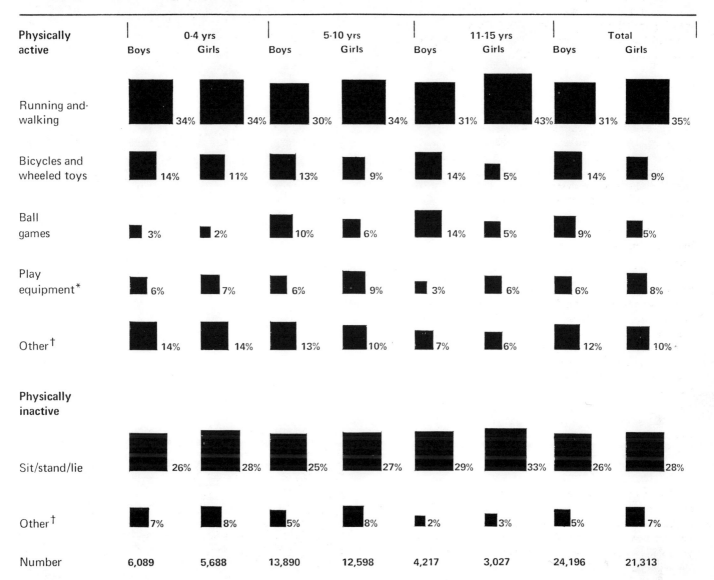

Physically active	0-4 yrs		5-10 yrs		11-15 yrs		Total	
	Boys	Girls	Boys	Girls	Boys	Girls	Boys	Girls
Running and walking	34%	34%	30%	34%	31%	43%	31%	35%
Bicycles and wheeled toys	14%	11%	13%	9%	14%	5%	14%	9%
Ball games	3%	2%	10%	6%	14%	5%	9%	5%
Play equipment*	6%	7%	6%	9%	3%	6%	6%	8%
Other†	14%	14%	13%	10%	7%	6%	12%	10%
Physically inactive								
Sit/stand/lie	26%	28%	25%	27%	29%	33%	26%	28%
Other†	7%	8%	5%	8%	2%	3%	5%	7%
Number	6,089	5,688	13,890	12,598	4,217	3,027	24,196	21,313

* Percentages were adjusted to exclude the numbers of children observed on those estates which did not have play equipment.

† Percentages were adjusted to exclude the numbers of children observed on those estates where the activity category was not divided into physically active and inactive.

Therefore totals exceed 100%.

145

69 Park Hill

70 St Mary's

69 and **70** Most groups of children seen out were of various ages and both sexes

71 Woodway Lane

72 Gloucester Street

71 and **72** Ball games were most popular with school-age children

Playing shops, hospitals, dressing up and playing with toys and books were some of the imaginative activities categorized as 'physically inactive' play

73   St Mary's

74   Woodway Lane

76   Acorn Place

75   Gloucester Street

77   Park Hill

78 St Mary's

79 Warwick Estate Adventure Playground

148

4 Play areas

91. It was one of the recommendations of the Parker Morris Committee[24] that all housing estates at higher densities should provide 20–25 sq ft of play space for every family bedspace. However a random sample of recently completed local authority housing schemes taken ten years later, in 1971,[13] showed somewhat surprisingly that of 94 schemes containing family dwellings only 27 provided space for play. The type of provision varied considerably from one authority to another, both in terms of space and of equipment. This was also true of the 15 estates on which play observations were carried out. The amount of space provided ranged from 0.1 sq ft per bedspace to 15.1 sq ft per bedspace (Figure 80), and the scheme built at the highest density with the least space about buildings had the most play space. The range and type of equipment also varied. There was the more conventional type of playground equipment, both moving and static, including swings and slides. Some estates had architectural equipment individually designed for each estate, and included mazes and stepping stones. (For a complete list of the equipment in each category, see Figure 81.) Ball-games areas were hard-surfaced and enclosed. They did not include large grassed areas subsequently taken over and used by the children for ball games.

92. Less than half of the estates provided more than two of the four types of provision shown in Figure 82 and they were all high-density estates. Of the four estates of houses, Woodway Lane had equipped play spaces, Fleury Road had designated play space but

no equipment (Figure 83), and Woodhouse and Gloucester Street had neither. This perhaps reflected the view that play spaces are less needed at low densities, where families live in houses with gardens.[25]

93. Apart from the adventure playground at Warwick, none of the play areas was supervised either full or part time by trained play leaders, nor did they provide for indoor play. At Winstanley Road and Acorn Place some of the play areas were at deck level or over garages (Figure 84). On all other estates the play provision was at ground level. At Canada the estate was adjacent to

80 Amount of playspace provided, by estate

Estate L = Low rise M = Medium rise Mx = Mixed rise	Sq ft of playspace per child bedspace	Sq ft of playspace per bedspace
Canada (Mx)	30.3 sq ft (5.0 sq ft)*	15.1 sq ft (2.5 sq ft)*
Park Hill (Mx)	30.2 sq ft	14.5 sq ft
St Mary's (M)	28.8 sq ft	12.8 sq ft
Winstanley Rd (Mx)	21.5 sq ft	10.2 sq ft
Edith Ave (M)	21.1 sq ft	9.6 sq ft
Acorn Place (M)	20.0 sq ft	9.8 sq ft
Woodway Lane (L)	19.7 sq ft	11.0 sq ft
Curnock St (M)	16.4 sq ft	8.7 sq ft
The Bonamy (M)	5.2 sq ft	2.7 sq ft
Fleury Rd (L)	2.4 sq ft	1.2 sq ft
Sceaux Gardens (Mx)	0.2 sq ft	0.1 sq ft

*This excludes park adjacent to the estate but included in the observation area.

NB—Although playspaces were provided on Warwick, separate information is not available for only that part of the Estate studied (see Appendix 2, paragraph 30).

81 Types of play equipment provided on the estates

Moving equipment	Static specialist equipment	Static architectural equipment
Swings (including cradle seats)	Tubular climbing frame	Mazes
Merry-go-round	Tubular climbing ladders	Play platforms
Whirling platform	Somersault bars	Concrete climbing frames
Rocking horse	Slides	Climbing blocks
Rocking boat		Climbing columns
See-saws		Wendy houses
Pendulum see-saws		Pyramid
		Tunnels
		Concrete slides
		Forts
		Mushrooms
		Stone seats
		Fairy circle (seats)
		Play shelter
		Play shops
		Play sculptures
		Toddlers' table
		Empty paddling pools
		Empty sand-pits
		Tree trunks
		Wooden play house

82 Types of play equipment, by estate

Estate L = Low rise M = Medium rise Mx = Mixed rise	Moving equipment	Static specialist	Static architectural	Ball-games area
St Mary's (M)	+	+	+	+
Winstanley Rd (Mx)	+	+	+	+
Canada (Mx)	+	+	+ .	+
Acorn Place (Mx)	+	+	−	+
Park Hill (Mx)	−	+	+	+
Warwick (Mx)	−	+	+	+
Curnock St (M)	+	+	+	−
Edith Ave (M)	−	−	+	+
The Bonamy (M)	−	+	+	−
Woodway Lane (L)	−	−	+	−
Sceaux Gardens (Mx)	−	+	−	−
Woodhouse (L)	−	−	−	−
Fleury Rd (L)	−	−	−	−
Royal College St (M)	−	−	−	−
Gloucester St (L)	−	−	−	−

83 FLEURY ROAD
The one play area was unequipped

84 WINSTANLEY ROAD
One of the play areas here was built over parking space

85 CANADA
Play area immediately adjacent to the estate

86 Percentage of children seen in play areas on each estate

Estate	%		No.
Park Hill	18		4,424
St Mary's	18		5,169
Curnock	15		2,846
Canada	13		3,780
Acorn	13		3,732
Winstanley	11		3,562
The Bonamy	8		3,163
Woodway	5		3,215
Sceaux	4		1,732
Edith	3		4,861
Warwick	3		4,773

a small park with a ball-games area and a play area equipped with conventional play equipment. We included this in our observations as it was not cut off from the estate by any roads and was used by the children as part of the estate (Figure 85).

94. At Park Hill and St Mary's the play areas attracted almost a fifth of the observed children (Figure 86). On five estates only a twelfth were seen in play areas, and on the remaining estates the play areas were even less popular. The adventure playground at Warwick, which attracted 12% of the children, was no more popular than the play areas at Canada, Curnock Street and Acorn Place, and less popular than those at Park Hill and St Mary's.

Play equipment

95. Few children were attracted to architectural equipment in play areas, (Figures 87 to 89). On estates where they had a choice of different types of equipment they preferred the conventional (Figure 90). At Park Hill, St Mary's, Acorn Place, Canada and Winstanley Road, far more children were seen in areas with conventional playground equipment, whether static or moving, than in those with specialist architectural shapes. At Woodway Lane, where only architectural equipment had been provided (Figure 89), less than one in 25 of the children was seen in the play areas.

Architectural equipment was unpopular

87 St Mary's

88 Winstanley Road

89 Woodway Lane

151

96. Conventional equipment was most popular with children of all ages. What was popular with one age group was popular with another, though the play areas at Park Hill containing sand-pits and climbing frames were more popular with pre-school children, and ball-games areas with over-tens. Even the over-tens played more on swings and roundabouts etc. than in ball-games areas. Surprisingly the ball-games areas were little used (Figures 96 and 97). Even at Park Hill, which had provided two ball-games areas, including a large area of 12,740 sq ft (the Parker Morris recommendation was 6,600 sq ft[24]), these attracted no more than a tenth of boys over ten. On all other estates ball-games areas were used considerably less by children of all ages.

90 Examples of the relative popularity of various types of play areas

Estates with areas of conventional equipment and ball-games areas and/or architectural equipment

St Mary's

	% total play in these areas
2 conventional areas	13.97
1 ball-games area	0.77
4 architectural areas	3.16
Total play	17.90%

Acorn Place

	% total play in these areas
2 conventional areas	12.68
1 ball-games area	0.38
Total play	13.06%

Canada

	% total play in these areas
1 conventional area	6.83
1 ball-games area	2.57
3 architectural areas	3.83
Total play	13.23%

Winstanley Road

	% total play in these areas
3 conventional areas	8.65
1 ball-games area	1.52
3 architectural areas	0.79
Total play	10.96%

Popular equipment

91 St Mary's

92 St Mary's

93 Canada

94 Winstanley Road

95   Winstanley Road

97. Interviews with children too, revealed that their own choice was for conventional equipment (paragraph 165) even though the children at St Mary's and Warwick were familiar with architectural equipment. Visiting parks and recreation grounds to play with swings and slides or to play ball was what most of the seven to 11s in Paddington and Oldham liked best. The Building Research Station report[7] also showed that when children between six and 11 were asked to write essays on 'Where I like to play' similar items of equipment featured prominently. Though the children's ideal was a large park with all their favourite equipment, this does not mean that they cannot get a considerable amount of enjoyment from even one carefully chosen item. This should be placed where as many children as possible can enjoy its occasional use, for instance, on paths to schools and shops, and where the disturbance to adult and elderly households will be minimal.

98. We are not the first researchers to have discovered that children use conventional playground equipment more than architectural. The Building Research Station research team reported that items more traditionally associated with playgrounds 'consistently attract a high level of usage, even where other less conventional items are available. A number of the architectural items are little used.'[7] And Holme and Massie too found that 'swings, slides and gymnastic items are high on the list and are preferred and used more frequently by children than the fantasy type of equipment, unless these also provide scope for gymnastic activity'.[3]

99. Some people may feel however that there is little educational and developmental advantage in conventional equipment, as children cannot change or manipulate it, and spend very little time using any one item. It is perhaps overlooked that such equipment is an aid to physical development and that young children need opportunities to practice climbing, balancing etc. There seems little point in providing equipment which, while it may be more potentially constructive, is rarely or scarcely used by the children.

154

96 and **97** Ball-games areas were not very popular

96 Edith Avenue

97 Winstanley Road

Cost of play areas

100. Further, in terms of value for money, architectural equipment can prove very wasteful. One play area at Canada, for example, consisting of a concrete maze, cost £2,248* for materials, paving and drainage, and attracted only 2% of the children (Figure 98). Yet at Acorn Place a play area of swings and slides cost £1,320 and attracted 7% of the children (Figure 99). Eleven per cent of the observed children played in the main play area at Oldham with swings, slides and fort, paddling pool and climbing frame, and which cost £6,270 (Figure 100). At Warwick the eight play areas, consisting mainly of concrete structures, cost £24,783 and attracted only 3% of the children (Figures 101 and 102).

---

*The costs quoted are not actual scheme costs, but are a comparable valuation based on prices ruling for average local authority schemes in early 1972. They therefore eliminate the many variables between individual schemes.

99 ACORN PLACE
This area was much cheaper and was better used

98 CANADA
The costly maze was little used

100 ST MARY'S
This area was very well liked by the children

155

101

102

101 and **102**   WARWICK ESTATE   These play areas were unpopular
and expensive

156

101. The popularity of the play areas was therefore not related to their cost. Some of the least expensive play areas were the most successful, and some of the most expensive the least used (Figure 103). For instance, the play areas at St Mary's, with the lowest cost per sq ft, were among the most used. The cost per sq ft of play space ranged from 47p to £1.74.

likely to be provided by older brothers and sisters. Therefore there may be disadvantages in providing play areas which segregate children of different ages.

103 Cost and use of play areas, by estate

Estate	Cost per sq ft* £	Percentage of use %		No.
Winstanley	1.74	11		3,562
Curnock	1.58	15		2,846
Acorn	1.32	13		3,732
Canada	0.95	13		3,780
The Bonamy	0.95	8		3,163
Warwick	0.92	3		4,773
Edith	0.87	3		4,861
Sceaux	0.75	4		1,732
Park Hill	0.74	18		4,424
Woodway	0.50	5		3,215
St Mary's	0.47	18		5,169

*   The costs per sq ft quoted in the table are not actual scheme costs, but are a comparable valuation based on prices ruling for average local authority schemes in early 1972. They therefore eliminate the many variables between individual schemes. They include the cost of: construction; play equipment; seats, litter bins and lighting; enclosing walls, fencing and ballustrading; planting; paving, grassing and turfing; drainage and general excavation.

Amount of play space

102. However, the success of play areas was related to the *amount* of play space provided, proportional to the number of children living on each estate. Park Hill and St Mary's provided the most space for play and these were two of the three estates whose play areas were the most used. On the third estate – Curnock Street – though there was less play space per resident child, there was an above-average amount of conventional equipment. A significant relationship was found between the use of play areas and the number of items of conventional equipment in them. Thus Curnock Street, and to a lesser extent Acorn Place and Winstanley Road, compensated somewhat for their lack of play space by providing, in certain play areas, not only the type of equipment which children enjoyed using but enough of it to attract the children.

Location of play areas

103. Large groups of children were more often seen in play areas than in locations close to the dwellings such as roads, paved and access areas and gardens (Figure 104). It would seem that the well-equipped play areas provided a social centre where children of all ages and of both sexes could meet their friends and play together. Few under-fives were seen accompanied by adults in play areas and any informal supervision of young children was

157

104   Play locations, by size of groups, at Fleury Road, Acorn Place, Park Hill, Sceaux Gardens, Canada and Winstanley Road

Play locations	Children alone	Children in groups of 2-4	Children in groups of 5-10 or more	Children with adults	Total %	No.
Roads, pavements, etc	29%	52%	13%	6%	100	1,734
Paved areas	27%	51%	18%	4%	100	5,018
Grassed areas	13%	51%	35%	1%	100	1,524
Play areas	18%	48%	35%	—	100	2,539
Unorthodox areas	13%	59%	27%	1%	100	393
Access areas within buildings (5 estates)	28%	54%	16%	2%	100	6,398
Private gardens (5 estates)	29%	63%	7%	1%	100	224
Planted areas	15%	55%	28%	2%	100	272
All areas	24%	52%	22%	2%	100	18,102

NB — The 108 children seen in the library at Winstanley Road are excluded because it was impossible to tell which children were in groups.

105 Canada

106 St Mary's

105 and 106 Large groups of children were more often seen in play areas than in other areas close to home

107 EDITH AVENUE
At the time of the observations the sand in the pit had not been renewed for three years

104. There are also disadvantages in providing play areas which are too far from home. 'However good the neighbourhood play facilities are, some provision on an estate, at least for the younger age groups, is essential.'[7] Apart from parental concern about letting children stray too far, during school term at least, with all the competing activities which take place inside the home, the children have little time to travel far to play spaces (paragraph 170). A child's play environment is extremely circumscribed and neighbourhood provision, however near, is no realistic substitute for play areas which children can use casually at any time without relying on adults or older brothers and sisters to take them there.

Siting of play areas within housing estates

105. Not only are play spaces needed on all housing estates but their careful siting within the estate is crucial. Part of the success of the main play area at St Mary's may have been not only that it provided the type of equipment the children enjoyed, but that it was a large centrally-placed area with safe access to the children's homes nearby. Yet though the family dwellings should be adjacent to play spaces, designers should resist the temptation of seeing play areas as a focal point of interest for old people, particularly if their living rooms are immediately adjacent to play areas. Adult and elderly households dislike the noise and disturbance from young children, and the loss of privacy this produces.[13,14,15,16] A successful play area will be a noisy place where all age groups meet, and in the event of conflict between the needs of childless households for peace and the young for noise, it will usually be the children who lose. All too frequently play equipment is removed or locked up after complaints from adults.

Maintenance and management of play areas

106. Some play areas proved white elephants not only because of the type of equipment provided but also because of the lack of maintenance. At St Mary's, sand had originally been put in the 'fairy circle' of stone seats, but as it was not completely enclosed the sand spilled over onto the surrounding paving, creating a constant headache for the caretaker, and a rapidly diminishing supply of sand (Figure 108). The sand has now been completely removed, and the stone circle little used (Figure 109). The brick 'castle' at Woodway Lane for some unknown reason was provided without drainage. This soon became known as 'the mucky pool' and a favourite 'aiming' target for little boys (Figure 110). After complaints from the residents it was filled in and paved over (Figure 111). At Edith Avenue the three sand-pits costing a total

of £2,557 had been filled with sand when the scheme had been first occupied, three years before the time of the observations. Since then the sand had not been renewed (Figure 107). The little sand that remained was in a very poor condition. Less than 1 % of the children played there.

107. It is essential that at the design stage of schemes the architects find out from the people responsible for the maintenance of play equipment – usually the housing manager or local authority engineer – whether maintenance and management of the type of equipment they are hoping to include is feasible or not. Sand-pits and paddling pools give children pleasure, but need daily attention. This can be part of the daily cleaning routine of schemes large enough to have daily caretaking staff to clean and maintain other communal areas. Raking out a sand-pit will take no longer than sweeping the stairs. At Park Hill, for example, the estate caretaker rakes and cleans the sand-pits each day and the sand is changed every six months. Here the sand-pits were well used, particularly by the pre-school children. Experience at St Mary's would suggest that paddling pools, apart from regular maintenance, also require some form of adult supervision. Mothers on this estate found that without supervision the children were getting wet and muddy in cold weather and the smaller ones were at risk of being pushed in by the older ones. It was therefore agreed that the estate caretaker would only fill the pool on exceptionally hot days and at the same time keep an eye on the children. Our observations took place on two such hot days and the pool was in great demand.

108

109

108 and **109** ST MARY'S
The sand-pit at St Mary's used to be well used but because of its design the sand spilled over on to the path to the annoyance of tenants. The sand was therefore removed and the pit paved over

159

108. Most items of conventional playground equipment need occasional oiling and repainting and regularly checking for wear, damage and replacement. None of the housing managers or borough engineers responsible for such equipment on the schemes we studied regarded this as an onerous duty. Play equipment was regarded like any other item of property on the estate for which the local authority was responsible, and cleaned and maintained accordingly. No distinction was made to us about moving and non-moving equipment; responsibility for reporting faulty equipment was in some cases with estate officers, in others with rent collectors, or even tenants. The British Standards Institution recommends that equipment '. . . should be inspected by a responsible representative of the purchaser at weekly intervals' and that '. . . a log book be kept for each item of apparatus and that the person(s) responsible for maintenance should be required to certify, by signing the log book each week, that the equipment is not in need of repair'.[26]

110

111

110 and 111 WOODWAY LANE
The 'castle' was not provided with drainage and soon filled up with stagnant water. It was later filled in and paved over

109. There did not appear to be problems of insuring against injury on different types of play equipment; in most cases equipment was covered by general third-party insurance. Accidents occur wherever children play, though there are those who would say that children suffer more accidents on conventional equipment. Official accident statistics do not reveal how many children are hurt while playing on play equipment. However we can find little evidence from elsewhere that children are more liable to have accidents on conventional equipment. There seems little point in denying children access to what they enjoy using, particularly as it may be the child who is bored through lack of adequate play facilities who is accident-prone.

110. Seats for mothers should be provided in play areas and should regularly be checked for wear and tear along with the equipment. Litter bins will also help to ensure that the play areas are kept tidy. Lavatories, wash basins and drinking fountains should be within a reasonable distance of play areas and should be kept in working order, especially where children have to go up flights of stairs or up in lifts before reaching home. It is a common complaint that lifts are fouled by children using them as lavatories.

Landscaping

111. Play areas need careful landscaping, and attention given to their appearance. The appearance of housing estates is one of the most important factors influencing the residents' overall satisfaction.[13,14,15,16] All too easily play areas can be an eyesore of asphalt. Yet the work of landscape architects such as Mary Mitchell in Birmingham and Blackburn, and Patrick Dawson in Basildon, shows that they can be made attractive, especially if a landscape architect has been involved in their design from the early planning stages of the whole estate. 'It is not his function to be called in at a late stage to titivate the architect's plans with trees and shrubs.'[27]

112. Natural features such as mounds and existing trees should be retained wherever possible and advantage can be taken of surplus soil from excavation of the rest of the estate (Figures 113 and 114). If slides are built into mounds they not only add to the attractiveness of the play area but are, in addition, the safest way of providing them. The large play area at St Mary's and the grassed areas at Winstanley Road are examples of areas where a rolling topography has greatly added to the attractiveness of the estate.

112 ST MARY'S
The pool was only filled on very hot days

Play areas need not be an eyesore of asphalt

113 Basildon New Town

114 Basildon New Town

115 St Mary's

115 and 116 Grass planted very close to equipment becomes badly worn. Slides should be flanked by hard surfacing

116 Gorse Ride, Finchampstead

117

117 and 118 Granite setts and tree trunks have been used in the landscaping of these play areas at Queen's Park Flats, Blackburn

118

119 Gorse Ride, Finchampstead

113. Experience at St Mary's has shown that grass planted very close to equipment will get badly worn (Figure 115). This has been avoided in a later scheme at Gorse Ride, Finchampstead. Hard surfacing such as granite setts can be flanked by grass, thereby avoiding unnecessary acres of flat concrete (Figure 116). Mary Mitchell has enhanced the appearance of play areas by the use of granite setts and tree trunks (Figures 117 and 118). A variety of surfacing materials as used throughout Winstanley Road estate helps to create an attractive environment. Synthetic materials are now available which very often are pleasanter to look at than concrete and have the additional advantages of drying quickly after rain and of being less hard to fall on. If the guide-lines given in paragraph 71 regarding the provision of planted areas are followed, there is no reason why planting should not be provided in play areas.

114. In schemes where there are no facilities for indoor play it is essential that play areas should be sheltered from wind and cold. Such areas are social meeting places and the children have no wish to stand around talking to their friends in exposed open spaces. Mounds and thick planting of evergreens not only look attractive but also act as windshields. Play areas can be sheltered by sinking them below the level of the buildings.

Ages of children using play areas

115. Two-thirds of the children using play areas were between five and ten, and the rest were divided fairly equally between the other age groups. Clearly the range and types of play areas included in our sample did not succeed in attracting large numbers of either the very young or the secondary age children. For pre-school children in particular we must consider what more can be done for their needs, as we know they are not allowed far from their own homes. Few parents seem to have adopted the approach of accompanying their young children themselves. On six of the estates for which this information was available, less than 2% of pre-school children seen in play areas were with adults. On most of the estates more under-fives played on doorstep locations such as access areas than in play areas (Figure 120). Again supervised play facilities may be the answer. These will be discussed in more detail in paragraphs 182–208.

120 Where the 0–4 age groups played on those estates which had play areas

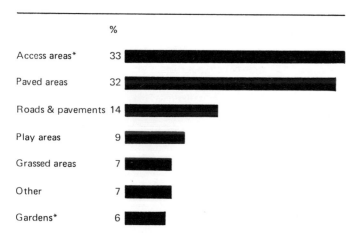

	%
Access areas*	33
Paved areas	32
Roads & pavements	14
Play areas	9
Grassed areas	7
Other	7
Gardens*	6

Number = 8,419

* These percentages were adjusted to exclude the numbers of children observed on the estates which did not have locations in these categories. Therefore the total exceeds 100%.

116. The fact that never more than a fifth of a child's time was spent in play areas shows clearly that the designer's primary concern should be to plan estates with the other four-fifths of a child's outdoor leisure time in mind. Children play everywhere on an estate. It is unrealistic to suppose that play areas will prevent this entirely. However the Building Research Station research[7,8] found that playgrounds did have some effect in attracting children away from roads and access areas, and we too found that where playgrounds were sparse or ill-equipped the under-fives played more on roads than in the play areas. The provision of play space should be seen in terms of adding to the child's enjoyment of his leisure time and his range of experience, providing a place where he can meet his friends, and helping to keep him away from the roads.

Standards for children's play space

117. A recently issued circular laid down standards for the provision of play space in all new local authority schemes.[9] To assist in meeting the extra costs of these standards, local authorities are now eligible for special subsidisable allowances added to the Housing Cost Yardstick which sets the cost limit for a scheme.[28]

118. The new standards differ from the previous recommended standards[25] in that they require play space to be equipped, and to be provided in housing schemes at all densities. In this they are reflecting some of the research findings discussed in this bulletin; namely that play space to be used and enjoyed by children should be equipped with conventional playground items; and that play space is needed at low as well as high densities. In high-density schemes where children have to live off the ground and therefore play outdoors less, it is hoped that play space will attract them outside. At low densities where it was found that children play more on roads and pavements than in gardens, well-equipped play areas can succeed in attracting children away from roads. And at all densities and in all types of schemes, parents express the need for adequate play facilities for their children.

119. The amount of play space laid down in the standards, and the level of the allowances, are based on actual costs incurred on the more popular schemes examined and on the significant relationship between the proportion of children using play areas and the amount of play space provided. The decision to base the amount of play space on child bedspaces rather than all bedspaces in a scheme has resulted from the finding that this more accurately reflects the likely resident child population. At the same time it avoids the overprovision of play space on schemes where there are a large proportion of small dwellings suitable for childless households who are likely to be disturbed by children playing.

5 Adults' attitudes to play

The views of mothers

120. Two-thirds of all the mothers interviewed (paragraph 10) found their children's play either a 'great problem' or 'rather a problem' (Figure 121). There was considerable variation in attitudes within all types of building form, showing that as with other aspects[13,14] the character and success of individual schemes is not necessarily determined by physical factors (Figure 122). However, it did seem that at all densities their children's play was less of a problem for mothers living in houses (Figure 123).*

121 **Attitudes of the different household types to play**

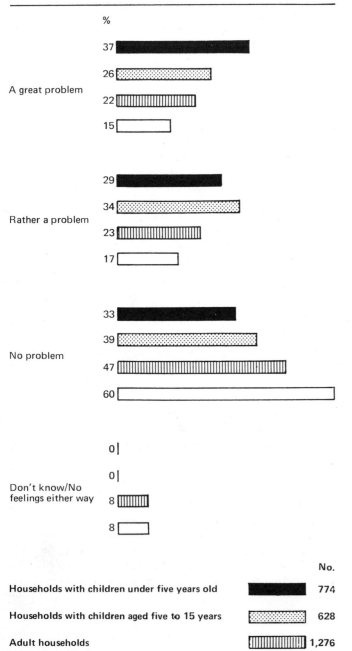

The fact that play was significantly less of a problem for mothers living at lower than at higher densities (Figure 124) was partly due to the prevalence of houses at these lower densities.

121. At densities of over 120 bspa, where it is more difficult to accommodate families in houses, no one type of building form emerged as more satisfactory than any other one, and dwellings on the tenth or higher floors were no more likely to produce problems than those between the first and the tenth. In general multistorey schemes, except those with deck access, produced more problems than schemes with only houses. However, as there were only two schemes in the sample with deck access it would perhaps be rash to conclude that at very high densities mothers will find play less of a problem in deck-access schemes. The only conclusions that can be drawn are that not only do children play out more if they live on the ground, but their mothers too will find their children's play less of a problem.

122. Figure 125 shows the types of play problem experienced by mothers. Overwhelmingly the main cause of complaint was the lack of play facilities near at hand. 'There is nowhere for the children to play' was also a frequent grumble. Two-thirds of the mothers felt that the facilities on or near their own estate were unsatisfactory. When they were asked how things could be improved, far the greatest demand was for more and better play areas near to home (Figure 126). The Building Research Station research showed that until children are about nine or ten a great many of them are not allowed off the estate by themselves.[7,8] Even in Stevenage where many of the areas are traffic-segregated, Holme and Massie found that almost two-fifths of the under-tens were not allowed out alone.[3]

123. However, one should avoid the temptation of concluding that providing play areas on estates would solve all the play problems mothers admit to. Where play facilities had been provided they did not significantly reduce the number of housewives finding play a problem though they were less likely to complain that the facilities were inadequate. In fact a wide range of seemingly relevant variables did not correlate with this issue.†

---

*Many fewer children lived in ground-floor flats than lived in houses or in flats above the ground. Although it did seem that children's play was more of a problem to mothers in ground-floor flats than in houses it is difficult to know if this would have been confirmed in a larger sample.

†The percentages of mothers finding play to be a 'great problem' or 'rather a problem' did not correlate with: (a) whether estate had play areas or not; (b) whether conventional equipment had been provided or not; (c) whether play provision was regarded as being satisfactory or not; (d) whether children were thought to be safe from traffic or not; (e) whether housewives suffered from 'nerves' in the last month or not; (f) whether housewives suffered from undue irritability or not.

	%		No.
HOUSES AT BELOW 70 b s p a			
Sunningdale, Delves Lane	19		21
Phase 2. Mannersway/Derek Gardens	22		9
Brennard Close, Brennard Road, Warley	43		7
Hillview, Station Lane, Greatham	44		18
Sherbourne Ct; Sherbourne Rd. Site; Sebastopol	50		6
Lockeridge Rd. Station Rd., Bere Alston	57		14
Langley Rise, Section 4	68		25
Torlands Estate, Green Lane, Tavistock	75		12
Wissett Rd. Housing Estate	76		8
Fleury Road	78		28
Leen Valley, Phase 2	84		13
HOUSES AT 70 b s p a AND ABOVE			
Tanhouse	35		106
Houghton Green Central Area	43		51
Capehill	50		78
Milton Road	53		30
East Road	54		26
Harts Lane Phase II	60		20
St. Mary's	66		73
West Smethwick	75		96
East Dulwich Grove	78		23
Low Stakesby Estate (Rosedale Cl. & Fountains Cl.)	78		40
Acorn Place	84		33
DECK ACCESS			
Chalkhill Redevelopment Phase I	57		43
Park Hill	65		82
BALCONY ACCESS			
Winstanley Road	43		66
Lefevre Road Stage II	74		34
Sceaux Gardens	84		18
Acorn Place	86		43
WALK-UP BLOCKS			
St. Mary's	41		29
Bakewell Street, Coalville	67		5
Canada	69		16
Howard St., Sedgley Rd. West	78		14
Baker St., St. George's Scheme (Cheviot Cl.)	83		11
'Canterbury' — Lewisham Park Housing	84		6
CORRIDOR BLOCKS			
Oppidans Road Development	66		12
Winstanley Road	72		42
Sceaux Gardens	81		38
POINT BLOCKS			
Civic Centre, Phase II (Galton Tower, Broad St.)	58		7
Winstanley Road	71		21
Canada	73		51
Northwood Tower, 71 Marlowe Rd., Walthamstow	78		9
Gough Road, Lee Bank	93		17
Grays South Devt. Phase I. The Echoes Site	95		23
Castle Vale Shopping Centre	100		9

123 Percentage of mothers finding play a problem, by building types

Building types	Number of estates	%		No.
Low-density houses	11	56		161
High-density houses	11	61		576
Deck access	2	61		125
Balcony access with lifts	4	72		161
Walk-up blocks	6	72		81
Corridor blocks	3	73		92
Point blocks	7	81		137

124. One possible explanation is that mothers were recording more than 'play' problems in answer to this question, and reflecting instead a whole range of difficulties of bringing up young children; problems which the provision of play facilities alone do not necessarily resolve. For instance, significantly more mothers with at least one child under five than with older children were concerned that play was a 'great problem' (Figure 121). This perhaps reflects the greater strain of looking after pre-school children generally, and the need to keep a more watchful eye on them when playing.

124 Percentage of mothers finding play a problem, by density

Density in bed-spaces per acre	Number of estates	%		No.
0– 40	2	32		39
41– 80	12	63		236
81–120	8	58		373
121–160	8	76		441
161–200	6	71		211
200+	4	92		56

125. Some of these anxieties could no doubt have been partly relieved by supervised play facilities (paragraphs 182–208). Although few mothers actually mentioned the need for supervision, this was implicit in some of the suggestions made to improve the situation (Figure 126). Sand-pits, sports fields, youth clubs etc., all need people to organise and maintain them. The presence of responsible adults would no doubt have helped to reassure the two-fifths of the mothers who felt their children were not safe from traffic when they played outside.

126. Besides traffic worries, researchers have also found that parents expressed anxiety about rough play and bullying, accidents and molestation.[3,7] It is likely that these problems too would have been much alleviated by adult supervision.

The views of households without children

127. Although children's play was considerably more of a problem for residents who had children of their own, it is as well to remember that even for those without young children, play creates difficulties. Almost half the households without children under 16 (adult households) and a third of those where more than half of the family were over pensionable age (elderly households) felt children's play was a 'great problem' or 'rather a problem' (Figure 121).

128. On the whole the households without young children made the same types of complaint as the mothers. The lack of adequate facilities near at hand was the main grievance (Figure 125). This was partly a belief particularly held by elderly residents that with enough play areas of their own the children would be less nuisance. Two-fifths of the complaints of the elderly and a third of those of the adult households referred to the noise nuisance or damage caused by children when playing, especially when they played too close to the dwellings. Although some felt it was up to the parents or other adults to keep a closer and stricter watch over their offspring, many felt that better play facilities would have gone a long way to alleviate these problems (Figure 126). It is essential that in providing play areas they are not sited too close to the dwellings of households without children, otherwise the problems of noise will merely be aggravated (paragraph 105). As a high priority childless households demand privacy and quiet.[13,14,15,16]

129. Like those with children, adult and elderly households found children's play more difficult to cope with where they lived on schemes built at very high rather than at low and medium densities. Yet as with all household types, there were considerable variations between different schemes built at the same density. The only clear pattern to emerge was that houses at densities below 40 bspa produced by far the fewest problems, and that houses built at high densities produced as many problems as other building forms. This would indicate that at high densities, unlike the mothers' problems many of which could be solved merely by living on or near the ground, the problems of households without children could actually be increased by living on the ground if this meant their living in close proximity to families with children. For those households, living in a multi-storey building could be preferable if it increased their chances of peace and quiet.

Reasons given	Families with young children	Adult households	Elderly households
Not enough play facilities in area/ nowhere to play	75%	56%	56%
Children not safe from traffic	16%	10%	5%
Play areas not safe	9%	2%	3%
Children play too close to dwelling/ are a nuisance	8%	33%	41%
No supervision	5%	1%	1%
Older people complain	5%	2%	2%
Differences in age groups/nowhere for particular age group to play	5%	4%	2%
Difficult to keep child in sight	3%	1%	1%
Other	2%	14%	13%
Number	329	536	318

NB — Percentages do not add up to 100% as mothers could give several reasons for play problem.

Suggestions made	Families with young children	Adult households	Elderly households
Better play areas on estate	60%	28%	18%
Swings, roundabout, slides, sandpit	30%	4%	4%
Should be separate play areas for younger children	8%	—	—
Facilities for ball games needed	8%	10%	10%
Parks needed	8%	—	—
Supervision needed	4%	14%	10%
Recreation centre/a nursery/play centre/ youth club/adventure playground needed	2%	3%	5%
Other	13%	8%	11%
Number	192	273	133

NB — Percentages do not add up to 100% as mothers could give several suggestions for alleviating the play problem.

b - Play in Older Areas

127 The steep cobbled roads and pavements in the older area of
Oldham made very active games, particularly with wheeled
toys, difficult for young children

The need to create play space

130. In providing for children's play in new housing areas the
main need is for architects, planners and housing managers to
plan for the requirements of the children at the design stage of
new schemes and new communities. In this way it is possible
from the outset to allocate resources and the right amount of
space in the most suitable places.

131. In older areas making the right provision may be more
difficult. Many of the older residential areas with 19th-century
legacies of congestion and overcrowding and high population
densities have the least public recreational space and specifically
of play space per head of the population. As Holme and Massie
showed,[3] Southwark has 1.5 acres of public recreational space
per thousand of the population, compared with 9.8 acres in
Gloucester. In Bradford there are 2,300 children to every play
space compared to 400 in Stevenage.

132. In renewal of older areas, ten or even 15 years may seem to
a planner to be quite a short period. Improvements to the existing
environment, such as new play space, may not seem worthwhile,
but for a child growing up even five years is important. As Arvid
Bengtsson, the Swedish playground expert, remarks, 'If we cannot give the child all that it has the right to claim, we must at
least give it all we can reasonably provide. The possible future
redevelopment of old towns by no means relieves us of responsibility for the present. There are many possibilities if we look
around for inspiration! It is initiative, not opportunity, that is
sometimes lacking.'[29]

133. Though the overall proportion and pattern of physically
active play for five to tens and 11 to 15s in the older area of
Oldham was no different from that on the new housing estates,
significantly fewer pre-school children were engaged in it (Figure
128). No doubt a contributing reason for this was that the steep
cobbled roads and pavements made very active games, particularly with wheeled toys, difficult for young children (Figure
127). It must not be forgotten that all children irrespective of
where they live need sufficient space for ball games, play with
wheeled toys and other energetic pursuits. So there is an urgent
need to create new open spaces for play and recreation and to
make better use of existing ones in all older areas that are short
of such spaces. Some suggestions are given below.

128 **Pre-school children seen out who were engaged in physically
active play**

	%		No.
Low-rise estates	72		4,332
Medium-rise estates	61		4,694
Mixed-rise estates	63		2,751
Older area, Oldham	53		1,760

169

The older area of Oldham

129

130

129 and **130**   The active play of the school-age children was similar
to that on the new estates but fewer pre-school children
were engaged in it

170

Waste and derelict land

134. In many of the inner areas of large cities, demolition, road schemes and industrial decay, have created large areas of waste ground. The older area of Oldham, less than a mile square, had over 50 derelict houses, and in one corner whole blocks had been cleared away. Almost a tenth of all observed play activities took place on waste areas (Figure 131), as many as in gardens and second in importance to roads.

131 Where the children played in the older area of Oldham

	%	
Roads & pavements	54	
Gardens	9	
Waste & derelict land	9	
Paved areas	7	
Access areas	7	
Wild areas	5	
Play areas	3	
Unorthodox areas	3	
Grassed areas	0	
Other areas	3	
Total	100%	
Number	362	

redevelopment[30] and one such area is now used as a football pitch. This method has cut the costs from the usual £500 per acre for such work to £60 per acre, thus removing the often-heard argument that high costs on temporary sites would not be warranted.

136. For young children, particularly the under-fives, a small playground with, say, a swing and a slide and seats for the mothers could well be located in a space left by the clearance of only one or two houses at the end of the terrace. In Exeter this has been done in Newtown improvement area, and is proving very successful (Figures 134 and 135). Now with the new Slum Clearance Subsidy[31] there is a greater incentive for local authorities to make use of their cleared slum sites for such schemes.

137. On less temporary sites, the planners should be prepared to think ambitiously of their potential. In Stoke-on-Trent for example, spoil tips, clay workings and abandoned railways have been converted to recreational uses, including a forest park, playing fields and a sports stadium.[32] In the Lower Swansea Valley a ten-acre derelict site is being used among other things for a covered games stadium and an ice rink.[33] More ambitiously still the Lee Valley Regional Park is slowly transforming huge areas to recreational uses in which playgrounds and playing fields are prominently featured.[34]

138. Not all long-term reclamation schemes are dependent on such far-reaching planning decisions and large sites. In Lancashire the Pretoria Tip in Atherton was treated by planting trees in balls of soil, and is now widely used for children's play and for walking. Moreover, landscape architects like Mary Mitchell have shown how with imagination and foresight fairly small decaying landscapes can be transformed into pleasant recreational areas well-used by both children and adults (Figures 136 and 137). For instance at Nuneaton a silted muddy pond has become a large fishing lake and a dominant feature of Camp Hill playground.[35]

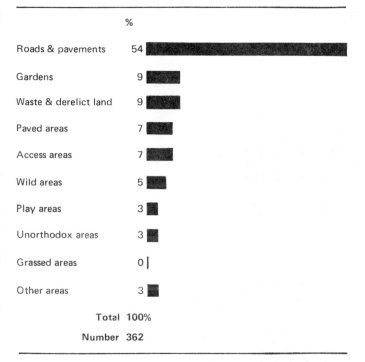

132

133

132 and **133** At Oldham derelict houses and sites were used for play

135. As those areas are therefore likely to be used by children, they should be made varied and interesting, and free from obvious dangers. They should be made as attractive as possible to both children and adults. Even sites which are only going to be vacant for a short time can be made less of an eyesore by removing derelict houses, rubbish etc. and by grassing wherever possible. At Liverpool University the Botany Department has developed techniques for carrying out low cost grassing of sites awaiting

134

135

134 and 135   As part of an area improvement scheme at Newtown,
Exeter, a small derelict site has been made into a
playground

136

137

136 and **137**   A derelict site at St Aidan's, Blackburn, transformed into a children's playground

The older area of Oldham
Over half of all play took place on roads and pavements

138

139

Play streets

139. Totally* or partly† restricting traffic through pressure from residents or the efforts of community workers and planners is becoming more common as a means of creating play space that is at least safe from traffic. Already it is usual for children to play in such areas. In the older area of Oldham, over half of all activities took place on roads and pavements (Figures 138, 139, 143 and 144) – even more than the proportion on roads on the estates of new houses (Figure 142). They were by far the most important location for nearly all activities. As with the new areas of housing, the roads and pavements with the doorstep were the places for play closest to the dwellings. When adults were observed with children it was most likely to be on the doorstep.

140. Play streets should only be considered where there is no through traffic as it is almost impossible to prevent vehicles from taking short cuts while the children are playing. Care also needs to be taken that in diverting traffic away from the play street other areas and other children are not exposed to more traffic. A run-down area with low car ownership such as the area we studied in Oldham, where the roads were often steep and cobbled, is unlikely to expose children to many dangers. Traffic in Oldham was on the whole slight and slow-moving.

141

*The Town and Country Planning Act 1971[36] gives powers for closure of streets to vehicular traffic.
†In the Road Traffic Regulation Act 1967[37] (as amended by Part IX of Transport Act 1968[38]), highway authorities are empowered to make an order prohibiting vehicles from using a road to be used as a children's playground.

142 **Percentage of children seen playing on roads and pavements**

	%		No.
Older area, Oldham	54		6,953
Low-rise estates	39		10,806
Medium-rise estates	11		21,206
Mixed-rise estates	9		13,498

140

140 and **141**   A play street in Notting Hill, London – part of a summer play scheme

141. Moreover, as traffic is diverted from a particular road so will more children be attracted there. In the older area of Oldham two-thirds of all ball games took place in the road, and even a few extra children playing football in a narrow street of terraced houses make a good deal of noise. Experience from four general improvement areas has shown that, though families with young children may support proposals for new play areas, many residents are likely to oppose them unless they can feel there will not be too much noise and disturbance.[39] Play streets should only be considered where there are few adult and elderly families living in them.

143

144

143 and **144**   The older area of Oldham. Cobbled roads and little traffic

Dual use of school facilities

142. Since the war the idea of the Village College, which was first developed in the 1940's by Henry Morris, Cambridgeshire Director of Education, has been taken up by local authorities in a variety of ways. The common aim has been to make school facilities available to the community out of school hours. In addition, in recent years local education authorities have been encouraged when embarking on new educational building schemes to pool capital resources with other local authorities and voluntary organisations so as to provide comprehensive recreational facilities, such as sports centres and swimming pools.[40]

143. Because of their size secondary schools are normally the centres for such developments, but many successful schemes have been based on primary schools.[41]

144. It is not only in planning new schools that these ideas are feasible. Making existing school facilities such as playgrounds and playing fields more readily available, where this can be done under proper supervision and without excessive wear and tear of pitches, would go a long way towards filling the gaps in the neighbourhood provision of recreational facilities.

145. It is not only the outdoor space belonging to schools which should make a valuable contribution. As shown in paragraph 192 indoor space for play is badly needed by children of all ages. The Inner London Education Authority for example, has for many years used its schools for youth clubs, holiday centres and after-school play centres. On the Warwick Estate, the ILEA ran a play centre and junior club in one of the primary schools every after-noon and evening after school (paragraphs 176 and 177). In spite of operating in cramped Dickensian conditions, these play schemes allowed a wide range of activities well appreciated by the children we interviewed. Of children between seven and 11 who attended the play centre, most lived nearby or actually attended the school in which it was held.

146. One of the reasons that so many children did not go to the play centre was that they did not know about it. This was especially so for children who did not live on the estate or attend the school. Unless *all* schools in an area are going to make out-of-hours provision for play, those that do should publicise this as much as they can, perhaps by circulating to all the other schools in the neighbourhood the range of facilities available and the hours of opening. At present ILEA leaves it to the schools concerned to publicise their play centres and supplies head teachers with lists of current schemes. But the authority is continually reviewing its policy on publicity.

Public parks and recreation grounds

147. From the children interviewed, visiting parks and recreation grounds was a favourite occupation. Most of them appreciated such facilities as play equipment, boating lakes and ball-game areas in parks. A recent survey of the use of open spaces in London indeed showed that young children are frequent visitors to parks.[42] Much can be done to make parks and recreation grounds more attractive to children and to make better use of the space.

148. Lady Allen, in describing the role of the Play Parks run by the Greater London Council (see also Appendix III), said they were a 'means of extending play opportunities into the hitherto "sacred land" of the public parks'.[43] In the local park about a quarter of a mile from Gloucester Street the children were allowed to play on the grass on Whit Mondays only! Without doubt there are many parks which could spare a corner away from the flower beds and the sitting-out areas to be used as play areas, whether they are used to provide conventionally equipped playgrounds or to echo the success of the Play Parks in widening the range of play activities.

149. Alexandra Park in Oldham, about which the children spoke with such enthusiasm, is a good example of how in a park of modest size and amenities the Council has gone out of its way to cater for the needs of young children (Figures 145 to 150). As Figure 148 shows, the paddling pool is much used in hot weather. There is a boating and fishing lake, a small zoo and a wide range of conventional equipment throughout the park.

Alexandra Park, Oldham

145

146

147

148

149

150

The Emslie Horniman Pleasance Recreation Ground
Here there was play equipment for the younger children and space for the older ones to play ball, as well as a pleasant place for adults to sit

151

150. The observations at the Emslie Horniman Pleasance Recreation Ground in Kensal Town, at that time run by the Greater London Council, showed how even on a small site (3.4 acres) a valuable amenity for the area can be provided. On the nine days during which observations took place an average of about 300 children attended the recreation ground each day. The ornamental lily pond and a planted sitting-out area provided an attraction for the mothers. A third of all pre-school-age children seen in the recreation ground were with adults compared with only a twentieth on the new housing estates. In a rather depressing area of high-density housing estates, slum dwellings and acres of waste ground cleared for redevelopment, this small recreation ground provided play equipment for the younger children and space for the older ones to play ball as well as a pleasant place for adults to sit (Figures 151, 153 and 154).

151. During part of the observation period a play scheme was organised at the recreation ground. On average there were 11 or 12 voluntary helpers a day, who organised a wide variety of activities. Although the supervised play scheme did not succeed in attracting significantly more children to the recreation ground, it did disperse the children (Figure 152). A quarter of the supervised activities took place on a previously unused area of waste ground (Figures 155 and 156). After the play scheme finished it again became unused.

152. Where there is a scarcity of play space, it may be worth the Council considering the cost of providing permanent, salaried playleaders to make better use of existing sites in areas where it is virtually impossible to create more play space.

152   Where the children played in the Emslie Horniman Pleasance Recreation Ground

Locations	Percentage before supervision	Percentage during supervision	Percentage after supervision
Play equipment	42%	22%	28%
Grass	28%	16%	39%
Pond area	8%	15%	10%
Waste areas	3%	27%	2%
Gravel area	13%	6%	11%
Shelters	2%	11%	3%
Paths	3%	1%	3%
Hard surface	1%	2%	3%
Walls, railings, fences	—	—	1%
Total	100%	100%	100%
Number	682	746	673

178

153

154

155

156

155 and **156** Waste ground next to the Emslie Horniman Pleasance Recreation Ground was successfully used for a play scheme

Space under motorways

153. As part of the Notting Hill Summer Play Project, play schemes have been set up in space under the Westway Motorway every summer since 1968 (Figures 157 to 159). These have been very successful, and have provided in one of the most congested areas of North Kensington large areas of safe play space suitable for play in all weathers. The schemes have been so successful that in 1971 an adventure playground was set up permanently beneath part of the motorway.

154. This relied on adult supervision for its success and showed that ingenious ways can be found of using all available areas for children's play needs. In the absence of the ideal, children will enjoy and put to good use second-best alternatives.

Safe pedestrian access to play space

155. There is no doubt that many existing playgrounds could be more used if safe pedestrian access was provided across major roads. The location of playgrounds, an inheritance maybe from Victorian times, may now bear little relation to new building and new roads, and the present child population may find it extremely difficult to get to the play spaces.

156. Not only do children make most use of playgrounds within a very short distance from home,[3] but they are most likely to visit them if they are not cut off by busy roads and insufficient pedestrian crossings. A study of an adventure playground in Stevenage showed that children who did not have to cross busy roads came from further afield to visit it.[44] This is confirmed by our own findings of children attending the Warwick Estate Adventure Playground. Children, particularly small ones, generally cross major roads with parents,[3] yet only two-fifths of children visiting playgrounds are actually accompanied by adults. It seems highly probable that there are many who never or rarely use playgrounds or recreational play spaces if they are cut off by major roads.

The Housing Act 1969 and the Urban Aid Programme

157. The suggestions made here for creating more recreational space for children's play have represented measures of environmental improvement, however small, in areas of existing housing. The Housing Act 1969[45] and the Urban Aid Programme[46] are two examples of government measures for aiding such improvements.

158. The Housing Act 1969 provides for improvements carried out in a general improvement area to qualify for grants from central government. Residents are encouraged to put forward their own priorities for improvements which can then be incorporated into the area proposals. Already it is becoming clear that in some areas improving facilities for children's play has been recognised as a priority. For example, in the Woodland Walk and Tyler Street Improvement Area in Greenwich an adventure playground was one of the main proposals put forward by the Residents' Association. The play area at Exeter Newtown was also added to the scheme as a result of a survey of residents' attitudes to environmental proposals which showed that many residents considered additional play space was needed.

159. The Urban Aid Programme, set up under the Local Government Grants (Social Need) Act 1969,[47] aims to encourage additional expenditure by local authorities on education, health and welfare services in areas of special social needs; Exchequer grant at a rate of 75% is paid on approved schemes. The scope of the Programme is very wide; so far as children's play facilities are

The Notting Hill Summer Project
This play scheme under the Westway Motorway was originally run during school holidays. It has proved to be so successful that it now operates all year round

157

158

159

concerned it includes, for example, grants to voluntary play groups and adventure playgrounds, including staff and advisers; the provision or extension of playgrounds and open spaces; and grants to holiday play schemes of the kind mentioned in paragraph 204 below. It is interesting to see that money available under the Urban Programme is being spent on trying to correct, through play, some of the disadvantages in which some children are placed by virtue of their social and physical surroundings.

160. However, the demand and need for improved play facilities is by no means confined to general improvement and deprived areas, where residents and councils already think in terms of improving the environment and attempting to make-good areas of physical and social deprivation. In recent research concerned with a Family Advice Service Centre on a housing estate built in 1939, one of the problems about which tenants generally were most vociferous was lack of play space.[48] But for the presence of the social worker, the discontent would not have been translated into a complaint to the Council nor into subsequent practical action. There must be many such areas, not identified as problem areas, where local authorities might think of means of creating more open spaces for children in some of the ways outlined earlier. As so much of children's play is spontaneous, short-term, and takes place near to home, improvements for play should be looked at street by street.

C – The Children's Choices

160 **What the children in Paddington and Oldham liked about where they lived**

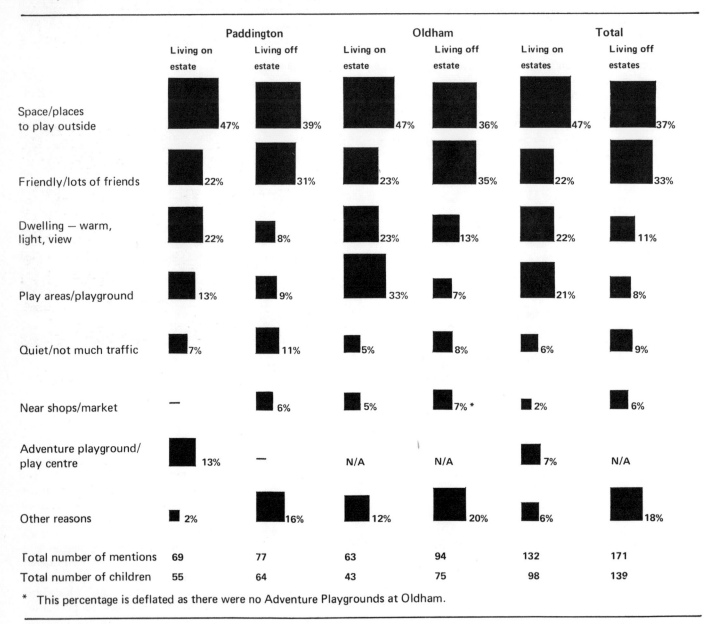

	Paddington		Oldham		Total	
	Living on estate	Living off estate	Living on estate	Living off estate	Living on estates	Living off estates
Space/places to play outside	47%	39%	47%	36%	47%	37%
Friendly/lots of friends	22%	31%	23%	35%	22%	33%
Dwelling — warm, light, view	22%	8%	23%	13%	22%	11%
Play areas/playground	13%	9%	33%	7%	21%	8%
Quiet/not much traffic	7%	11%	5%	8%	6%	9%
Near shops/market	—	6%	5%	7% *	2%	6%
Adventure playground/ play centre	13%	—	N/A	N/A	7%	N/A
Other reasons	2%	16%	12%	20%	6%	18%
Total number of mentions	69	77	63	94	132	171
Total number of children	55	64	43	75	98	139

* This percentage is deflated as there were no Adventure Playgrounds at Oldham.

Reasons for interviewing children

161. As adults we make decisions for children for the good of their health, education or recreation. This does not always mean that these decisions reflect the children's own desires or that they will like or appreciate our decisions. This is largely unavoidable, but if children are to get the most out of their play some attempt should be made to find out what they want.

162. One way of doing this is by watching children at play since this tells what children do and where, as opposed to what their parents think or say they do. But observing children can only tell us what children are actually doing within a limited geographical area. It tells us nothing about why they are playing there, or their preferences. So we decided to interview a sample of children in two of the observation areas – Oldham and Paddington. These areas were chosen for two reasons. First, in both of them, within the catchment areas of the local schools there were both new local authority estates and slum dwellings awaiting clearance and renewal. We hoped to see whether the play habits and expectations of children living in the slum dwellings were any different from those of children living on the new estates where provision was made for safe play; and also whether the children from slum dwellings made use of the new estates for play. Secondly, we wished to see what use the Paddington school children made of some of the supervised facilities available on the Warwick Estate – the adventure playground and the play centre – and to ask what they thought of them.

163. One hundred and thirty children from Oldham and 125 from Paddington between seven and 11 were selected at random from three primary schools in the areas immediately surrounding the estates. Each child was interviewed separately and in confidence, the interviewer using a prepared questionnaire. Response to all questions was high; even the youngest children answered fully. There was a high level of consistency in all that the children said, the reliability of which was backed by the observation data. There was also a high degree of comparability in the children's responses in the two areas, which suggests that the findings are fairly generally applicable to other children of the same age, living in similar social and physical environments.

161 Oldham

162 Paddington

161 and **162** The children were critical of poor housing conditions

The children's preferences

164. One of the interesting points to emerge from the interview was that young children care as much about their surroundings as adults. A fifth of the Oldham school children and two-fifths of those in Paddington, though they generally liked living where they did, qualified their answers by mentioning things they disliked. Poor housing, and living on busy roads, are just as likely to be noticed by children as adults, and like adults they too will appreciate modern homes, quiet streets and friendly neighbours. Play facilities were mentioned spontaneously by just under half of the Paddington school children and just over two-fifths at Oldham as something they liked about where they lived (Figure 160).

165. In both areas, significantly more children mentioned facilities and places for play as a reason for satisfaction if they lived on the new estate than if they lived in an older housing area. Play areas were specifically mentioned by a third of the children living on the St Mary's estate, which confirms our earlier findings that play areas with conventional equipment are popular with children (Figure 163). The play areas on Warwick Estate, though plentiful, were mainly equipped with static concrete structures, and only a tenth of the children thought they deserved a special mention (Figure 164). Their preferences were further revealed in answers to questions about their 'really favourite place to go' and favourite games. Going to the parks and playing with the swings and slides or playing ball were the clear favourites in both

areas, representing about half of the stated favourites. For children living on the St Mary's estate the largest play area took over to a great extent the role of the local parks as it had much the same sort of equipment and was referred to by the children as playing in the 'park' (Figure 167). The only activity which the main park provided and the estate did not and which the children much enjoyed was boating on the lake. Ball games were a favourite activity, particularly football. These were well catered for on the Warwick Estate, and at Oldham, on 'The Edge' a large area of waste ground. Children also played ball on a works playing field on 'The Edge' which was meant to be out-of-bounds (Figure 170). However, for children living in Paddington and not on the Warwick Estate playing ball mainly took place in the local parks, such as Kensington Gardens and the Paddington Recreation Gardens, though the children freely admitted to playing ball 'round the streets'.

166. The children who played on Oldham Edge seemed to have had more scope for imaginative activities than the other children. Playing there represented a measure of freedom not experienced in other places; 'up on the Edge nobody tells us off – plenty of places to play'. Although such places are not round every corner there must be many areas which if cleared, grassed and made safe would provide for the children the same sort of unrestricted environment as Oldham Edge for physical, vigorous play and giving rein to the imagination.

163 ST MARY'S
The conventional equipment here was well appreciated by the children

164 WARWICK
Few children thought the static concrete structures deserved special mention

184

165 **166**

165 and 166 ALEXANDRA PARK, OLDHAM

The children's favourite activities were going to parks to play with swings and slides or to play ball games

167 ST MARY'S

The children referred to the main play area here as 'The Park'

168   ALEXANDRA PARK, OLDHAM
Boating on the lake was particularly enjoyed by the children

169   WARWICK
A conventional ball-games area

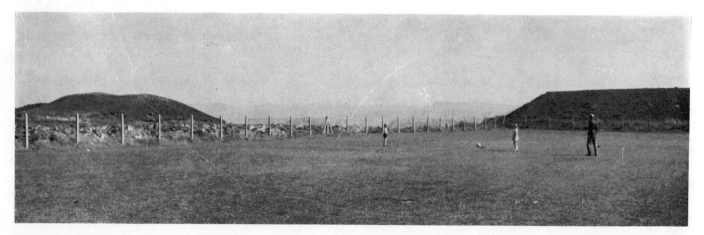

170   OLDHAM EDGE
A works playing field was used for ball games

171 PADDINGTON
The children here freely admitted to playing ball 'round the streets'

167. A quarter of the children interviewed in Paddington and a seventh in Oldham mentioned traditional games like tig and hide-and-seek which could be and were played anywhere out of doors. Interesting variations were noted; for instance, in Paddington a game commonly known as follow-my-leader was called 'run outs'. This less usual version involved following the leader for a bus ride, and running through large department stores in the West End grabbing items from the counters along the way. The Opies[49] observe that after a certain age children may be reluctant to admit that they like playing games. Only in one or two instances was this the case with the children interviewed. Up to the age of 11 at least, most children spent a good proportion of their time in traditional games handed down from generation to generation and they spoke with enthusiasm of such things as 'in and out of the dusty bluebells', 'pom poms' and 'ping pong poison'.

After-school activities

168. To get some idea of what the children were doing when they were not outside, and what proportion of their time was spent indoors, they were asked what they normally did when they came home from school, what they had done the night before and what they would do that particular evening. No mention was made of play specifically, in order to learn as much as possible about the child's total activities.

169. In both areas most children spent their time after school playing, but some children spent time on household chores. Other studies confirm this and indicate that this increases with age, particularly for girls.[3,7,8,50] A fifth of the Oldham children and a quarter of the Paddington ones mentioned some task like looking after the baby or getting the tea which had to be done apart from playing. A very few children in each area did not mention any play activities at all but had a hard evening routine of getting the tea, looking after brothers and sisters and cleaning the house. It is interesting to note, and this is discussed in paragraphs 178–181, that all of these six children came from troubled homes and their head teachers described them as being from 'problem families'.

172

173
172 and **173** OLDHAM EDGE
Children enjoyed the freedom of roaming 'The Edge'

187

170. Although the interviewing took place in November, half of the children in Oldham and a quarter in Paddington, where it snowed during the interviewing period, played outdoors for some of the time. It is unlikely that these outdoor activities such as tig, hide-and-seek and ball games took place far from home, sandwiched as they were between the few hours remaining between coming home from school, having tea, going to bed and indoor activities which took up a greater proportion of the children's time. In fact one can probably assume that on weekdays at least, when children are not observed outside, they are indoors rather than outdoors further away.

171. The Building Research Station study[7] found that, even during the summer holidays, children frequently mentioned indoor pursuits as the way their time was spent 'yesterday'; and in Holme and Massie's study[3] of children's activities in Southwark and Stevenage, seven of the eight activities engaged in by more than half of the children were basically indoor and non-participant ones; these were:

WATCHING TELEVISION   LISTENING TO THE RADIO
LOOKING AT COMICS   DRAWING WITH A PENCIL
READING BOOKS   READING NEWSPAPERS
READING JOKES OR FUNNY SAYINGS

As with the children in these studies, watching television was a major pastime with the Paddington and Oldham children and mentioned by over four-fifths of them.

172. The pattern which emerged from the children's account of activities was thus one of almost continuous play, but divided sporadically between inside and outside the house. Yet the fact that even in snowy winter weather a quarter of the children played outside after school when it was already getting dark shows that outside play is an important part of their evening activities.

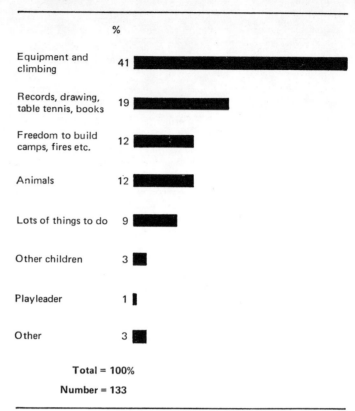

174   What the children liked about the Warwick Estate Adventure Playground

%

	%
Equipment and climbing	41
Records, drawing, table tennis, books	19
Freedom to build camps, fires etc.	12
Animals	12
Lots of things to do	9
Other children	3
Playleader	1
Other	3

Total = 100%

Number = 133

The Warwick Estate Adventure Playground
The children liked climbing on the wooden structures, in many cases built by themselves

175

The adventure playground

173. One in ten of children living on the Warwick Estate and one in 50 of children living nearby mentioned spontaneously the Warwick Estate Adventure Playground as a favourite place to play. However, when the children were asked specifically whether they went to the playground two-thirds of those who lived on the estate said they did. Less than a third who lived off the estate visited the playground, and not very regularly, and mainly during school holidays. The main reasons for not going were that it was too far and too dangerous because of the traffic; again showing how very localised play facilities need to be in order to be well-used. To the children the adventure playground was not a neighbourhood facility which they would make a special effort to visit like the parks, but a home-based estate playground, mainly used by those near at hand.

177

174. Using equipment and climbing ranked as the most popular activities at the adventure playground (Figure 174). The equipment was not the purpose-built conventional variety but large wooden structures built in many cases by the children themselves (Figures 175–177). Over a tenth of the children enjoyed the freedom to make things, build camps and make fires and another tenth said there was 'lots to do'. A fifth of what the children did was indoor pursuits such as playing records, table tennis, drawing and painting.

175. The main criticisms of the playground were that it was dangerous, that the other children were bossy, and that it was dirty and muddy: a few children wished there were fewer restrictions. These criticisms give an interesting insight into children's preferences. Getting dirty and meeting dangers are not liked or needed by all children. Wherever possible, however, play leaders will try to reconcile the personality demands of different children.

176

The play centre

176. The play centre on Warwick, like the adventure playground, was most used by children living nearby. Half of the children living on the estate went there, as opposed to a quarter living in the surrounding area, who attended irregularly. The most popular activities were the organised games and playing with the scooters and bikes provided by the centre (Figure 178); indoor activities – including painting, drawing, buying food and playing table tennis and billiards – accounted for over a quarter of the favourite ones.

178 What the children liked about the play centre on the Warwick Estate

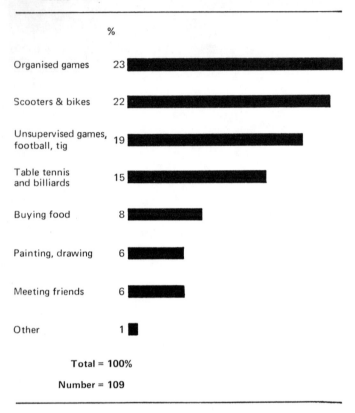

%

	%
Organised games	23
Scooters & bikes	22
Unsupervised games, football, tig	19
Table tennis and billiards	15
Buying food	8
Painting, drawing	6
Meeting friends	6
Other	1

Total = 100%

Number = 109

177. The main reasons for not going to the play centre were much the same as those for not going to the adventure playground, namely that it was too far, they weren't allowed to go, or the other children were too rough. A higher proportion on the other hand said they didn't know of it (paragraph 146).

Effects of home background on play habits

178. It is difficult to judge whether the quality of play differed according to where the child lived. Certainly the impression gained by the interviewers was that most children's enjoyment of their leisure was unaffected by whether they lived on a new estate with amenities for play or in an older slum area. Possibly the children in the slum area had to make a special effort to seek out opportunities for recreation.

179. The difference that did emerge however was between children from 'normal' or 'abnormal' backgrounds. In Oldham and Paddington an attempt was made to assess the home circumstances of the children by getting the head teachers to fill in a short questionnaire. Details such as the number of children in the family, parental interest in school work, whether the child had free school meals, whether the child had one or both parents, and his school attainment, did give us a picture, albeit crude, of a small proportion of children in both areas who came from difficult or unhappy homes.

180. Four out of five children in Paddington and five out of eight at Oldham who could think of nothing they liked about living where they did came from 'abnormal' home backgrounds. In asking about favourite places for play and favourite activities, it became evident that a few children spent little time playing with others, had few friends and played outdoors less than other children. Those with difficult backgrounds spent a higher proportion of their time doing household chores than other children, and three children from each area spent all their time after school in housework. A seven-year-old boy in Oldham described his evening as 'I go into the back and play with dad's lorry, light a fire, clean up house, have a cup of coffee, go and make beds, go and meet me mum, go to dad's work, get money, bring him chips. At 11 o'clock get him his supper.' A West Indian girl talked of sweeping the bedrooms and stairs, making something for her brother and sisters to eat and then washing the plates.

181. Although our evidence is limited it does appear that social background is a major determinant of the extent to which play facilities will be used. This raises the question of what type of play provision could be relevant to such children.

190

Appendix I Activity and location coding

Activity coding
Physically active*

(1) *Running or walking* — E.g. running, fighting, tig, chase, hide-and-seek, skipping, jumping etc. Walking or wandering, whether purposeful walking to shops etc. or wandering round site with little obvious purpose.

(2) *Ball games* — E.g. football, cricket, pig-in-the-middle, ball against wall.

(3) *Wheeled vehicles* — E.g. bikes, trikes, go-carts, roller skates and any toys on wheels on which children can ride.

(4) *Playground equipment*

(5) *Other†* — Pursuits which do not fit into any of the above categories, e.g. imaginative games, cowboys, cops and robbers.

Physically inactive*

(6) *Sitting, standing, lying etc.*

(7) *Other†* — Pursuits which do not fit into category 6, e.g. imaginative games, playing house, painting, play with toys, jig-saws, card games.

Location coding

(8) *Roads, pavements and garage courts* — Pavements immediately adjacent to roads have been classed with the roads on the grounds that children playing on these pavements would be in some danger. Many activities took place on roads and pavements concurrently.

(9) *Paved areas*

(10) *Gardens*

(11) *Access areas* — These included access balconies and decks, open areas under buildings, interior corridors, staircases and lift landings.

(12) *Grassed areas*

(13) *'Unorthodox areas'* — These included tops of walls and railings, garage roofs, trees etc. (i.e. places where children were not supposed to be).

(14) *Planted areas*

(15) *Play areas* — At Warwick this category included the adventure playground.

(16) *Wild areas* — At Warwick a waste building site was included in this category.

(17) *Other areas* — This included the library at Winstanley Road, the public park adjacent to Canada (excluding the play facilities which were included in category 15) and the underground car park at Curnock Street.

---

*Activities were not categorised as 'physically active' or 'physically inactive' for observations on the first three estates – Gloucester Street, Woodhouse and Woodway Lane.

†Originally, these categories were broken down into 'imaginative games', 'own toys', 'unorthodox' and 'other'. However, it became clear that observers could not reliably differentiate between them.

Appendix II Description of observation areas

A Low-rise estates

Gloucester Street, Sheffield

1. This small scheme of 39 houses is an infill site in a slum clearance area about a mile west of Sheffield city centre. Although most of the dwellings are adjacent to roads, tenants have access to a central open grassed space from their garden without going near a road. There are linked paved areas connecting dwellings and roads at the back of the houses all of which have private gardens.

2. There are no play areas. The nearest open space is a public park about a quarter of a mile away which can be reached only by crossing some busy roads; in this park ball games are prohibited on every day except Whit Monday.

Woodhouse Estate, Sheffield

3. Woodhouse Estate, an estate of family houses, forms part of a larger housing development about four miles south-east of Sheffield city centre. At the time of the observations the sloping site, bounded to the north by a brook, was surrounded by a considerable amount of open countryside. The site is trisected by a distributor road, which carries a bus service, and an access road. Only a few of the houses lead directly on to roads, with the majority in terraces at right angles to the road. There is a separate network of pedestrian paths and all the dwellings have private gardens.

4. No play areas are provided.

Woodway Lane, Coventry

5. This estate has two-storey houses (all with private gardens) and a few old people's bungalows. It is three-and-a-half miles north-east of Coventry city centre, bounded on one side by a brook and some rough open space. It has no through roads, and pedestrian paths are sited at the front of the houses away from the roads. All the dwellings back on to roads or culs-de-sac which are directly accessible from the gardens.

6. Six small play areas are provided, all with brick structures or logs. A factor which influenced the form of play areas was the local authority's intention of developing the rough ground to the west of the site as an open space and neighbourhood play area.

Fleury Road, Sheffield

7. The dwellings at Fleury Road are part of the Gleadless Valley Estate on the outskirts of Sheffield. The estate is on a steeply sloping, south-facing hillside overlooking a large wooded open space in the bottom of the valley. By grouping the terraces of dwellings close together, large open spaces have been created which have been mainly grassed and this, together with the open surroundings, gives the estate a semi-rural setting. The estate consists entirely of houses half of which have garages beneath at the front. All the houses have small paved yards at the rear, and about half have private front gardens; most of the others have private balconies. There is one through road and several access roads. Some of the houses open on to roads at the rear and all front on to pedestrian paths.

8. There is one small, unequipped play area.

B Medium-rise estates

St Mary's, Oldham

9. This estate was the first redeveloped site in a slum clearance area. Surrounded by derelict houses and industrial premises, old occupied houses and cleared areas, it is situated close to Oldham's town centre. About a third of the dwellings are houses with private gardens and the rest are deck-access flats. The estate is mainly traffic-segregated with four, short, access culs-de-sac. The houses, where the majority of children live, are at right angles to the road and open both ways on to extensive pedestrian paths and paved areas. There is a high proportion of grassed, common open space.

10. There are seven play areas on the site. Four of these consist of concrete structures; one has swings: another a slide, paddling pool, swings, a fort and play house: the other is a ball-games area. The nearest open space at the northern end of the site is a wild area known as Oldham Edge. The nearest park is more than half a mile away on the other side of three main roads and the town centre.

The Bonamy, London SE1

11. Situated in Southwark in an area characterised by small industrial development, a railway goods yard, a canal, and a few 19th-century terraced houses, The Bonamy Estate is divided into two by the Rotherhithe New Road. Observations were made only on the northern part, which is connected to the remainder of the estate by a footbridge, giving access to a shopping centre, community buildings, and a public house. Apart from a service road at one end, the estate is strictly traffic-segregated, the dwellings running across the site to form a series of paved pedestrian ways and small courtyards. There are grassed and planted areas raised above the level of the walkways and level grassed areas on the periphery of the site. Most of the ground-floor dwellings have private patios and those at the upper levels, large roof terraces.

12. On the half of the estate where observations were made there is one play area consisting of a climbing frame, slide, swings and sand-pit. At the time of the observations the swings were without seats and the sand-pit empty. There are no parks in the area.

Curnock Street, London NW1

13. This estate in the London Borough of Camden, consisting largely of maisonettes in four-storey blocks but with one six-storey block of flats and nine two-storey houses, is in an area of mixed residential and small light-industrial development adjacent to the main shopping centre in Camden High Road. It is entirely traffic-free, but the outer blocks face busy roads on two sides of the estate. The blocks are arranged to form four courtyards, each with extensive paved and planted areas. None of the dwellings have private gardens or balconies but the ground-level dwellings all have a side-screened section of paving which is contiguous with the access-way paving. Seven shops (unlet at the time of the observations) and a public house are incorporated in the scheme.

14. Each courtyard has a play area with swings, conventional static equipment and architectural features. Across a busy road is a large kickabout area and a main road would have to be crossed to reach the nearest park to the estate.

Royal College Street, London NW1

15. Closely surrounded by other flats, two colleges, a school and a hospital, this estate of flats and maisonettes is next door to Curnock Street and also in the London Borough of Camden. It is traffic-segregated apart from a service road which bisects the site between two of the perimeter roads. A long covered pedestrian way runs alongside the service road giving access to shops. A community hall is provided on the site. All dwellings have recessed balconies except those at ground level which have access to shared but enclosed grassed areas. A few have private gardens.

16. There is no special provision for children's play.

Edith Avenue, Washington New Town

17. The site of this estate is bounded by 19th-century terraced housing, a railway and slag heaps, and some more recent new development of two-storey terraced houses. The estate has access culs-de-sac, leaving the central area traffic-free with dwellings forming a series of well-landscaped courtyards linked by pedestrian paths. Some ground-level dwellings have completely private gardens; some have gardens arranged in pairs, each pair being divided only by a path; and some others have only enclosed greens shared between several dwellings. Upper-level dwellings all have balconies and most of them are served by an 8 ft-wide access deck. At the time of the observations there was one shop on the site.

18. There are three ball-games areas, three with sand-pits and paddling pools (empty at the time of observations) and three separate sand-pits. There are no parks close to the estate.

Acorn Place, London SE15

19. This estate of houses, maisonettes and flats is in a largely residential area in Southwark close to the Peckham shopping centre beside the busy A21 road to the Kent coast. There are, however, only two access roads on the estate itself. The dwellings are arranged to form a series of paved courtyards, with planting. The houses have private gardens and some also have private balconies; most of the flats have no private open space. An existing pub, 11 shops, a surgery and three laundries were included in the estate. The only grassed area is a small strip at the southern end of the site.

20. There are three playgrounds on the estate. One of these, a roof over a group of garages, is unequipped and was intended as a kickabout area but it is not enclosed. The other two are equipped with moving and conventional static equipment. One of these is partially under cover. There are no parks close to the estate.

C Mixed-rise estates
Park Hill, Sheffield

21. This estate, a redevelopment of a slum area, is in an area of mixed residential, industrial and commercial uses on a steep hill overlooking Sheffield's town centre and station. The whole estate consists of four to 14-storey deck-access slab blocks, which are linked together at every third floor by the deck systems to form one unit. These 10 ft-wide decks are large enough to take small service vehicles. None of the dwellings has a private garden but all have private balconies. The estate is traffic-segregated and all the blocks face away from the roads. There are large expanses of paved areas and wide stretches of grass in the space between the blocks. Two schools, four pubs, 31 shops, a tenants' meeting hall, a police sub-station and a laundry are included in the site.

22. There are three large playgrounds with sand-pits, climbing frames and concrete structures; a narrow bowling alley, and two ball-games areas. Although there are no parks nearby, there is an extensive grassy area sloping down from the estate to the main railway station.

Sceaux Gardens, London SE5

23. Part of this estate in Southwark fronts on to the busy Peckham Road, but much of it is separated from roads and located in an old area with some new residential development. It was built on the site of a hospital with well-established gardens, which have since become overgrown. A large central pedestrian precinct is a major feature of the estate. All the bungalows, which are occupied by elderly residents, have small private gardens, but none of the other residents has a private open space except for the narrow fire-escape balconies in the internal corridor blocks. Six shops and a communal laundry are on the site.

24. There is one tubular climbing frame.

Canada Estate, London SE16

25. Situated in the London Borough of Southwark not far from the southern end of the Rotherhithe tunnel, adjacent to the Surrey Docks, Canada Estate is in an old area of mixed residential and industrial use. There is only one through road, mainly used by estate traffic. Much of the open space is paved but there are several large grassed areas. None of the flats in the two 21-storey point blocks has a private balcony but in the cluster blocks ground-floor dwellings have private gardens and those above, private balconies.

26. Three concrete play structures are provided, and the estate is adjacent to a small park with a ball-games area and a play area equipped with moving and conventional static equipment. A short distance away but over a main road is the larger Southwark Park.

Winstanley Road, London SW11

27. Located in the London Borough of Wandsworth, in one of London's inner suburbs, this estate is adjacent to Clapham Junction Station; it was an early stage of a large-scale renewal of a largely residential area. There is only one through road on the estate and it receives little traffic; the remaining road area consists of culs-de-sac. The site is intensively developed and much of it is paved with a variety of materials. There are only a few grassed areas, which are rather inaccessible to children. Some of the ground-floor dwellings have private gardens and the dwellings in the point and internal-corridor slab blocks have private balconies. The remaining residents have no open space. Four shops, a children's library and six workrooms are included in the estate.

28. There are eight play areas dotted about the estate. Three of these are equipped with play sculptures, two with climbing apparatus made of wood, metal and concrete and one with a concrete Wendy house and shops. There is a ball-games area and an area built over parking space, equipped with moving and conventional static equipment. Although there are three parks in the district, none of them is within a mile.

Warwick Estate, London W2

29. This, the largest estate where observations were made, is situated in North Paddington in the City of Westminster, in a slum clearance area bounded to the north by the Grand Union Canal and to the south and south-west by the busy Harrow Road. It is not traffic-segregated and most of the dwellings face on to roads. Some of them have gardens if they are on the ground floor

or balconies if higher up, but others have no private open space. There are several large grassed areas. Three schools, two churches, an old people's home, a fire station, three pubs and 12 shops are included in the site.

30. There are eight small play areas with concrete structures or somersault bars. Away from the main part of the estate is a small extension with three small play areas – one including swings. This section was excluded from the observations because it was separated by the very busy Harrow Road. Observations were made on an adventure playground on the estate which was run by a voluntary organisation with the leaders' salaries financed by the Inner London Education Authority.

D The older area, Oldham

31. The area is adjacent to the St Mary's Estate in Oldham (see paragraphs 9 and 10 of this Appendix). It stretches from Oldham Edge (a large area of rough open ground) in the north to the town centre in the south, and includes derelict waste areas and small-scale industry. It is bisected by one busy main road, but most of the other roads are steep and cobbled, with little and slow-moving traffic. Most of the housing is due to be cleared for redevelopment, and consists of 19th-century terraced dwellings. Few of them have private gardens, but many have small back yards opening on to unkempt alleyways. Some of the slightly larger houses have very small front gardens but most front doors have direct access on to the narrow pavements.

32. There is no specific play provision in this area, but at the time of the observations the Territorial Army hut on Oldham Edge (since demolished) had some simple gymnastic equipment, sometimes used by the children. Also on Oldham Edge is a small playing field prohibited for general use. The nearest park is on the other side of the town centre.

E The Recreation Ground, London W10

33. Emslie Horniman Pleasance is a recreation ground in Kensal Town, in the Royal Borough of Kensington and Chelsea. There is a housing estate to one side of the park and a primary school on the other. To the south lies the main British Railways line out of Paddington.

34. The park, which has a park keeper but no formally supervised facilities, contains an equipped play area. At the time of the observations this contained several swings, a see-saw, two merry-go-rounds and a pendulum see-saw. It was chosen for observations because during the summer of 1969 a supervised play scheme was organised there, so it was possible to carry out three observation surveys, before, during and after the scheme was in operation. The intention was to assess the effectiveness of play supervision in terms of patterns of activity and general use of the facilities and to see how these changed during the period of supervision.

35. During the period of supervision there was an average of 11 to 12 playleaders a day on the site, two or three of whom were qualified playleaders while the remainder were voluntary helpers. A church hall was used when it was raining and a waste area adjacent to the park was utilised. The first observation study was carried out in early July, the second in August and the third in September.

References

1 FLETCHER S S F *Froebel's chief writings on education* Edward Arnold 1912 p 50

2 GIDDENS A Notes on the concepts of play and leisure *Sociological Review* Vol 12 March 1964 pp 73–89

3 HOLME Anthea *and* MASSIE P *Children's play: a study of needs and opportunities* Michael Joseph 1970

4 McLELLAN J *The question of play* Pergamon 1970

5 MILLER S *The psychology of play* Penguin 1968

6 PIAGET J *Play dreams and imitation in childhood* Heinemann 1951

7 BUILDING RESEARCH STATION National Building Studies Research Paper 39 *Children's play on housing estates* (Vere Hole) HMSO 1966

8 BUILDING RESEARCH STATION Design Series 46 *Children's play on housing estates: a summary of two BRS studies* (Vere Hole *and* A Miller) The Station 1966

9 DEPARTMENT OF THE ENVIRONMENT Circular 79/72 (Welsh Office 165/72) *Children's playspace* HMSO 1972

10 DANISH NATIONAL INSTITUTE OF BUILDING RESEARCH *Children's use of recreational areas* (Jeanne Morville) Copenhagen: The Institute 1969 In Danish

11 WOHLIN H *Outdoor play and playspaces* Stockholm 1961 In Swedish

12 JEPHCOTT Pearl *Homes in high flats* Oliver and Boyd 1971 p 55

13 DEPARTMENT OF THE ENVIRONMENT *Quality monitoring: a pilot survey of the quality and performance of local authority housing in England and Wales* To be published

14 DEPARTMENT OF THE ENVIRONMENT Design Bulletin 25 *The estate outside the dwelling: reactions of residents to aspects of housing layout* HMSO 1972

15 DEPARTMENT OF THE ENVIRONMENT Design Bulletin 22 *New housing in a cleared area: a study of St Mary's Oldham* HMSO 1971

16 DEPARTMENT OF THE ENVIRONMENT *Medium-rise high-density housing* To be published

17 MUSSEN P H *and others* *Child development and personality* New York: Harper and Row 1963

18 NEWSOM J *and* NEWSOM Elizabeth *Four years old in an urban community* Allen and Unwin 1968

19 ACKERMANS E *The vicinity of the home used as a play area* Netherlands Institute for Preventive Medicine 1970 In Dutch with an English summary

20 OFFICE OF POPULATION CENSUSES AND SURVEYS Social Survey Division *Children and road safety: a survey amongst mothers* (Judy Sadler) HMSO 1972 p 76

21 SANDELS S *Small children in traffic* Stockholm 1969 In Swedish

22 EDINBURGH UNIVERSITY Architecture Research Unit *Aspects of traffic separated housing layouts: Stevenage* Stevenage Development Corporation 1970

23 BUILDING RESEARCH STATION Current Paper 39/68 *The location of primary schools* (P H Levin *and* A J Bruce) The Station 1968

24 MINISTRY OF HOUSING AND LOCAL GOVERNMENT *Homes for today and tomorrow* (Parker Morris Report) HMSO 1961

25 MINISTRY OF HOUSING AND LOCAL GOVERNMENT Circular 36/67 *Housing standards costs and subsidies* HMSO 1967 p 14 para. F

26 BRITISH STANDARDS INSTITUTION BS 3178: Part 1: 1959 *Playground equipment for parks: general requirements*

27 LADY ALLEN OF HURTWOOD *New playgrounds* Housing Centre Trust 1964 p 27

28 DEPARTMENT OF THE ENVIRONMENT *Housing procedures manual 1972* To be published

29 BENGTSSON A *Environmental planning for children's play* Crosby Lockwood 1970 p 59

30 LIVERPOOL UNIVERSITY *Low cost grassing of sites awaiting redevelopment* (A D Bradshaw) 1970 Unpublished

31 DEPARTMENT OF THE ENVIRONMENT *Fair deal for housing* Cmnd 4728 HMSO 1971

32 PLANT J W *and* ROBINSON L K *Programme for derelict land reclamation* Stokc-on-Trent City Council 1970 Unpublished

33 HILTON K J *The lower Swansea valley project* Longman 1967

34 LEE VALLEY REGIONAL PARK AUTHORITY *Lee Valley regional park* The Authority 1969

35 Current Work No 2 Camp Hill, Nuneaton *Journal of the Institute of Landscape Architects* February 1967 pp 8–11

36 TOWN AND COUNTRY PLANNING ACT 1971 c 78 section 212 HMSO 1971

37 ROAD TRAFFIC REGULATION ACT 1967 c 76 HMSO 1967

38 TRANSPORT ACT 1968 c 73 HMSO 1968

39 DEPARTMENT OF THE ENVIRONMENT Area Improvement Note 3 *Improving the environment* HMSO 1971

40 DEPARTMENT OF EDUCATION AND SCIENCE Circular 2/70 *The chance to share* The Department 1970

41 DEPARTMENT OF EDUCATION AND SCIENCE Architects and Building Branch Design Note 5 *The school and the community* The Department 1970

42 GREATER LONDON COUNCIL *Surveys of the use of open spaces* Vol 1 The Council 1968

43 LADY ALLEN OF HURTWOOD *Planning for play* Thames and Hudson 1968 p 92

44 STEVENAGE DEVELOPMENT CORPORATION Social Relations Department *Survey of children's play 1968/1969* First report Unpublished

45 HOUSING ACT 1969 c 33 HMSO 1969

46 HOME OFFICE Circulars 225/68, 34/69, 117/70, 51/71 (Welsh Office 29/71), 161/71 (Welsh Office 128/71), 247/71 (Welsh Office 235/71), 91/72 (Welsh Office 98/72)

47 LOCAL GOVERNMENT GRANTS (SOCIAL NEED) ACT 1969 c 2 HMSO 1969

48 LEISSNER A *and others* *Advice guidance and assistance: a study of seven family advice centres* Longman 1971

49 OPIE Iona *and* OPIE P *Lore and language of school children* Oxford University Press 1959

50 HIMMELWEIT H T *and others* *Television and the child* Oxford University Press 1958

51 BLOOM B S *Stability and change in human characteristics* J Wiley 1964

52 PRINGLE Mia Kellmer Policy implications of child development studies *Concern* November 1969 pp 40–48

53 PRINGLE Mia Kellmer *Deprivation and education* 2nd ed. Longman 1971

54 CRELLIN E. *and others* *Born illegitimate* NFER 1971

55 DEPARTMENT OF EDUCATION AND SCIENCE *Children and their primary schools* (Plowden Report) HMSO 1967 Vol 1 para. 55

56 BERNSTEIN B *Social class and linguistic development in education economy and society* New York Free Press 1961

57 PRINGLE Mia Kellmer *and others 11,000 seven-year-olds* Longman 1966

58 DAVIE R *and others From birth to seven* Longman 1972

59 BERNSTEIN B *and* YOUNG D Social class differences in conceptions of the uses of toys *Sociology* Vol 1 May 1967 pp 131–140

60 ASSOCIATION OF MULTI-RACIAL PLAYGROUPS *Occasional Papers 1–4* The Association (Now known as Priority Area Children)

61 HOME OFFICE *Criminal statistics England and Wales* Table A *Criminal offences known to the police* Annually HMSO

62 TORONTO PSYCHIATRIC HOSPITAL Forensic Clinic *The forensic clinic study* (J W Mohr) Unpublished

63 BURTON L *Vulnerable children three studies of children in conflict: accident involved children, sexually assaulted children and children with asthma* Routledge and Kegan Paul 1968

64 HERBERT J *Bandley Hill Children's Play Association Stevenage* The Association 1967 Unpublished

65 DEPARTMENT OF THE ENVIRONMENT *High density housing project at Granby Street, Bethnal Green for the Greater London Council: proposals for the community building* 1971 Unpublished

66 NOTTING HILL SOCIAL COUNCIL An unpublished Report

67 NORTH KENSINGTON FAMILY STUDY COMMITTEE *Play for the under fives* The Committee 1966

68 GORDON Ira J *Parent involvement in compensatory education* University of Illinois Press 1970 Chap III

69 EDUCATION ACT 1944 c 31 Section 53 HMSO 1944

70 NATIONAL HEALTH SERVICE ACT 1946 c 81 HMSO 1946

71 HEALTH SERVICES AND PUBLIC HEALTH ACT 1968 HMSO 1968

72 CHILDREN'S ACT 1948 c 43 Section 46 HMSO 1948

73 CHILDREN AND YOUNG PERSONS ACT 1963 c 37 Section 1 HMSO 1963

74 CHILDREN AND YOUNG PERSONS ACT 1969 c 54 HMSO 1969

75 PHYSICAL TRAINING AND RECREATION ACT 1937 c 46 Section 4 HMSO 1937

76 NURSERIES AND CHILD-MINDERS REGULATION ACT 1948 c 53 HMSO 1948

5

HOUSING THE CAR (1)

Dimensions and Multi-storey parking

I Dimensions

1. The purpose of this bulletin is to answer some technical questions that have been asked about the problems of parking and garaging cars in residential areas. It does not cover road design.

2. Its conclusions are not necessarily valid for areas other than residential, nor does it answer questions of policy or overall design.

3. There are a number of reference books, mostly of American origin, dealing with the more general aspects of car parking and garaging. This bulletin assumes some familiarity with the better known of these,[1] and concentrates on the particular problems of cars in residential areas and on the smaller European car.

4. Car ownership and the size of car owned will vary from district to district. This bulletin can only concern itself with general trends and should be modified in the light of local knowledge. With this reservation, it is true to say that the size of vehicle owned is not directly connected with the income of the owner. Large cars are often cheaper, secondhand, than smaller ones and are a familiar sight in low-income districts; vans and lorries are also often seen at the homes of the drivers. While average British car sizes have remained relatively static over recent years, there is no certain guarantee that they will continue to do so. Size is as much a matter of fashion as anything else. However, the bulk of the existing stock of six million or so garages are probably less than $5 \cdot 000 \times 2 \cdot 500$. This must be a powerful influence in maintaining existing maxima.

5. Where lock-up garages are closely associated with particular houses, each will have to accommodate any car likely to be owned. Where lock-ups are grouped, it is possible for them to be allocated according to the size of the car owned; this gives some flexibility.

6. Many local authorities provide larger garages for higher-income tenants. This is as much to provide incidental storage and workshop space as to allow for larger cars. There is a considerable demand for such space throughout the entire range of income levels, but its provision lies outside the scope of this bulletin except where it directly affects basic requirements. Information on space requirements for such incidental storage is given in Design Bulletin 6, *Space in the home* (page 77).

Vehicle sizes

7. From statistics on new registrations of cars[2] it is possible to draw conclusions about the size distribution of the car population. Over 95% of new registrations will fit within a rectangular plan envelope of $4 \cdot 750 \times 1 \cdot 800$ and it is suggested that where possible this should be the standard car size considered in new construction.

8. The functional factors of road space and garage sizes inhibit the construction of cars longer than the 95% figure quoted above. The larger models are either luxury cars of special character or imports, largely of USA origin. The largest British car in general production is the Rolls-Royce Phantom VI and this might well be taken as representative of the 5% that are larger than the standard size. To be on the safe side, at least 10% of the places provided overall should be for cars larger than the standard size.

[1] e.g. RICKER: *Traffic design of parking garages;* BAKER AND FUNARO: *Parking;* VAHLEFELD AND JAQUES: *Garages and service stations.*

[2] SOCIETY OF MOTOR MANUFACTURERS AND TRADERS LIMITED: *New registration of new motor vehicles in Great Britain, Northern Ireland and the Isle of Man.* Six-monthly.

Comparative table of 'design' car sizes

	Key to Figure 1	small design car	standard design car	large design car
% of new registrations production falling within these limits		50% approx.	95% approx.	100%
% places to be provided		not more than 25%	residue	not less than 10%
length	A	4·100	4·750	6·100
width	B	1·600	1·800	2·000
height	C	1·500	1·700	(2·200) see para. 10
door opening clearance:	D	*		
full		1·200	0·900	see para. 9
normal		0·500	0·500	
minimum		0·400	0·400	
wheelbase	E	see para. 9	0·900	see para. 9
(worst cases)	F		2·900	3·700
	G		1·100	see para. 9
driver's sight:				
front	H	1·800	2·500	see para. 9
rear	J	2·300	2·700	
nearside clearance:				
normal	K	0·200	0·200	see para. 9
minimum (piers etc.)		0·150	0·150	
turning circle: (diameter)				
kerb	M	11·000	13·000	15·000
wall	N	see para. 9	14·000	see para. 9
ground clearance	P	0·130	0·100	(0·050) see para. 10

* a rather larger dimension is shown for the small design car than the standard because of the 'two door' models fitting within the envelope.

Over 90% of new registrations will fit within an envelope of 4·700 × 1·700, and about 50% within 4·100 × 1·600. Where, and only where, some flexibility in place sizes is possible and where there are pressing demands on space, some could be designed to accommodate a smaller vehicle. As there is no control over dimensions it would be unwise to commit more than a small proportion of the stock of places: say 25% for the 4·100 × 1·600 small envelope. A certain number of these smaller places could be designed for a specific best-selling small car if it seems likely to remain popular. But the number of places at risk should not exceed, say, 5%—possibly for filling odd corners, since when the particular model of car goes out of production or 'grows' it may be difficult to find replacements of the same size.

9. The 'standard' envelope discussed earlier has been further detailed in the Table above. The 'standard design car' incorporates the features of current cars fitting within the envelope that make most demands on the designer. Dimensions of a small and a large design car have also been given. The code letters refer to Figure 1. Certain dimensions are not itemised because the way in which they could become critical varies with the overall characteristics of each car body and it is not possible to give generalised answers that are meaningful.

10. Certain large design car dimensions above are in brackets, because they apply to specialised vehicles. These often have one feature making serious demands on the designer, while all other dimensions are similar to normal private cars. The minimum ground clearance quoted applies to one model of sports car, which in other respects presents no problems. The height feature is more complex. A considerable number of light commercial vehicles are used as private cars. They can be either in standard form or else as a 'motorised caravan' or 'mini-bus'. In terms of length and width these are comparable with private cars, but they

are considerably higher and therefore liable to foul 'up and over' doors on domestic garages and the overhead structure in multi-storey parks. The 'motorised caravan' conversion is frequently rather higher than its van equivalent, due to an extensible roof construction. It is difficult to generalise on heights since some of these conversions are produced by small local firms. However, as a guide, one popular example has a van height of 2·020 and a conversion on it has a height of 2·160. The length of this example is 4·500 and the width 1·960. As this particular van has sliding doors its effective width is less than for a car of the same width with hinged doors. It is difficult to obtain figures for the number of such light commercial-type vehicles in private use: indeed the proportion will probably vary from area to area. Local usage should, therefore, be investigated. Some suitable places may be needed in addition to the 10% allocated for large private cars.

11. Although commercial vehicles are not the concern of this bulletin, commercial-type vehicles, as the previous paragraph suggests, are often used for private transport. As these vehicles increase in size the problems grow more acute: fortunately their private use becomes rarer. The model mentioned before has a long wheel base version, whose length is 5·350; width 2·060 and height 2·210. Caravan conversions of this are thought to be rare. At the extreme, and put in here for comparative purposes only, since the question of lorry parking is outside the scope of this bulletin, the maximum permitted sizes of commercial vehicles are:

Rigid chassis   11·000 × 2·500
Articulated   15·000 × 2·500

and a typical commercial chassis has a turning circle of 30·000. There is no restriction on height, but buses are normally about 4·500 high: bridges with clearance less than 5·000 are regarded as 'low'.

The maximum permitted weight on any two-wheeled axle is, at the time of writing, 10 tons (Imperial) (Metric equivalent about 10 000kg) which is, of course, enormously different from that of a car and may require heavier foundation works.

Further information on such vehicles is given in the Ministry of Transport's publication *Design of roads in urban areas*.

Garage sizes

12. (See Figure 2)

(a) Dimensional Co-ordination

Where garaging is an integral part of a building structure containing residential accommodation, it will normally follow the recommendations of Design Bulletin 16, Figures 2, 3 and 4, and its Addendum *The Dimensional Framework and Component Size* (page 7). Independent structures for car garaging will normally conform to the requirements of BS 4330.

(b) General

Because of the requirements for dimensional co-ordination, slight reductions in the minimum dimensions for single car garages suggested in the first edition of this bulletin have been made. The 4% or so of 'largest in the range' standard cars can normally use these spaces, but require rather more care.

A more desirable series of minimum dimensions for garages has been added, for guidance where space is relatively cheap to provide: these will reduce the inconvenience to drivers of larger cars. The dimensions are based on the second preference modular grid (of 0·100) for non floor-supporting walls. Where the walls are

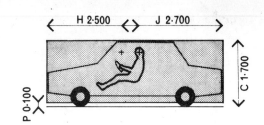

1 The 'standard design car'

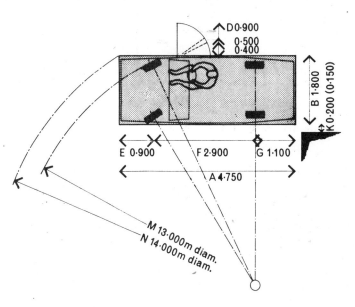

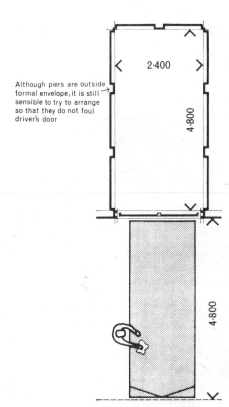

Although piers are outside formal envelope, it is still sensible to try to arrange so that they do not foul driver's door

2 The standard garage

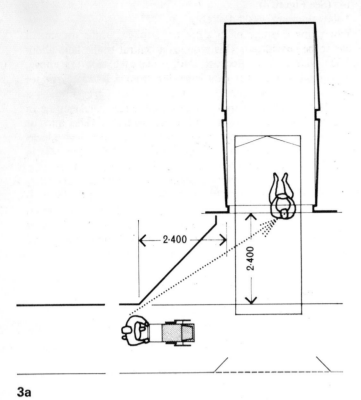

3a

floor-supporting the first preference grid will normally be followed: this will result in spaces above the minimum (i.e. 2·700 × 5·100).

(c) Clear width for a standard design car

minimum 2·400

applied as —standard car width 1·800
                nearside clearance 0·200
                door opening—minimum 0·400

desirably 2·500

(d) Garage door clear opening

minimum 2·200
desirably full width

(e) Clear length for standard design car

minimum 4·800

applied as —standard car length 4·750
                clearance at front 0·025
                clearance at rear 0·025

desirably 4·900

Forecourt sizes

Forecourt to road or footway
13. (See Figures 2 and 3)

(a) Depth
The minimum depth normally recommended is 4·800, though 5·400 is desirable. This allows the car to stand outside the garage for cleaning or unloading (Figure 2). Where standing space is available elsewhere this figure can be reduced to not less than 2·400. This minimum is required between the garage doorpost and the back of a footway or boundary of a road for the driver to be able to see in either direction down the road before the car begins to cause an obstruction (Figure 3). Where side-hinged doors that do not open fully back are used, their dimensions should be measured, treating them as obstructions to the field of view. With side-hinged doors the forecourt should, ideally, be deep enough for the doors to be opened with the car already standing on the forecourt.

(b) Width
Normal angular sightlines will be needed, to be kept clear of high (over 1·050) obstructions. For a footway this clear zone should have a length along the footway of not less than 2·400 (Figure 3). For a minor road or cul-de-sac where the traffic speed is not likely to exceed 23km/h, the relevant figure, measured along the kerb of the road, should be 20·000. Where traffic speeds are higher, greater distances will be needed and this may suggest that garages are better placed elsewhere.

(c) Exceptions
There are situations where there is effectively no traffic movement, or the movement is unusual in direction: for example, the end of a cul-de-sac. The sightlines and forecourts suggested above may be inappropriate in these situations.

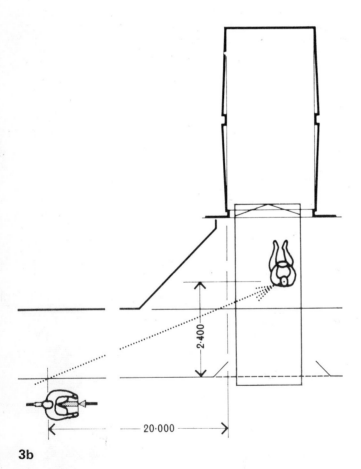

3b

202

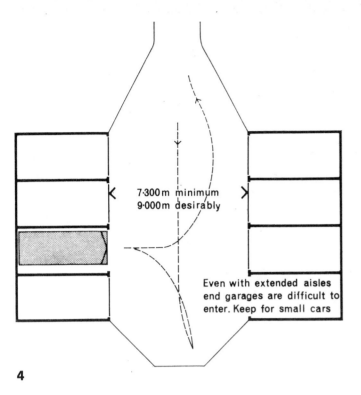

7·300m minimum
9·000m desirably

Even with extended aisles end garages are difficult to enter. Keep for small cars

4

Forecourt to a wall or other garages opposite

14. (See Figure 4)

7·300 minimum, 9·000 desirably

Where any quantity of lock-ups are banked, traffic movement has to be considered. This requires a central traffic lane about 2·500 wide and a forecourt 2·400 wide each side (as above, paragraph 13) so that cars emerging from a lock-up can see traffic moving along the lane. The resulting 7·300 width is a standard highway dimension: that of a two-lane carriageway. In this width the standard design car can 'in one' reverse into, or drive out of, a lock-up. 'In three' it can drive forward into a lock-up. Where lock-ups and forecourt form part of a building (as in a multi-storey garage) the preferred dimension next above, i.e. 7·500, will usually be chosen. Where, for any reason, cars may need to reverse direction between the faces of garages, a minimum of about 8·000 will be needed to complete a 'three point turn' (Figure 5). The standard design car requires about 9·000 to drive forward into a minimum lock-up 'in one' and this is a more desirable distance where space is not at a premium.

Forecourt to curb opposite

15. (See Figure 6)

6·700 minimum, 8·100 desirably

Slightly less space is required where there is a low kerb opposite rather than a wall as cars can overhang.

Reduced minimum dimensions for small design car

16. (See Figure 4)

Forecourt to road or footway	1·800 deep
Forecourt to wall opposite	6·100 deep
Forecourt where turn is required	6·700 deep

NB. End lock-ups are difficult to enter (Figure 4) and need special consideration. In addition all the forecourt dimensions quoted above assume adequate space elsewhere for casual parking, maintenance, etc. If this takes place in the forecourt much larger dimensions will be needed.

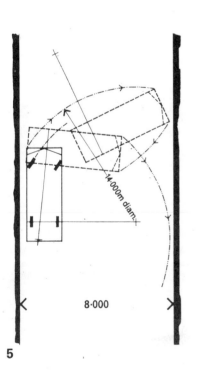

14·000m diam.

8·000

5

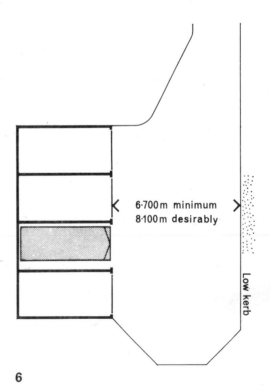

6·700m minimum
8·100m desirably

Low kerb

6

0°

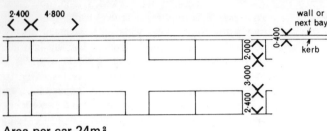

Area per car 24m²

7a

45°

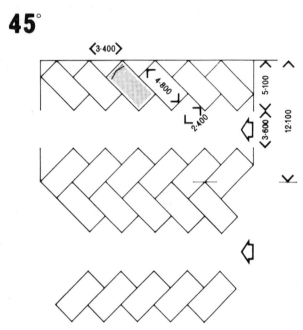

Area per car 24m² } + ends of row
If interlocking 21m²

note: car spaces can only be interlocked properly at 45°

7b

60°

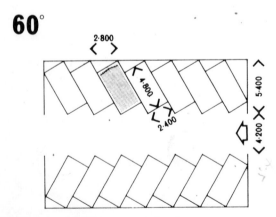

Area per car 21m² + ends of row

7c

Parking-bay sizes

17. (See Figures 7a–d.) Smaller dimensions can be used for open parking areas than for lock-ups, as turning movements and door opening movements can overlap into adjoining bays. It is not really possible to give precise minima for parking bays, as their use depends on the skill and patience of individual drivers. With repeated reversals a car can be manoeuvred into a space very little larger than its own physical dimensions, but this is hardly practical for a car park in regular use. In residential areas, with a normal proportion of unskilled drivers, it is essential that parking should be easy, otherwise parking space will not be properly used. For this reason it is recommended that dimensions in general be not less than those shown in Figures 7a–d. While these are larger than much current commercial practice, there will still be some difficulty with the occasional very large car, but in residential areas it should be relatively easy to allocate special bays for large cars.

18. The width of the parking bay, the angle of parking and the width of the aisle are interconnected. Figures 7a–d show recommended dimensions for a few parking angles. Parking at right angles to the kerb remains the most popular, but angle parking is useful for narrow sites, as the overall 'bin' width (two lines of cars and an aisle) can be very much less than that for parking at right angles.

19. Necessarily the narrow aisles with angle parking should be one-way. This gives a slight safety advantage and also enables cars to be driven forwards into bays—some drivers find it difficult to reverse into a confined space, particularly if that space is not square with the kerb. The irregular outside edges of angled parking can be both extravagant of space and a design difficulty, so that the areas quoted in Figures 7a–d should be tested against the actual site conditions.

90°

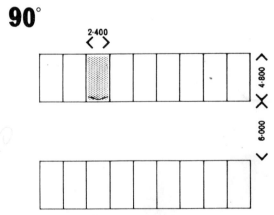

Area per car 19m²

7d

II Multi-storey parking garages

20. This part of the bulletin is planned as a summary of the design problems peculiar to multi-storey parking garages serving purely residential areas, and as an introduction to the general problems of parking garages. There are several books available (see Bibliography) dealing with the design of garages serving commercial areas, and they discuss more fully the general problems, although it should be noted that some of these are American, with dimensions for typical American-sized cars. The dimensions in this bulletin have all been related to typical British car sizes (see paragraphs 7, 8 and 9).

21. The general use of multi-storey parking garages in Great Britain is fairly recent; their use in residential areas is very recent. But the rapid growth of car ownership will make them much more common within a few more years. At the moment their function seems to require certain design solutions; but their novelty, and, indeed, the comparative novelty of car ownership, produce problems and attitudes which require other solutions. There are not yet sufficient examples of all these solutions in practice, and the growth of ownership and familiarity with ownership will in time modify them. This bulletin must, therefore, be regarded as interim.

22. Ease of use is quite as important a design target as the number of parking places. A garage that is difficult to use will never be successful. This applies as much to detailed design, e.g. the appearance of ramps, as to the basic plan. Some useful comments on operation are contained in Road Research Note LR 221. However, in residential areas where cars are allocated particular parking places, it is not essential for every car to be able to use every parking place in the garage, since some parking places can be arranged to accommodate the few unusually large cars.

Selection of type of garage

23. A single building as large as a multi-storey parking garage will be influenced by the basic planning problems of the site. These will dictate the shape and, probably, the internal planning. For this reason the diagrams show only the basic principles and not a comprehensive list of all variations, and for this reason too it is not possible to recommend one type only on theoretical grounds. However some theoretical factors should be considered at the selection stage.

24. For management reasons, discussed later, it is desirable that multi-storey garages in residential areas should be split up into individual lock-ups. Where this is done, the construction of the cage, however open it is, will interfere with the normal casual sightlines that a driver who is unparking his car has over and through adjacent cars. Traffic flow near the entrance or exit in such garages can be considerable at peak hours (if a 400-car garage half-empties in one hour the average interval between cars will be 18 seconds), particularly bearing in mind the unusual nature of the aisles and ramps. There is a real risk of accidents and congestion between cars travelling in the aisles and cars leaving lock-ups. This can be reduced either by use of clearway ramps as defined below in paragraph 26 or by making aisles one-way only. Except for small garages with light traffic, these factors favour garage designs based on Figures 10 to 13, 15 and 16.

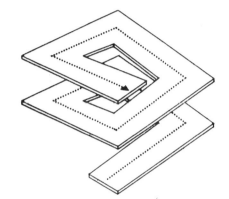

8

General layout of multi-storey ramp garages

25. Some multi-storey garages have been built to considerable heights, but they necessarily involve long journeys along steeply-sloping ramps and produce disinclination to use the higher floors. In residential areas where land costs are not particularly high this consumer resistance will be the limiting factor and parking floors on the top of high garages are unlikely to be fully used. The maximum height in any particular case will be influenced by design factors such as the ease of using the ramps and the ease of pedestrian access to the higher floors. For example, if one of the higher floors of a multi-storey garage links directly into one of the higher floors of the building it serves, it will be more popular than if the pedestrians have to descend to the ground. In commercial garages, four or five floors above ground is reckoned a reasonable maximum. In residential areas half this, i.e. two floors above ground, might be thought a reasonable maximum at present. There should be no special difficulty in constructing hem with provision for putting on extra floors if required.

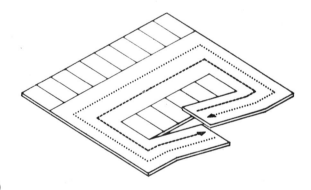

9

Descriptions

26. Types of garages can be described as follows:
Sloping floor: Where the floor on which the car is parked is sloped so that the aisle between the parked cars forms a gradual ramp leading on to the next floor (Figure 8).
Ramp access: Where the floors are level and separate ramps lead between them (Figures 9, 10, 11, etc.).
Clearway: Where the ramps are entirely separate from the parking floor (Figures 12 and 13). Some designs incorporate this on the 'out' ramp only.
Adjacent parking: Where the aisles between the parked cars are used as ramps (Figure 8) or as links between the ramps (Figures 9 and 10).

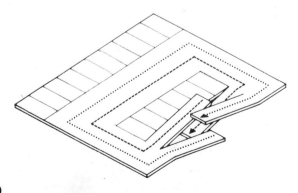

10

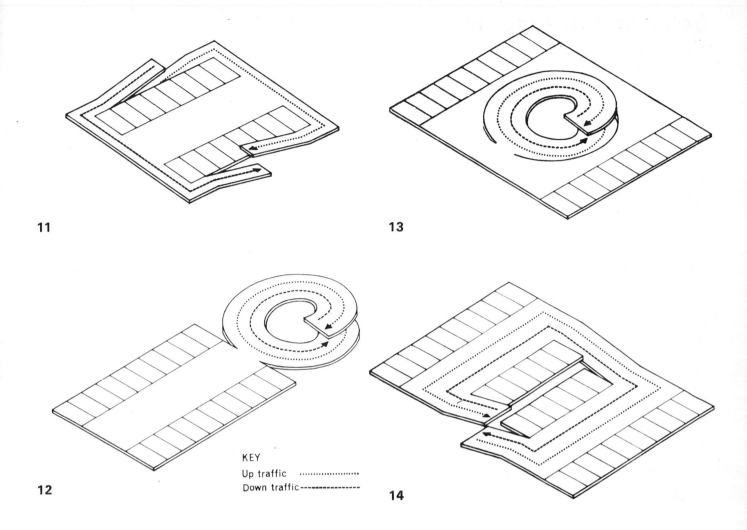

11

13

12

KEY
Up traffic ....
Down traffic -----------------

14

Ramp access garages, one-level floors

27. Figures 9, 10 and 11 show how changes in ramp design affect the functioning of the garage. Figure 9 is one of the least sophisticated designs, incorporating two-way traffic on aisles with adjacent parking. Figure 10 rearranges the ramps in what is known as opposed formation (crossing like scissors) in order to make the aisles one-way, while Figure 11 shows how they can be rearranged to give a 'clearway' design with no through traffic on the aisles. Figures 12 and 13 show different ways of using circular ramps. Both are 'clearway' ramps, but in Figure 12 they are outside the garage structure: in Figure 13 they are inside.

Ramp access garages, split-level floors

28. Split-level designs offer advantages in some circumstances. Figure 14 shows the basic unsophisticated design. In Figures 15 and 16 the ramps are rearranged so that the aisles become one-way. If the aisles are kept one-way rigidly, it is necessary, in designs like Figure 15, for unparking cars to drive up half a storey before descending, which is liable to lead to confusion.

29. In split-level garages ramps tend to cost less than those with one level, but there is likely to be some waste of space at ground level on flat sites because of the half-floor. These garages have a minimum width of two 'bins' (i.e. two aisles, four lines of parking places, usually about 30·000 wide, although for garages for residential areas only this dimension could be somewhat reduced by careful design) which restricts the sites for which they are suitable.

30. Ramp details for a design based on the diagrammatic principles of Figure 16 have been worked out in more detail in Figure 18. This shows how a floor to half-level-floor ramp can be accommodated in the roughly 10·000 occupied by two lines of cars, a feature that makes this type of garage unusually economical. Theoretically some ground space can be saved by tucking the bonnets of cars under the tail of the cars on the half-floors above, but this makes the design of the garage inflexible if car shapes change at any time in the future to a 'forward drive' or van-type silhouette. Even with present shapes bonnets can get trapped and damaged under the upper floor, and there is some risk of personal injury too.

Sloping floor garages

31. Necessarily this type of garage has to be arranged in some form of continuous spiral as in Figure 8. It also has a minimum width of two 'bins' (as paragraph 29) which again restricts the sites for which it is suitable. It is necessarily of the adjacent parking type, but the use of the parking aisle as the access ramp does lead to considerable economies in cost. In commercial garages of this type it is quite common to arrange for an 'expressway' ramp as the exit.

32. This type of garage is ordinarily economical in land since no space is used for separate ramps, though on the lower floors of large garages, where traffic is considerable, it may be necessary to widen the aisle and so take up more room. The natural slope

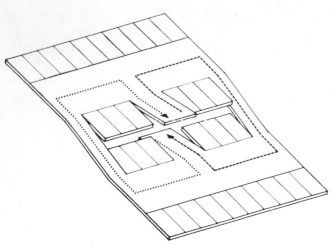

15

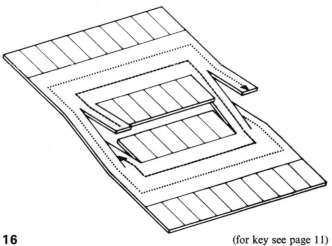

16

(for key see page 11)

of the land is unlikely to take up all the waste space at the ground created by the long shallow ramp, and it may be necessary partially to sink a semi-basement section of parking to get full use of the site.

Attendant and mechanical parking garages

33. A number of commercial ramp garages rely on the use of skilled parking attendants to park cars closer than they would normally be parked by their owners and to double and treble bank the cars. To run such a garage efficiently requires a large labour force at peak times (one man for about 30 cars) and shifts covering 24 hours. The capitalized cost of such a force puts the garage up to the cost of a mechanical parking garage, with which it is competitive. The mechanical parking garage itself uses machinery to pack cars tightly, and while most types are cheap in labour, they are at present very expensive in capital cost—over twice as much per car as the ordinary ramp garage. Both methods are more suitable for unusually difficult or very expensive sites (of the order of £250,000 per hectare) and are not likely to be generally used in residential areas.

Sloping sites

34. On steeply sloping sites two-level garages can be produced quite economically by a system of cut and fill to make terraces. The principles will be seen in Figure 17. The economy is in using the ground to carry the aisle instead of, as in the more usual two-storey type, using a suspended floor for the upper aisle. Clearly there is some saving of space in placing one lock-up over another, but Figure 17 shows why this type is not as space-saving as the more usual two-storey type.

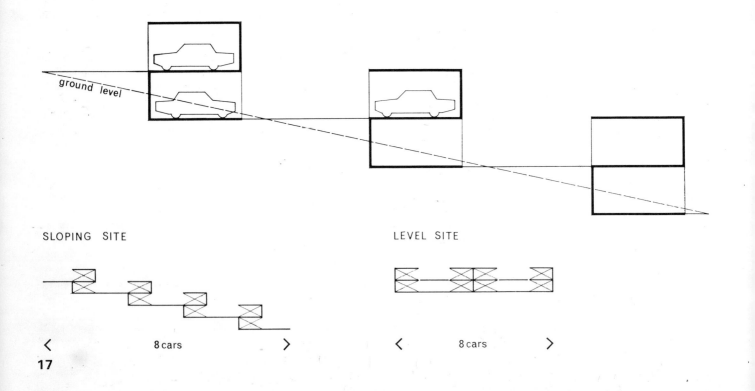

SLOPING SITE

LEVEL SITE

< 8 cars >

< 8 cars >

17

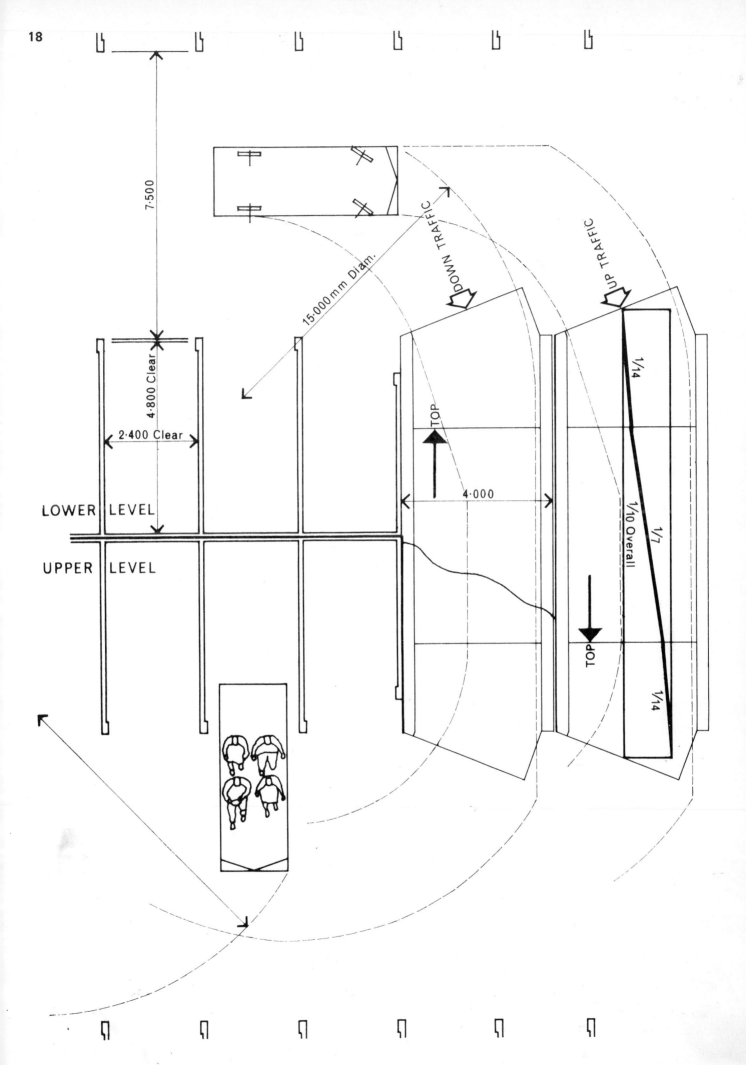

18

7·500

15·000 mm Diam.

4·800 Clear

2·400 Clear

LOWER LEVEL

UPPER LEVEL

DOWN TRAFFIC

UP TRAFFIC

TOP

TOP

4·000

1/14

1/10 Overall

1/7

1/14

Structural fire requirements

35. The fire resistance of garages, as of other buildings, is controlled by the Building Regulations 1965 and subsequent amendments.[1] This note is not intended to be an interpretation of these requirements, but as background information for use in discussion with the authorities who will be administering the Regulations. Multi-storey parking garages have many unusual features and particular examples may justify some relaxation of the Regulations. Circular 17/68 discusses some of the issues considered before relaxations are granted. It should be noted that the Circular is specifically concerned with open garages and not (as paragraph 8) with multi-storey private lock-up garages.

36. In addition to the control under the Building Regulations it is usually thought necessary for garages containing over about 20 cars[2] to be licensed under the Petroleum (Consolidation) Act 1928, the Petroleum Spirit (Motor Vehicles, etc.) Regulations 1929, and subsequent amendments. In addition, the 1929 Regulations contain certain other requirements applicable to nearly all garages. The licensing authority (normally the District Council) may attach such conditions as they think expedient to the licence.

Fire risk

37. The fire risk in well-designed and properly run parking garages is not very great. The modern car seldom catches fire in ordinary use, and the structure of the garage is a negligible risk. However, there are two most common sources of danger. The first is car maintenance by individual owners, within the garage itself—open bonnets, lighted matches, blowlamps, welding apparatus. This risk can be reduced by prohibiting such operations, and the taking of cans of petrol into the garage; and by providing a servicing area elsewhere. The second is incendiarism, possibly by children. To eliminate both these risks entirely will require constant supervision, which is normally out of the question, but some supervision will be needed, probably by the estate caretakers. In addition, it is desirable that doors to lock-ups (where used) should have some part made of open wire mesh so that the contents of the lock-ups can be under control. Fire fighting is discussed further in paragraphs 80 to 87.

Fire resistance

38. The fire severity in a parking garage due to the cars alone is not very great. The Ministry of Works' Post-war Building Study No. 28 (see Bibliography) calculated the fireload density as falling well within that for which a fire resistance of not less than one hour is suggested. Subsequent research work (for example Fire Note 10) has confirmed that the basic requirements need not be very onerous. It is not always possible to rate the required fire resistance of the structure simply on a count of the contents—the risk to the surroundings, for example, has to be

considered—but, nevertheless, the fire resistance necessary to resist collapse is unlikely to be as high as the four hours that is frequently required by simple application of Regulation E5, particularly with open-sided car parks. Although general guidance on possible grounds for relaxation of the Building Regulations are given in Circular 17/68, a brief commentary here may be helpful.

39. There are cases where a higher resistance than that called for by the cars alone will be necessary. Where there must be no possibility of collapse (for example, where the garage is supporting a large building complex) a safety factor will be required in the resistance, and, in addition, it may be necessary to take precautions against explosion. This is discussed further in Post-war Building Study No. 28. Following the 'Ronan Point' disaster, more recent work on resistance against explosions has been done, and some conclusions incorporated in the Building Regulations (5th Amendment) SI 1970 No. 109. The Building Study is mainly concerned with a particular example, the underground garage, where the enclosing effect of the walls produces a greater heat intensity. If mechanical means are used to park cars closer together than normal, or if the structure of the garage is combustible, or if the garage is used also for the incidental storage of household goods, the fire severity will also be increased.

40. Circular 17/68 considers the circumstances where there is unlikely to be a spread of fire from one car to another and therefore no danger of collapse. But the cost saving in not providing a fire resistance sufficient to prevent collapse in the event of a fire may have to be weighed against the disadvantages (such as increased insurance and the possible loss of all the cars). It would also be necessary to ensure that the provision and construction of the means of escape were fully adequate in the circumstances.

41. The cube and area of even a small multi-storey garage are necessarily large compared with other types of buildings although, as explained earlier, the fire danger in such garages is not very great. The value of providing fire break compartment walls has to be weighed against the possible inconvenience in operation and local factors such as the availability of the fire brigade, the degree of supervision, and the risk to surrounding buildings, and areas considerably larger than those required by good practice in other uses may well be permissible.

42. The possibility of heat being radiated from openings in the face of the garage on to adjoining buildings will be taken care of in the normal way by the boundary requirements of the Building Regulations (or as relaxed as suggested in Circular 17/68).

---

[1] At the time of writing (1971) the production of a consolidated version of the Building Regulations is under consideration. References should be altered appropriately on publication.

[2] The actual criterion is 60 gallons of petrol, assumed to be contained in the tanks of 20 cars at three gallons per car.

Floor construction

Floor loading

43. Floor loading requirements are given in the Building Regulations.

Structural aspects

44. Structural aspects are covered in the relevant Codes of Practice, but particular note should be made of the need to waterproof floors. Cars can carry quite a lot of water in the form of snow and ice, so that all floors must be waterproof. Parking garages in residential areas will require a higher standard of waterproofing than commercial garages since the cars will be exposed to leakage from above for longer periods. This can normally be achieved by careful control of in-situ concrete, with patching afterwards if and where trouble develops, but precast floors may require a 0·075 grano or 0·100 concrete (0·019 × 1:2:4) screed, in some cases with a membrane such as polythene. In addition, an adequate floor slope (2%) into drains of suitable design (petrol interceptors) is essential.

45. Obtaining a reasonable degree of waterproofing will involve ensuring a high quality concrete, adequate compaction, the presence of steel to control cracking (with adequate cover to all steel), limitation in size of panels, and the provision of watertight movement joints. The same applies to a concrete roof for normal use. For roof gardening, where the water is likely to stand, a membrane will probably be essential.

46. Asphalt does not possess a great flexibility to movement of the underlying structure, so that expansion joints with guttering systems will still be needed even where it is used. Asphalt is also liable to soften under oil drips from standing cars. While this process is not likely to be rapid, protection by means of a tile or similar surface finish may be necessary where failure cannot be tolerated.

47. Floor finishes should be moderately rough. Smooth finishes become slippery with grease and so dangerous to pedestrians; very rough finishes present maintenance problems. Recommended concrete finishes are wood-float or broom or lightly pattern-tamped. Sodium silicate treatment, or something similar, will prevent dusting of cement screed surfaces.

Floor planning

48. For garages in residential areas there are management advantages in providing each car with a lock-up wire cage. This form of construction will not alter the fire risk and, as it is cheap compared with the basic cost of the structure, it can be provided for a relatively small increase in the rent (about 15%). It considerably reduces the risk of theft or damage to the car and makes the parking place a much more marketable proposition. The alternative is to enclose the whole of the ground floor of the garage by a secure fence with lockable gates for entrance and exit, each tenant having a key. This is less satisfactory, as it leaves cars open to accidental damage from other cars and relies on each tenant properly locking the gates. In time, as garages become more numerous and more widely used, such

thief-and-vandal-proofing may become unnecessary, as it already is in America, but at present it seems both to be necessary and demanded by tenants.

49. Where lock-up cages are not provided, or seem likely to be removed within the life of the structure, the use of clear-span floors has operational advantages, obtained at an extra structural cost of some 15%. The absence of intermediate columns makes manoeuvring easier and also makes it possible to change the parking bay width or angle if at any time in the future car sizes change. By using pre-stressed concrete and taking advantage of the relatively light loading of private cars it is possible to span the 15·000 of two lines of parked cars and the aisle between with a reasonable depth of structure.

50. Where lock-up cages are provided there is less reason why intermediate columns cannot be used. Interlocking plans with angle-parked cars can still be used, but construction is probably easier if parking is at 90° to the aisles, in the more usual way.

51. There are obvious advantages in limiting the plan width of each column as much as possible, but they will still be wider than the frame for the wire partitioning. The length in plan of each column is unimportant provided it does not foul the driver's door when the door is opened.

52. In open garages, columns, where used, should ideally be set back from the aisle about 0·500 to give more manoeuvring space at the critical point. Where lock-up cages are used the width of the cage door is, if the doors are 'up-and-over', fixed by the column, since the door in the open position would otherwise foul the column, and there is no reason therefore why the column could not come forward right up to the aisle.

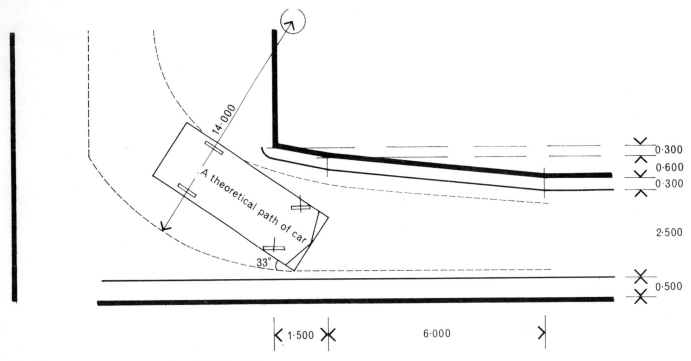

19 Flare at ramp entrance from 7·300 aisle

Ramp design

53. The gradient on straight ramps should not exceed 1 in 10 normally, or 1 in 7 for short lengths. On circular ramps it is measured on the centre line and preferably should not exceed 1 in 12. A transition length of at least 3·000 at half gradient, or on a vertical curve, is necessary at the top and bottom of ramps and the corners can be further rounded-off in construction. The effective headroom at these points should be carefully watched as the car 'bridges' across its wheelbase at the end of the ramp. For parking ramps, i.e. designs where the parking floor is gently sloped to act as a ramp as well, the gradient should not exceed 1 in 25.

54. It has been found that where ramps are two-way, i.e. with no separation between up and down lanes, drivers prefer not to pass on the sloping portion. They tend to swing wide at corners using the full width of the ramp as a single lane. In all but the smallest garages, therefore, it is recommended that up and down lanes are separated by a kerb at least 0·300 wide (more on corners or curved ramps), or are physically separate.

55. The dimensions in the paragraphs below are rather less than those normally quoted for garages designed for the larger American-type cars. While many such cars could use these ramps it is assumed that they will be allocated spaces on the ground floor. Where they are not or where there is a real risk of their using the ramps, American practice should be followed (see Bibliography and paragraph 3).

Straight ramps

56. The minimum width of straight ramps should be 2·500, with a 0·300 wide kerb 0·100 high on either side. End sections, on which cars are starting or completing a turn, should be flared to greater widths, and the outside kerb on such a section should preferably be 0·500. The flaring depends on the required turn and will be governed by the inside turning circle of the car. This is not, of course, a perfect circle since it is modified by the geometry of a car's turning and by the time the driver takes to turn the steering wheel to the required amount. The minimum amount required will be slightly different at the entrance and exit of the ramp. Where, at the exit, all the turning movement is normally made off the ramp, a flare of about 0·600 over the length of the transition gradient should give the driver adequate freedom. Where any turning movement is made on a ramp the width of that part should be increased as for curved ramps. At the entry the flaring should be rather longer as the rear wheels of a car turning into a straight line follow a gradual curve into that line.

57. Figure 19 shows a theoretical curve followed by such an entry from a 7·300 wide aisle and a flare which will accommodate this, made in straight sections for ease of construction. It will be noted that this flare is to accommodate the straightening-out movement of the car, the major part of the turn being completed in the aisle. Where the aisle is narrower than 7·300

20

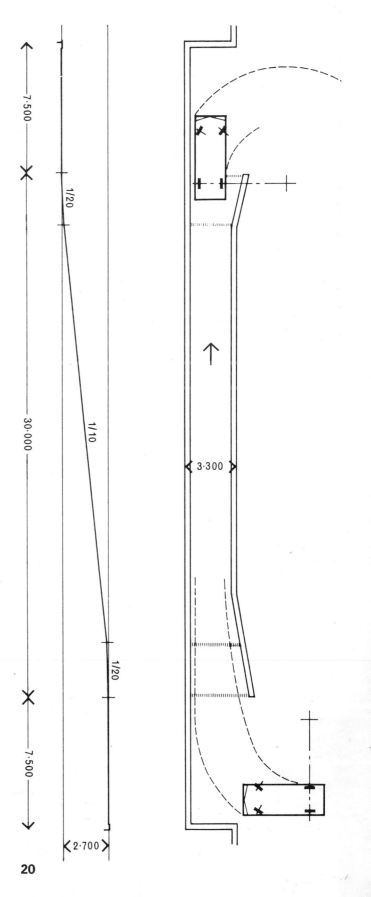

it may be necessary for the ramp to accommodate rather more of the turning movement proper. The relevant parts of the ramp and the aisle should then have at least the dimensions quoted for circular ramps i.e. they should be able to accommodate within their area a path of the relevant width and radius. Short ramps are often made overall to the maximum width of the flare as the saving in space and materials in following minimum standards is outweighed by the constructional difficulties.

58. Figure 20 shows the approximate area required by a straight ramp.

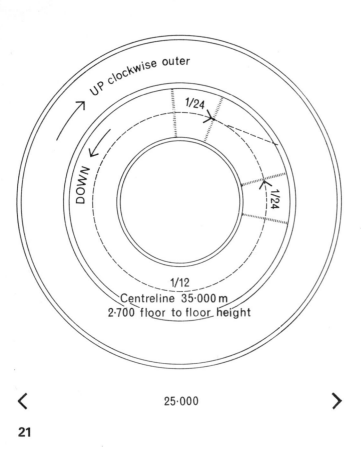

25·000

21

Curved ramps

59. The minimum radius of the outside kerb of an 'up' ramp should be 9·000, of a 'down' ramp 8·500. The minimum width at minimum radius should be 3·500 between kerbs. This could be reduced to 3·100 minimum, preferably 3·200, at 12·000 outside kerb radius. The inside kerb radius should not be less than 3·500, since otherwise cars can enter the curve at too sharp an angle. Superelevation up to 1 in 10 can be incorporated to make turning easier. The kerb separating ramps should be at least 0·500, and the outside kerb on any ramp preferably 0·500, wide. Greater dimensions will be necessary if there is any real risk of larger American cars using the ramps (see paragraph 55).

60. It is recommended practice to make climbing cars use the outside ramp. For Great Britain, where the 'keep left' rule is enforced, this means that spirals should be clockwise up the building.

61. Figure 21 shows the approximate area required by concentric ramps.

Access

62. Garages should not open immediately on to a busy road. The gradients in the outgoing direction should be so arranged that cars can pause on the level before entering a highway. In the incoming direction there should be enough space to allow cars to pull clear of the road before starting on the slow climb up the ramps. Where cars are likely to arrive in bunches a small reservoir space clear of the road may have to be provided. Reservoirs of the scale planned for commercial garages (where it is necessary to issue tickets) are not needed.

Headroom

63. Urban garages in the U.S.A. are designed with a minimum headroom of 2·300, lower ceilings having been found to damage car aerials. Parking garages will only be used by regular customers, and they might be expected to remember to lower the aerials before entering, but some will undoubtedly forget. If a 'loading gauge'—in the form, perhaps, of a metal rod with a bell hung on chains—is fixed at the entrance as a reminder, it is possible to reduce the minimum headroom to dimensions corresponding to the usual headroom for lock-up garages, say 2·100. This would apply under beams and ramps: as a general ceiling height it might be too oppressive. (It will be remembered that effective headroom under ramps can often be less than the actual headroom due to the 'bridging effect' of the car.)

64. A small number of vehicles, of the motor caravan type, are considerably higher than the general run of cars and may need to be considered separately. This could be done by giving the ground floor of the garage a higher minimum headroom, say 2·300. All low headroom points should be clearly marked with the relevant dimensions, making allowance for the 'bridging effect' of the cars at ramp ends.

Details

Construction of lock-ups

65. Lock-ups, when they are provided, can be made out of heavy chain link mesh or expanded metal on wood studs. Alternatively the walls can be made solid out of concrete and used as a load-bearing structure. 'Up-and-over' or 'slide-and-fold' doors should be fitted, as side-hung doors will obstruct the view along the aisles and are also liable to be damaged.

66. In designing the walling, and in particular the walling at the end of the lock-up (possibly the external wall of the building) damage by carelessly driven cars should be considered. This implies either a replaceable or a very strong wall or fence. Damage will be reduced if each lock-up is provided with a precast concrete block that can be adjusted by the tenant to a suitable position to act as a kerb to stop the wheels of the car.

67. All fittings on parking floors should be placed where they are not likely to be damaged by carelessly driven cars—in particular, building services such as water pipes should not encroach on the design areas either horizontally or vertically.

68. No object in the design areas should be between 0·100 and 1·000 high, as such objects are not visible when reversing a car, but are high enough to damage bumper or bodywork. This may involve making some parapet walls higher than they would otherwise be.

Pedestrians

69. Only the largest commercial garages are thought to warrant separate access for pedestrians within the parking floors themselves. It is, however, common sense to arrange where possible for pedestrians to enter and leave the garage at the opposite end from the entry and exit for cars. The car ramps should not be used as normal means of access from floor to floor by pedestrians, although they can be used as emergency fire exits. Staircases should be provided instead, and at least partly enclosed to prevent ice making them dangerous in winter. Stairs used as means of escape should be separated from the garage by a fire-resisting enclosure of the required resistance. It may be necessary to use external balconies as links between residential accommodation and the multi-storey garage in order to obtain complete fire separation between the two. Drivers who are disabled will need the usual special consideration.

Fire exits

70. Although the actual provision of fire exits is not within the powers of the Building Regulations, any proposals will be looked at by the licensing authority, and by the Department in considering whether to relax the Regulations. Some guidance on this is contained in Circular 17/68 (in particular paragraph 6(6)).

Fittings and services

Fittings

71. All fittings should be of exterior quality. They should be placed out of the way of cars (of car aerials in the case of overhead fittings) or otherwise protected.

Lighting

72. If artificial light is to be used for the interior during daytime the lighting of entrances and exits will require special consideration because of the transition from a high level of daylight to a comparatively low level of light inside. This might involve values of over 400 lux, or an arrangement of screens to break up the daylight progressively. Some brief notes on this, with further references, are in an article by Dr. D. A. Schreuder in *International Lighting Review*. The general level of lighting inside will also need to be higher than that required in a garage which only needs artificial light at night. The recommendations in the current (1968 revision) Illuminating Engineering Society Code are for a minimum level within garages of 50 lux and a limiting glare index of 28. This level is rather higher than that currently found in many commercial garages, which have minima of the order of 20 lux. This lower level at present appears reasonably acceptable functionally for night time use. However, it is generally thought that higher levels of illumination make policing easier and reduce vandalism. In addition illumination standards are continually rising: designs to low levels should, therefore, be capable of being revised. In main ramps the minimum should in any case be rather higher (minimum 50 lux).

73. The glare of exposed lighting units can be a problem, especially where they conflict with directional signs. They have to be mounted on the underside of the ceiling, which will be only just above eye level. The fittings chosen should, therefore, have a low surface brightness (such as fluorescent lighting) or give adequate screening of the light source. In one-way aisles the light sources can be hidden behind beams—care being taken that this does not produce undesirable shadows.

74. Lights should be screened so that they do not shine directly into adjacent bedroom windows. Higher levels of general illumination may also produce enough stray light to provoke complaints, which may involve more general screening. Besides an adequate level of illumination, columns and other obstructions should be picked out with paint of a contrasting colour.

Electrical

75. The electrical installation should conform to the requirements of the Institution of Electrical Engineers' Regulations for the Electrical Equipment of Buildings. According to the current edition (1966 with 1969 supplement) it would appear that, as the garages would be adequately ventilated, protection of cables against fire and explosion is not necessary. Regulation C10 requires that every fixed item of apparatus shall, unless of a totally enclosed or flameproof type, be fixed at a height above the general floor level as required by the authority administering the statutory requirements. Reference should also be made to British Standard Code of Practice C.P.321, Electric Wiring Systems.

76. There is some demand by car owners for electrical points in each lock-up for lighting, battery charging, and frost protection heaters. Cost has, up to the present, ruled out such provision. However, where portable apparatus, i.e. handlamps, heaters, etc., with flexible leads, is used, it should be adequately protected, properly earthed and shielded. Proper maintenance is essential. The use of a reduced voltage system for portable apparatus should be considered.

Signing

77. Directional signs should be of normal traffic engineering quality; they should be so placed as to avoid damage by car aerials.

Heating

78. Snow and ice on external ramps may cause difficulty in some areas. In most circumstances the normal methods of clearing will suffice, but where high exposure is combined with local labour difficulties electric heating may be necessary. Heating cables may be embedded in either concrete or bitumen surfacing. The local Electricity Board will be able to give advice on the details and the Road Research Laboratory has information on existing installations.

79. Running and capital costs will be fairly high, high enough to justify investigation of the alternative of providing a lightweight permanent cover to the exposed portion of the ramp. Where this can be provided cheaply, it may be competitive in total cost. As a first guide to the costs of a heating system, an installation in London has an installed load of 130 watts per m². The cost is, for capital—plus—operating, of the order of £0·30 per m² per year.[1]

Fire

80. Fire fighting equipment will be specified by the licensing authority to suit the particular requirements of the building being considered. 'Dry risers' will probably be required—in the Scottish Building Regulations[2] they may be required where any floor is higher than 11·000 above ground or is over 900m². They are normally placed within the protected enclosure of escape stairways. The inlet to such risers should be accessible to fire pumps—in Scotland within 18·000 of an access point, and no point in the garage should be more than 61·000 from an outlet. Where risers are not required the fire brigade will still require access to the garage for appliances, preferably along the whole length of one or two sides.

81. Portable equipment presents a difficult problem in an unsupervised garage, as it is likely to be tampered with. Where

---

[1] *Road Research Laboratory report LR* 303.

[2] But not in the English Building Regulations. This and following abbreviated summaries of Scottish Regulations are intended only as background for detailed discussions with the statutory authorities and not as either definitive requirements or a definitive interpretation of the legislation.

provided, it will probably consist of groups of one 2-gallon foam extinguisher and three sand buckets within 30·000 of any point.

82. Where a fire alarm system is fitted it is possible to link the fire fighting appliances to the alarm so that their removal sets the alarm off—possibly in a cupboard with the catch connected to the alarm system. Where this is not practicable the provision of such equipment may not be practicable either if the local authority think it is liable to be stolen.

83. Sprinklers or drenchers may be required in a few cases, perhaps where the garage consists of a large undivided area and is potentially dangerous to residential accommodation (for example where the accommodation is directly over the garage). Where sprinklers are required they should be of the 'alternate wet and dry pipe system' type. This type can be drained in winter to avoid freezing, compressed air providing the necessary link between the water mains or storage tank and the sprinkler heads. It would probably, depending on the degree of exposure, be desirable to have all the pipework galvanised. The cost of such an installation would be considerable, perhaps £30–£50 per car depending on the water supplies available in a 300-car garage, and it might also be necessary to increase the headroom in the garage to accommodate the falls to the pipes necessary to drain the system. Sprinklers will 'contain' a fire if it starts; drenchers along the outside of a garage will only help to prevent it spreading beyond the garage to adjoining buildings, but the cost would be rather less, say £5 per car to cover one long side of the garage. Normally sprinklers and drenches will automatically activate a local alarm bell and, at an additional cost (capitalized at about £2 per car) can automatically telephone the fire brigade. Where an estate has a 24-hour caretaker service this last facility may be unnecessary.

84. An automatic alarm system will provide less positive protection than sprinklers (the amount will depend on the fire brigade cover), albeit at less cost. This would capitalize at between £5 and £10 per car—one alarm head for two or three cars—depending on the fire brigade alerting arrangements.

85. Insurance premiums are reduced where automatic protection is provided (substantially for approved installations of sprinklers, but the original premium is small for buildings of such low risk and the reduction will probably have only a small effect, less than 10%, on the economics of installing this protection. However it must be emphasised that most garages are unlikely to offer immediate and substantial danger to residential accommodation and so will probably not require automatic protection.

86. There is little special risk in an adequately ventilated basement garage. Fire fighting access can be more difficult and needs to be carefully considered, and smoke vents, of an order of size of about 10% of the floor area, will be required, but in underground garages built under grass or paving, the risk of further involvement is negligible and the important factors to consider are solely the danger to firemen and the loss of parked cars.

87. It is prudent, where automatic protection is not provided, to make arrangements for the fire brigade to be called at any hour of the day or night, and these arrangements should be prominently displayed on noticeboards in the garage.

Ventilation

88. Ventilation in above-ground garages can be obtained either mechanically or naturally. Below ground it is necessary to rely in part at least on mechanical ventilation since petrol vapour being heavier than air tends to sink. However, the standard of ventilation needed is set by the emission from car exhausts of carbon monoxide gas, since this will require a higher rate of ventilation than that needed to cope with petrol vapour. In garages serving residential areas there will be one comparatively short period of time in the morning when the rush hour cars are starting from cold when it will require a higher rate of ventilation than is likely to be needed during the rest of the day.

89. The performance of mechanical ventilation systems can be specified fairly accurately. For example the Scottish Building Regulations[1] may require two independent mechanical systems, each capable of giving four air changes per hour. (The duplication is partly in case one system breaks down.) The performance of such a system is analysed in some detail in Post-war Building Study No. 28. The Scottish Regulations also describe some of the details of the required system; it should be independent of any other ventilating plant, should have at least one exhaust air outlet for every 190m², should extract at least two-thirds of the air from outlets not more than 0·600 above the floor level, and should have an independently powered warning system to instruct drivers to switch engines off if the system breaks down. It is normal practice in low pressure ventilation systems to provide any openings which present a risk of the spread of fire with steel dampers held by fusible links. In high pressure systems such dampers may not be practicable, and advice should be taken on the most suitable methods for the system.

90. It is more difficult to specify the requirements for natural ventilation, since it depends on so many variable factors. However, a considerable amount of guidance is now given in paragraph 6(5) of Circular 17/68.

Servicing

91. In any large garage there will be a considerable demand for the simpler types of car servicing—cleaning and washing—and some for more advanced mechanical repairs. It is desirable that neither should take place inside the parking garage itself: the first to avoid the floors getting flooded and the second to keep the fire risk down. A washdown area to take several cars is essential. It should be inconspicuous, and properly drained, and ideally it should have a standpipe fitted with a self-closing tap for filling buckets. Self-closing taps are normally run off service pipes, not direct off the mains. Areas for major servicing may be more controversial since they involve management problems; at the worst they may become back street car repair businesses. Where servicing areas are provided the minimum requirements will be a pit or ramp and, less essentially, an electric point and a lifting beam. They should, of course, have adequate fire separation from the parking garage.

---

[1] But not in the English Building Regulations.

Appendix: Car turning-circles

1. It is possible to calculate the space needed by a car doing various movements, but most people will find it easier to draw the movements and measure the results. Not too much credence should be placed on such theoretical results, however, as few drivers follow precisely theoretical movements. For example, on most cars it is possible, though not advisable, to turn from one full lock to the other without moving the car. In practice it is much easier, and better, to make the turn while the car is moving, and the small distance needed should be added to the theoretical distance.

2. Figure 1 shows the basic geometry of circle-turning. The centre of the circle is on the line of the back axle and all parts of the car turn around this centre. The front wheels of the car are linked (by a non-parallel motion) so that when the steering wheel is turned, they trace a path about this centre. In practice there are minor modifications to this simple geometry to provide good 'road holding'. When a car turns a sharp corner slowly it is possible to treat the path followed by each wheel as an arc of a circle with its centre on the axis of the back wheels. To the arc needs to be added, however, an introductory transition, while the driver turns the steering on to full lock, and an exit transition while he turns it back to the straight position. Thus the shape of the total curve is more complex.

3. For reasons of simplicity some books on traffic engineering show the total curve swept by the front wheels as a true arc with its centre on the extention of the front axle. This provides a rule of thumb for allowing for the introductory transition and is probably a reasonable representation for vehicles moving at normal road speeds. However, the path thus arrived at is by no means the minimum path and at low speeds the divergence can be of importance. At the ultimate, the front wheels can be turned to full lock while the car is stationary (or so nearly so as to make no difference) in which case the front of the car will go off sideways instantaneously as in Figure 22a. This is a manoeuvre sometimes adopted by experienced drivers. By starting from a position parallel and next to the kerb they manage to make a U-turn in a carriageway of less width than the turning circle diameter.

4. It is possible to consider the transition curves mathematically. The exit transition from the turn is of some interest to the designer since it creates problems where a car makes a turn into a narrow ramp. A flare is normally required at this point to accommodate the transition (some suggested dimensions being given in Figure 19).

5. Two cases can usefully be considered. The first is when the car is turned on the required lock until the body of the car points in the final direction. The front wheels are then turned abruptly to the same direction and the car proceeds, as in Figure 22b. The path of the rear wheels is then a circular arc moving directly into a straight line, and there is no problem in describing this.

6. The other is when a car is turned on the required lock until a front wheel reaches a particular straight line, like a kerb,

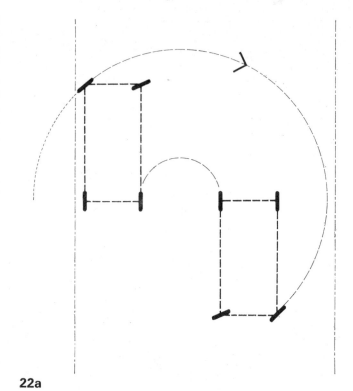

22a

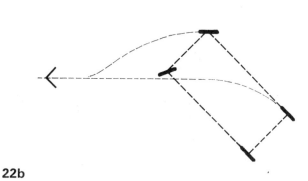

22b

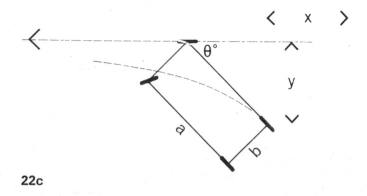

22c

218

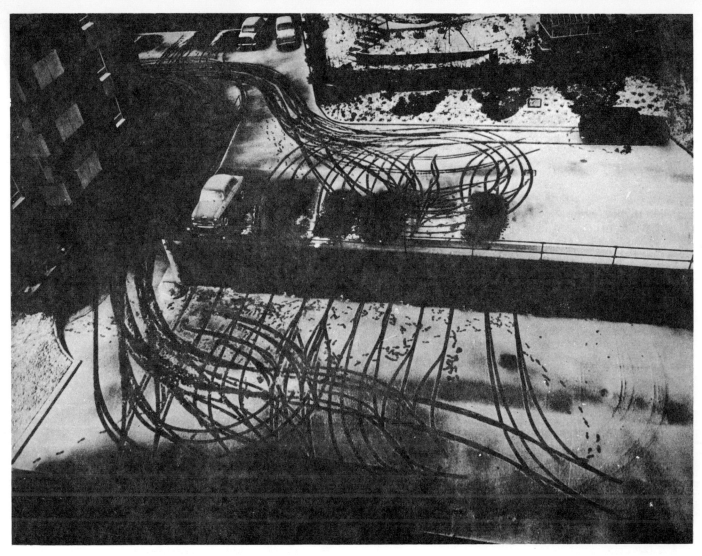

23

which leads in the final direction, and is then gradually straightened so as to follow this line. The back wheels (and, in association, the car body) then take more complicated paths. Initially they turn on a circle, as before, until the front wheel meets the line and begins to be straightened. They then follow curves of a complex character, gradually coming closer to the paths of the front wheels (Figure 22c). The position of the rear wheel on the same side as the front wheel which follows the straight line is given at any angular position[1] of the car by

$$X = a \log_e (\tan \tfrac{1}{2} \theta) + a \cos \theta + C$$

$$Y = a \sin \theta$$

Car movements at slow speeds will tend towards the second case in a confined place like a curved ramp entry, but factors such as the overall size of the car and the driver's attitude and skill will be important also.

7. The entry transition is discussed in some detail and a treatment suggested in *Strassenverkehrstechnik* (11 December, 1967), in an article entitled *Wirtschaftliche Aufteilung der Parkfläche von Parkhausen mit Rampenanlagen.*

---

[1] θ is the angle the car makes to the kerb at any point. It can take values only between 0° and the full lock angle of the outer front wheel in question. C is a constant whose value depends on the relative position of the origin and the commencement of the tractrix and *a* is the wheelbase. The position of the other wheels of the car can be derived by calculation or drawing.

8. Theoretic analyses of these kinds are of some value in early studies for designs departing from the dimensions suggested in the main text. There is, however, usually little difficulty in setting out a mock-up in an empty space (such as a large car park after hours) and testing it with 'representative' cars. It must, therefore, be emphasised that the results of theory should be tested on a full scale mock-up before being built. Figure 23, which shows some of the wide range of different approaches to garaging a car, will be of interest to those wishing to pursue the theory.

9. Turning circles quoted in tables are usually kerb-to-kerb dimensions, i.e. the diameter of the circle made by the outside front wheel. Detailed test reports often quote also the wall-to-wall circle, i.e. that made by the outside edge of the front bumper. They sometimes quote two dimensions for each—many cars are not quite the same on both locks.

Bibliography

General

1 AUTOCAR
Road tests and annual buyers' guide.
IPC Transport Press. Annual.

2 BEAZLEY (Elisabeth)
Design and detail of the space between buildings.
Architectural Press, 1960.

3 COCHRANE (T.)
Roads and paving: element design guide.
Architects' Journal, 9 November 1966, pp. 1173–1181.

4 FAIRWEATHER (L.) *and* SLIWA (J.)
AJ metric handbook, 3rd edition.
Architectural Press, 1970.

5 MINISTRY OF HOUSING AND LOCAL GOVERNMENT
Design Bulletin 5. *Landscaping for flats: the treatment of ground space on high density housing estates.*
2nd edition, HMSO, 1967.

6 MINISTRY OF HOUSING AND LOCAL GOVERNMENT
Homes for today and tomorrow (Parker Morris Report).
HMSO, 1961.

7 MINISTRY OF TRANSPORT
Roads in urban areas.
HMSO, 1966.

8 MINISTRY OF TRANSPORT: Mechanical Engineering Division.
Recommendations for siting and operation of controlled off-street car-parks.
The Division, 1970.

9 MOTOR
Specifications and prices of British and foreign cars.
IPC Transport Press. Annual.

10 SCHREUDER (Dr. D. A.)
Short tunnels.
International Lighting Review, Vol. XVI, No. 3, 1965, pp. 95–99.

11 SOCIETY OF MOTOR MANUFACTURERS AND TRADERS LIMITED
New registrations of new motor vehicles in Great Britain, Northern Ireland and The Isle of Man.
SMMT. Six monthly.

12 WHICH?
Road tests: special supplements.
Consumers' Association.

Multi-storey parking garages

13 ARCHITECTS' JOURNAL
Technical studies and design guides, various.
See in particular 22 and 29 June, 6 July 1966.

14 BAKER (G.) *and* FUNARO (B.)[1]
Parking.
New York: Reinhold, 1958.

15 KLOSE (D.)
Multi-storey car parks and garages.
Architectural Press, 1965.

16 MANZONI (Sir Herbert J.)
Public parking garages.
RIBA Journal, March 1958, pp. 147–159.

17 PIERCE (S. R.) *and others*
Planning: The architect's handbook, 8th edition.
Iliffe, 1959.

18 RICKER (E. R.)[2]
The traffic design of parking garages. Revised edition.
Saugatuck, Connecticut: Eno Foundation, 1957.

19 ROAD RESEARCH LABORATORY
Report LR 221: *Parking: dynamic capacities of car parks* (P. B. Ellson).
Road Research Laboratory, 1969.

20 VAHLEFELD (R.) *and* JACQUES (F.)[1]
Garages and service stations.
Leonard Hill, 1960.

Structural

21 BRITISH STANDARDS INSTITUTION
BS 4330: 1968. *Recommendations for the co-ordination of dimensions in building. Controlling dimensions* (Metric units).

22 FIRE RESEARCH STATION
Fire Note No. 10. *Fire and car-park buildings.*
(E. G. Butcher *and others*).
HMSO, 1968.

23 MINISTRY OF HOUSING AND LOCAL GOVERNMENT
Design Bulletin 16. *Co-ordination of components in housing: metric dimensional framework.*
HMSO, 1968.

24 MINISTRY OF HOUSING AND LOCAL GOVERNMENT
Co-ordination of components in housing: the dimensional framework and component size. Addendum to DB 16 and application of DC 10.
HMSO, 1970.

25 MINISTRY OF HOUSING AND LOCAL GOVERNMENT
Circular 17/68. *The Building Regulations*, 1965. *Multi-storey car parks.*
HMSO, 1968.

26 MINISTRY OF WORKS[1]
Post-war Building Studies No. 28. *Precautions against fire and explosion in underground car parks.* By a Joint Committee of the Department of Scientific and Industrial Research and of the Building Research Board of the Fire Officers' Committee.
HMSO, 1950.

---

[1] Out of print, but obtainable in some libraries.

[2] Not on sale in UK, but obtainable in some libraries.

27 ROAD RESEARCH LABORATORY
   Report LR 303. *Electrical road heating* (P. B. Ellson).
   Road Research Laboratory, 1969.

28 STATUTORY INSTRUMENT, 1965, No. 1373.
   The Building Regulations, 1965.
   169 pp., HMSO, 1965.

29 STATUTORY INSTRUMENT, 1966, No. 1144
   The Building (Second Amendment) Regulations, 1966.
   HMSO, 1966.

30 STATUTORY INSTRUMENT, 1967, No. 1645
   The Building (Third Amendment) Regulations, 1967.
   HMSO, 1967.

31 STATUTORY INSTRUMENT, 1969, No. 639
   The Building (Fourth Amendment) Regulations, 1969
   HMSO, 1969.

32 STATUTORY INSTRUMENT, 1970, No. 109
   The Building (Fifth Amendment) Regulations, 1970.
   HMSO, 1970.

33 STATUTORY INSTRUMENT, 1970, No. 1335
   The Building (Sixth Amendment) Regulations, 1970.
   HMSO, 1970.

34 STATUTORY INSTRUMENT, 1970, No. 1137 (S93)
   The Building Standards (Scotland) (Consolidation) Regulations,
   1970.
   HMSO, 1970.

5

HOUSING THE CAR (2)

Some medium density layouts

1 Introduction

Any housing scheme today has to provide for a steadily growing number of cars. The Buchanan Report[1] estimated (paragraph 45) that Great Britain's motor vehicle population could easily double within 10 years and nearly treble within 20.

This is not a trend that can be turned back or disregarded. We have to accept the car and plan for its increase. What we can do in housing schemes is minimise its visual intrusion; and, by separating it as completely as possible from pedestrians, keep it from making life dangerous and unpleasant. Only then can motorists and pedestrians, who are also sometimes the same people, enjoy the best of both worlds.

The main problem facing the designer of housing estates was succinctly posed in this passage from *Homes for today and tomorrow:*[2]

> '200. The overriding concern in designing with the car in mind must be to design for the pedestrian to stay alive. Since in a car-owning community a high proportion of the pedestrians and cyclists will be children, this will demand the segregation of pedestrian footpaths and cycleways from roads carrying motor vehicles, and preferably the organisation of these footpaths into a system leading from the quiet side of the houses to schools and shops and play spaces, so that children can go about their affairs with reasonable safety. Safety considerations also suggest the importance of arranging for cul-de-sac vehicular approach to residential development, so that vehicles adopt low speeds in the vicinity of homes and so that through traffic does not approach them at all.'

Safety is not, of course, the only consideration, even though it is the most important. Amenity, in its widest sense of pleasant living, is one; so is convenience, both for the driver with a car to garage or park, and the man, woman or child with an errand on foot; so is quiet; so is ease of getting to school or town or shops; so are sufficient open space and play space. The layout that is fair both to pedestrians and drivers will balance all these in the right proportions.

The purpose of this bulletin is to show how these 'user requirements' can be met by applying traffic separation[3] principles on the Radburn model, and to describe the special problems of house design and house grouping that they involve. It includes also some illustration of the way housing layouts that separate pedestrians and vehicles are developing in this country.

The bulletin is concerned with principles: it does not try to appraise particular schemes. It is hoped to do this later when more information is available on user reaction and capital costs.

The bulletin concentrates on medium density schemes of roughly 14 to 23 houses to the acre and providing for a car/dwelling ratio of 1, plus some allowance for casual and visitors' parking.

[1] *Traffic in towns:* A study of the long-term problems of traffic in urban areas (HMSO 1963; 50s.)
[2] Report of the Parker Morris Committee (HMSO 1961; 4s.)
[3] For the sake of brevity, the term 'traffic separation' is used throughout this bulletin, but applying only to residential areas, and not to the central areas of towns.

2 Background

As long ago as the late twenties over 21 million motor vehicles were registered in the United States, and the car had already become a disruptive factor in urban life. The grid layout of the typical American town, with its frequent intersections, added to the danger from traffic.

In 1928 a new system of planning, derived from the English garden city, began to be developed at Radburn in New Jersey. One of its aims was to secure safety from traffic without hampering the freedom of the car.

Roads were to be planned for vehicles only and not, as formerly, for general use. There was to be a complete and entirely separate pedestrian circulation system. A central area of parkland for recreation was an important feature. And, most revolutionary of all, the houses, which traditionally had always faced on to the roads with their main windows and sitting-out porches, were to face instead on to the pedestrian ways, and all access for servicing was to be on the vehicle side.

The intention was to build three residential areas, each of about $\frac{1}{2}$-mile radius, and to include a school and shopping centre, with generous car parking space attached.

These areas were to be connected with each other by safe foot bridges or underpasses, and each was to have a final population of 25,000. But the project was started at a bad time. The first 400 families moved in in 1929, almost on the eve of the Wall Street collapse. In the end only two neighbourhoods were completed before the venture became a financial casualty of the depression.

Even so, enough had been done to demonstrate the great possibilities of the 'Radburn idea'.

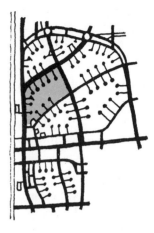

1 The original traffic separation layout at Radburn, New Jersey. (left) One of the completed neighbourhoods, (right) the block plan.

3 Traffic separation: basic principles

There are three essentials in any housing scheme which embodies the Radburn idea:

(a) roads for motor vehicles only;

(b) a separate footpath system;

(c) houses specially designed and grouped with separate access for pedestrians and cars.

These are the three basic principles of traffic separation. None of them is completely new or revolutionary in these days, but, used together, they can help to create a virtually new type of environment, and there is plenty of scope for variety and flexibility in combining them.

In a layout on the Radburn model or any development of it the neighbourhood is made up of several groups of houses, each group serviced from one access road for vehicles, which in turn is reached from a distributor road. The self-contained path system, independent of the vehicle roads, gives easy access on foot to every house and links houses with playgrounds, shops, schools and community buildings.

It has to be faced however that *absolute* separation of cars and pedestrians is impracticable, if only because bursting to get out of every vehicle is a would-be pedestrian; and because, except at a prohibitive cost in convenience and urbanity, it is impossible to keep children away from *every* spot where cars are likely to be. The Buchanan Report (paragraph 134) came to the conclusion, at any rate as far as shopping streets are concerned, that complete separation is not worth pursuing. And the same holds good for residential areas. Cars can be firmly canalised: but pedestrians have to be coaxed.

There are a number of successful developments in this country laid out on these principles. Examples are to be found at Basildon, Coventry, Cumbernauld, Northampton, Stevenage and Wrexham, among other places.

In some layouts, however, a number of things have not gone according to plan. There has been confusion over which is the main door, with visitors walking through the garden and entering through the kitchen or store, whereas brides and coffins go out past the dustbins. Alternatively, visitors may have to walk round to the front in the rain, having left their car on the other side. Children prefer playing on the hard surface of the cul-de-sac in wet weather rather than in the gardens or on the greens, and in any case they will play anywhere they can find the room, and not only where they are meant to. Postmen have got lost or had difficulty in finding the right house. It has proved difficult sometimes to ensure enough privacy. Some culs-de-sac with their garages and clothes lines are unsightly. In some layouts the turning circle at the head of the cul-de-sac is too small, making cars hard to manoeuvre.

In other words, like any new departure in design and planning, separating traffic from pedestrians throws up certain problems not all of which can be easily foreseen.

The bulletin deals in turn with the particular problems raised by the three basic principles described above, and illustrates ways in which some of them have been dealt with.

4 Roads for motor vehicles only

The essence of the Radburn idea is that, even if it is impossible to keep motor traffic and pedestrians completely apart, the two move on separate systems. The footpath system should make it unnecessary or unattractive for pedestrians to walk on or across roads. The road system should make it easy for cars to approach and service the living areas.

Any residential area laid out for traffic separation can take one of two basic forms, according to the demands of the site:

(*a*) a distributor road encloses or partly encloses, and defines, the residential area. Access roads are in the form of spurs which penetrate the site. Open space and the pedestrian network are then at the core. Most sites favour this form of layout. (Figure **2**.)

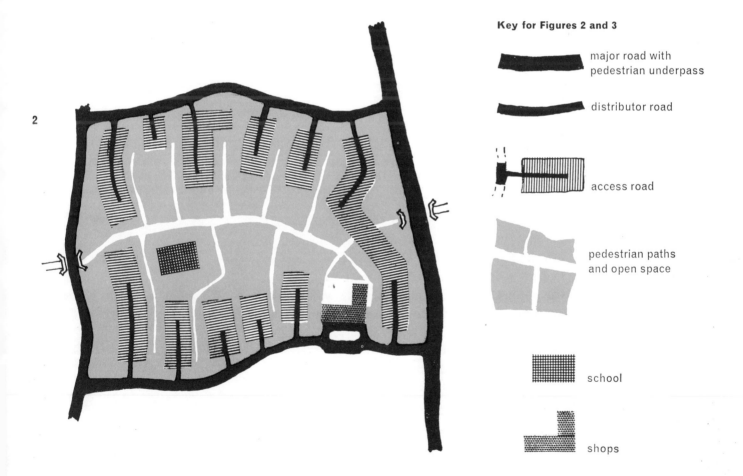

2

Key for Figures 2 and 3

major road with pedestrian underpass

distributor road

access road

pedestrian paths and open space

school

shops

3

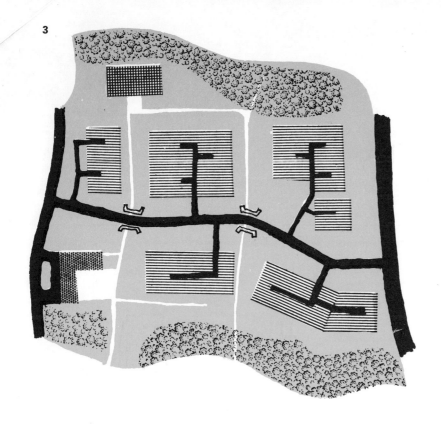

(*b*) where existing development, natural features or steep contours make an encircling route impracticable, the opposite occurs. The major distributor becomes a spine road with spurs on either side. To keep the path system independent more underpasses or bridges are needed. (Figure **3**.)

In either case the distributor road should connect directly with a free-flowing major carriageway bringing traffic conveniently into and out of the area. Bus stops which serve the area should themselves be served by pedestrian underpasses wherever numbers of people might otherwise have to make a dangerous crossing of the road at peak hours.

In general, motor traffic routes, including distributor roads, should be considered as lines of danger. The vehicle flow should be planned *for safety above all*. Routes should be made to fit in with the topography of the site. Junctions should be reduced to a minimum. Houses should not front on to traffic roads.

In travelling from one point to another *within the area*, pedestrians should have priority and the shortest route. This may mean sending cars round a longer way. Small parking lay-bys or spurs for visitors' waiting cars should be provided off the main line of traffic. These lay-bys should if possible give direct access to the pedestrian paths leading to houses.

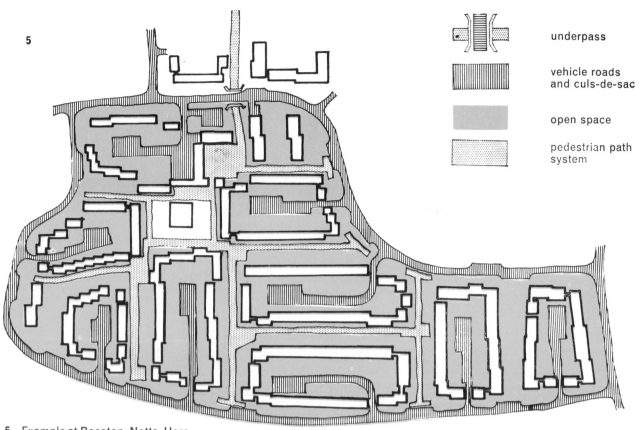

5 Example at Beeston, Notts. Here distributor roads completely enclose the residential area. Nursery school and shops are centrally placed on the path system, which is linked by an underpass to the next area.

6 Part of the traffic separation layout at Fairlands, Stevenage. The distributor road is a spine with cul-de-sac spurs on either side. Six underpasses are needed to make the path system run continuously.

underpass

vehicle roads and culs-de-sac

open space

pedestrian path system

0 50 100   200   300   400   500ft

5 A separate footpath system

In any traffic separation scheme the paths must be designed as a full-scale  pedestrian network that can be laid out at the same time as the roads and services. They must lead somewhere—to focal points like schools or shops, as well as to houses. And the path system should continue right to the edge of the area, and if necessary to points, such as a school or a rail or bus station, that lie actually outside it. In this way the residential area is connected to the town as a whole.

A path system should be as direct as possible, following any natural path lines unless there is a good reason (such as safety from traffic) for not doing so. Above all, it should be positive. People, and especially children, worry little about paths being dangerous as long as they are convenient, and a path system should make it *inconvenient* for pedestrians at any time to walk along or across any vehicle route, even if the cars have to be made to go a longer way round. Between houses the footpath system should usually be the shortest and easiest route—otherwise walkers will make their own.

Pedestrian movement has some of the characteristics of a stream or river. It follows the course of least resistance from point to point. For the fast walker with a purpose it may be a length of straight channel, widening at bends and junctions. Casual foot traffic sometimes prefers a meandering course, or it can fan out like a delta. But *every* path should reach a logical goal.

Paths must be efficient, but they should also be attractive: not only ramps rather than steps where prams are likely to be taken, and good lighting at night, but seats, planted areas and plenty of paved space for children to play on.

Underpasses or footbridges may be needed to avoid crossing of roads. Underpasses should be sited so that walkers use them as a matter of course, with changes of level as nearly imperceptible as possible: they should be well **8** lit and well drained, and large enough to avoid the appearance of a tunnel.

Likewise the footbridges: pedestrians should not be expected to climb and descend a flight of steps in order to use the bridge. If possible the road should be at a lower level: in any case the path should continue over the bridge with as little change of gradient as possible.

Where there are a lot of cyclists it may be necessary to provide specially for them, either adjoining the footway network itself, or by making a separate track system, as has been done in some of the new towns. In that case costs of underpasses can be kept down by letting the cyclist track and the footpath share them, with a curb between for safety.

7   A pathway at Hayesford Park,
Bromley, Kent.

8   A main pedestrian way at
Cumbernauld. Mature trees have been
retained.

9   A play space off the pedestrian way
through a house group at Lerwick,
Shetland.

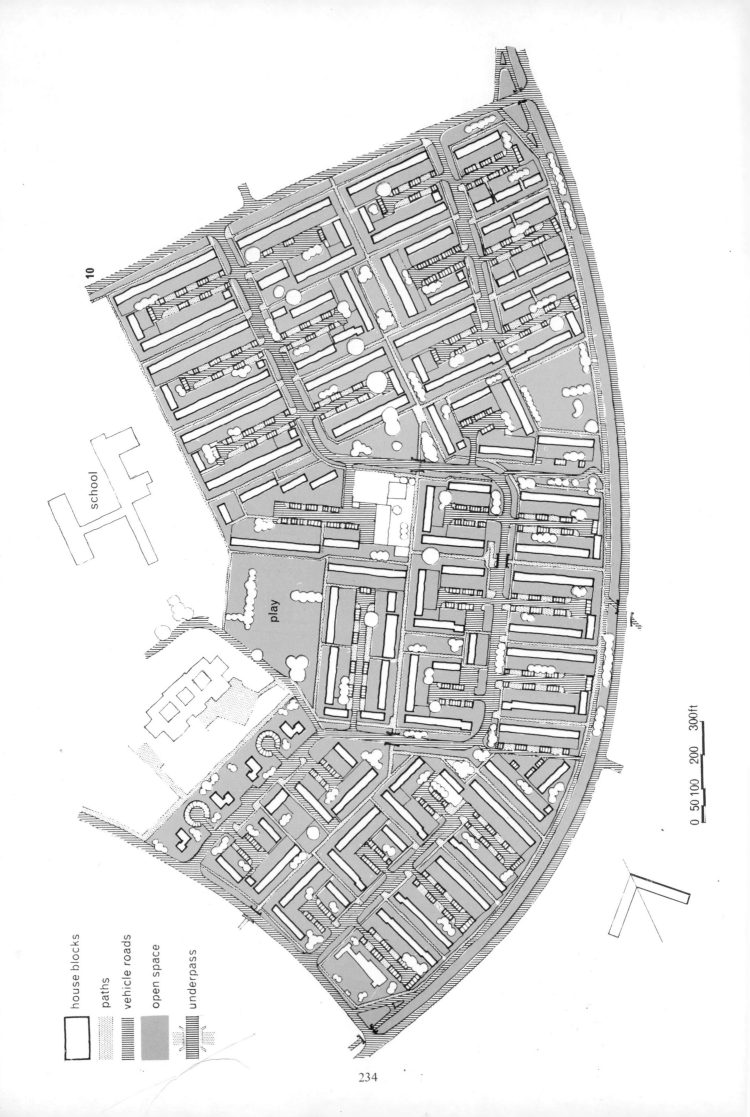

house blocks

paths

vehicle roads

open space

underpass

school

play

10

0 50 100   200   300ft

10 Example from Fairlands, Stevenage, where the distributor road takes the spine form. The plan shows the underpasses needed under the distributor road to approach the play area and school.

11 Example of a traffic separation layout from Cwmbran showing dominance of the central path system. Culs-de-sac are so aligned that the direction and flow along the main pedestrian routes is uninterrupted.

0 50 100 200 300ft

235

6 The grouping and design of houses

The essential housing component of a Radburn layout is a group of houses centred upon and sharing a vehicle access point from which they can all be serviced. The group should have cohesion and be recognisably part of the scheme as a whole, but there is plenty of scope for variety in the size and idiom of individual houses.

Analysis shows that any complete house group in a Radburn scheme is likely to conform to one of three basic types:

12

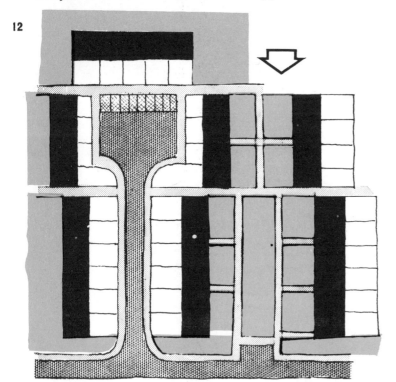

a The vehicle cul-de-sac

with a turning circle or hammer-head at the end of the carriageway, and with individual or grouped garages.

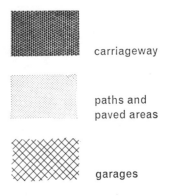

carriageway

paths and paved areas

garages

13

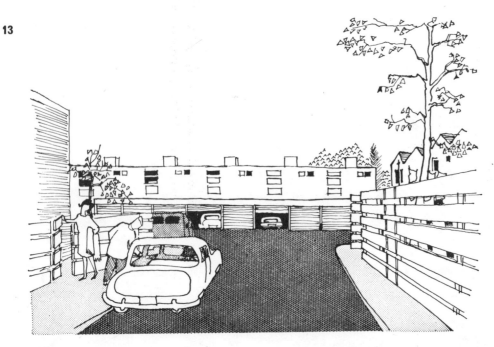

14

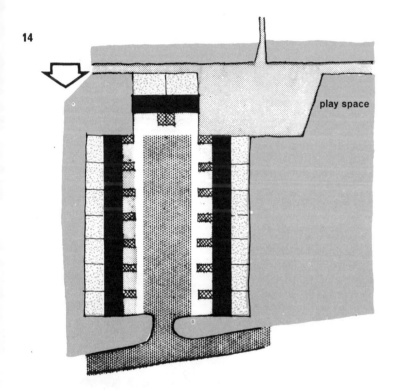

play space

b **The garage court** with the carriageway widened to form a single large enclosure for vehicles and grouped or individual garages.

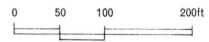

0   50   100   200ft

15

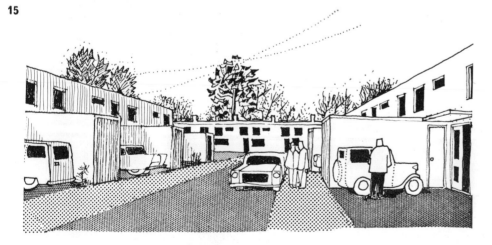

c **The pedestrian forecourt.** The head of the cul-de-sac or garage court is extended to form a paved pedestrian area from which each house is entered. Garages are grouped away from the houses

16   17

Variations on the pedestrian forecourt are:

18   19

c a **The pedestrian link** where a pedestrian way, lined with houses, forms a link between two vehicle access points.

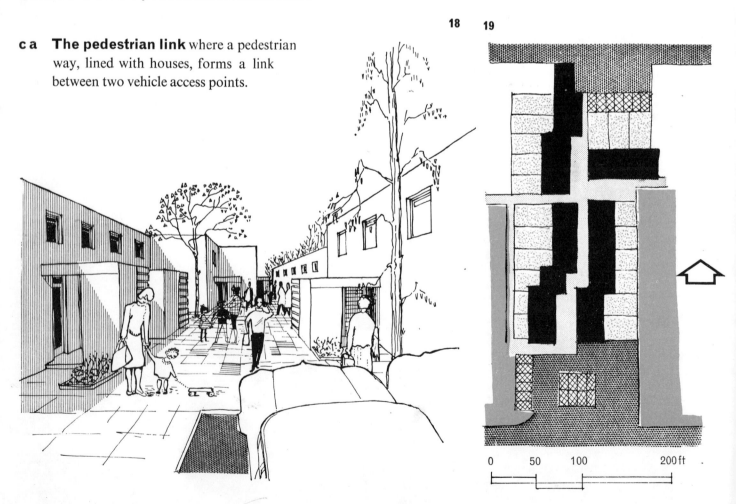

0   50   100   200 ft

c b The pedestrian passageway where at high densities the forecourt becomes part of a network of footways between houses.

20   21

Each of these types of house group caters for service access, i.e. access by
car as distinct from access on foot, in a different way, and they show different
solutions for housing the car—sometimes within the dwelling in a built-in
garage, sometimes in separate blocks a short walk away.

The next section of the bulletin discusses and illustrates these three types
of house group with variations of their basic house plan types.

6A   The vehicle cul-de-sac

In the earlier versions of the cul-de-sac form of house group, house terraces are placed back to back across the cul-de-sac and face each other across a landscaped open space which contains the path system, as shown in Figure **12.**

In this type of group (and in the garage court type also) the door for arrivals on foot opens directly on to the path system, while the door for arrivals by car opens on to the cul-de-sac (or court). If there are special lay-bys for visitors' cars, the visitor has the choice of either door.

This double access does away with the traditional distinction between 'front' and 'back' door. It is simpler for the architect to think in terms of a door which is primarily for pedestrians and a door which is primarily for those who have driven up in vehicles, and to regard both the 'front' and the 'back' of the house as equal in importance, and in the care and treatment they require.

This in turn leads to the characteristic, though not invariable, house for the cul-de-sac and garage court types of house group being called '*dual entry*'. In a cul-de-sac house group nearly all the houses are likely to be dual entry.

It is in the cul-de-sac type of layout that most of the difficulties instanced on page 228 have occurred, as well as certain others. Too much is apt to take place on the cul-de-sac side. The garden or small yard attached to each house is usually on this side, and callers from the cul-de-sac walk through it. Washing hangs out, bulk deliveries are carried in, and dustbins collected. The whole cul-de-sac area can easily become cluttered or squalid.

Recent designs have done their best to counteract these tendencies. Gardens can be placed on the path side, as in the original Radburn layouts: this gives more privacy and allows children to run out of the garden on to a path in complete safety. At the same time, enough space can be provided on the cul-de-sac side for an outdoor 'service threshold' where for example, dustbins can be neatly concealed, while a fence or external store can screen the clothes lines.

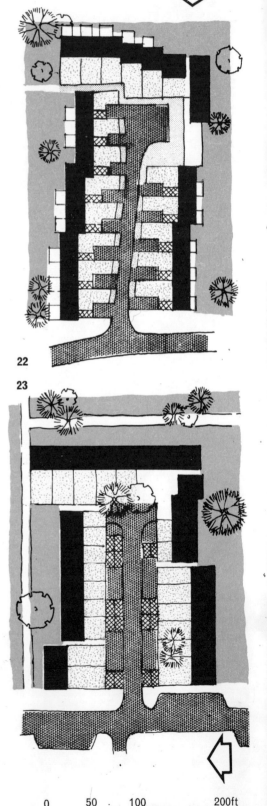

22

23

0   50   100   200ft

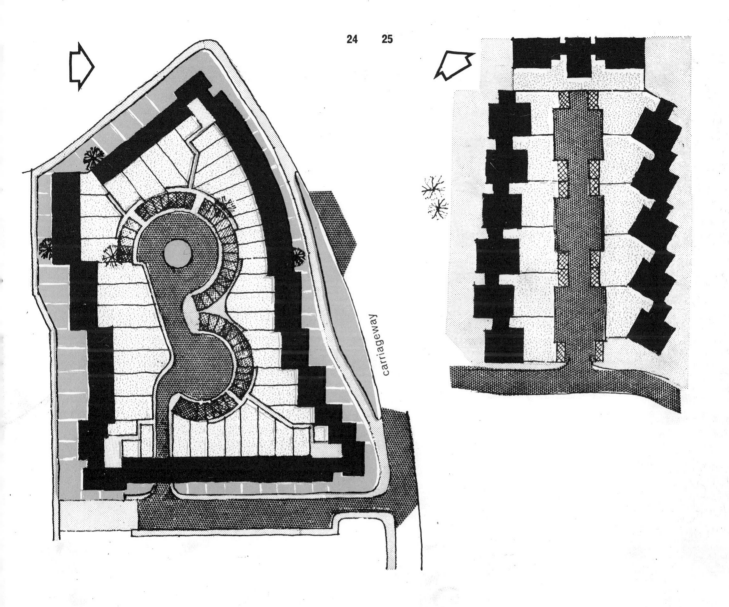

carriageway

22 Fairlands, Stevenage. Separate drive-in from the cul-de-sac to individual garages attached to terrace houses.

23 Almond Spring, Stevenage. Conventional form, but some screening of back garden, with garages.

24 Lee Chapel North, Basildon. A double cul-de-sac with generous provision for garages. A lay-by for visitors' cars is placed to enable visitors to approach houses easily on foot by the path system. The curved shape of the cul-de-sac facilitates street cleaning.

25 Park Area, Cumbernauld. A development of the cul-de-sac with lay-bys and grouped garages. Staggered single-storey house blocks give more privacy than earlier versions by reducing the overlooking from neighbours' houses. The private space is enclosed by high fences. Access gate for refuse collection.

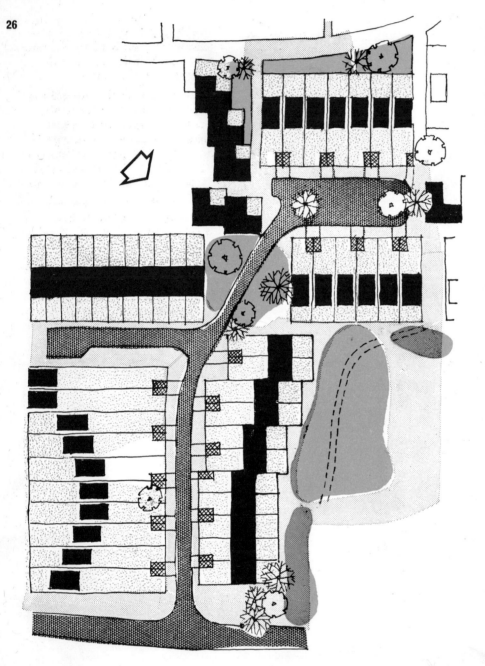

26 Project for a new village in Cambridgeshire. A branched cul-de-sac, 600 ft. in length from the distributor road, with open parking at its head. Garages are in pairs inside gardens and are entered direct from the carriageway. There is private garden space on both sides of the house. A low density layout (9 houses to the acre).

The vehicle cul-de-sac house

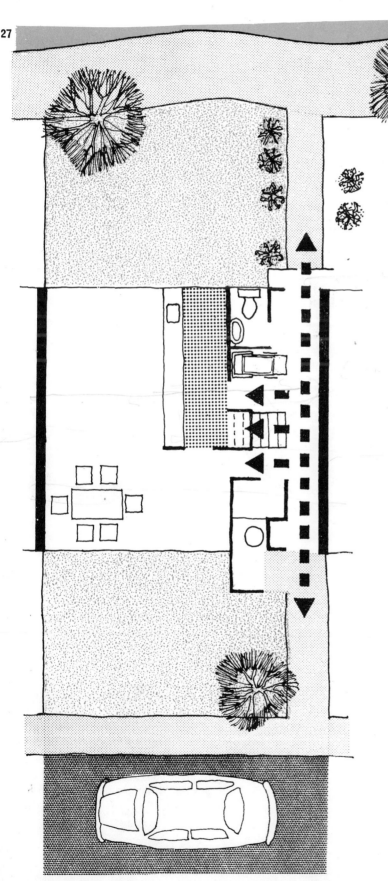

27

Figure **27** is a diagrammatic house plan suitable for the vehicle cul-de-sac form of house group. Both doors are equally important for receiving callers.

Callers at the door on the path side will naturally be visitors on foot who may have left their cars in a parking bay; postal and newspaper deliveries; and canvassers, salesmen, etc. The letter box will be in this door. The open space on this side may be publicly maintained.

The door on the cul-de-sac side will cater for all arrivals and departures by car, bulk deliveries from vans, and refuse collection. It can be entered without crossing the garden. Other points about this type of house are:

■ The baby's pram can be wheeled out on either side, whichever is sunnier, from the through hall.

■ Children may play either on the cul-de-sac side (provided that the garden or yard is adequately enclosed for safety) or on the path side where they can be under their mother's eye when she is in the kitchen.

■ The clothes line, which will naturally be on the cul-de-sac side, is easily reachable from the kitchen without carrying washing through the living area.

■ A recessed entry and a canopy protects callers from wet or cold at either side.

■ Callers approaching on the path side are directly visible from the kitchen.

| 0 | | | | | | 10 | | 15 | | 20 | | 25ft |

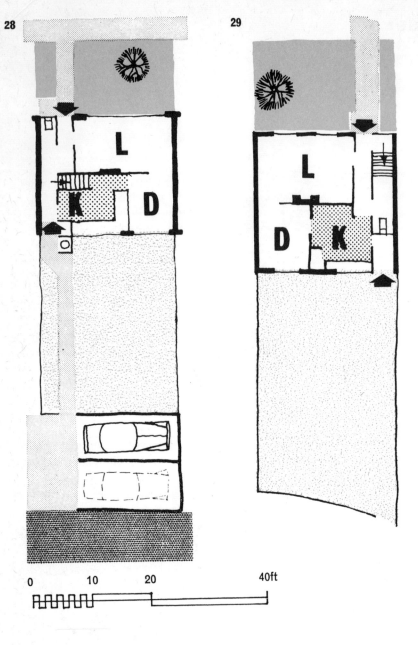

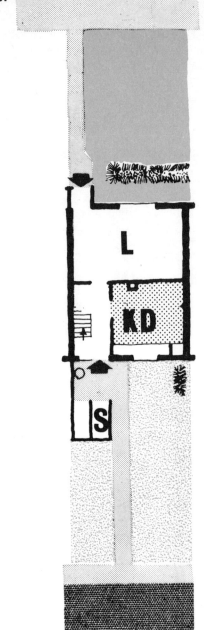

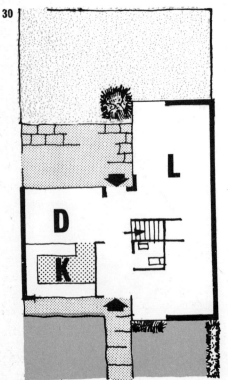

0   10   20   40ft

Variations on the basic house plan

28 Fairlands, Stevenage. A dual entry house with private space on one side only. The hall leads right through the house without going through any of the rooms.

29 Lee Chapel North, Basildon. Dual entry. Going through the house, you pass through the corner of the kitchen, but without crossing the working area.

30 Adaptable house designed by the Ministry of Housing and Local Government for the Ideal Home Exhibition 1962. Movable partitions enable this house to be adapted for entry into a central hall with access right through. The L shape allows for a small garden or court on the pedestrian side.

31 Wrexham. A dual entry house from one of the first traffic separation schemes designed in this country. Entrance direct into the living-room.

32 Fieldend, Twickenham. A scheme with enclosed private gardens on the cul-de-sac side, and a verge between fence and carriageway as an additional safety measure. The path side opens on to a publicly maintained green.

33, 34 Two schemes with direct entry from the path system. Corby (**33**) and Fox Hill, Nottingham (**34**).

32

33

34

6B   The garage court

Both the increase in car ownership and higher residential densities[1] make it necessary to provide for more cars in a given area. From this need a rather different type of grouping has emerged. The earlier cul-de-sac has been widened to create what has here been termed a 'garage court', and this is illustrated by the diagram and sketch on page 237. (Figures **14** and **15**.)

Space which in the cul-de-sac house group was used for gardens on the cul-de-sac side is now more likely to be used for garages, hardstanding or open parking for vehicles. This means that space available for gardens occurs generally on the path side of the house. As a counter-attraction to the larger hard surface of the garage court the main path should be widened at intervals to form equally interesting play spaces for each group of houses.

The garage court should have plenty of room for manoeuvring of vehicles, car washing and maintenance. Cars can be brought close to the houses. Visitors' cars can be accommodated on the hardstandings. All this, with the placing of the garden on the path side, is likely to increase the proportion of callers coming to the door on the garage court side, and so give more privacy on the path side.

Some of the callers on the garage court side will inevitably be pedestrians. A change of surface texture will help to keep them from passing too close in front of an open garage door when a car may be reversing outwards.

[1] See the Ministry's Planning Bulletin 2: *Residential Areas—Higher Densities* (HMSO 1962; 2s.)

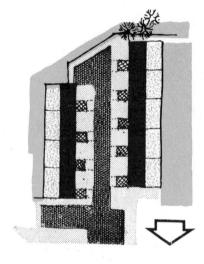

35

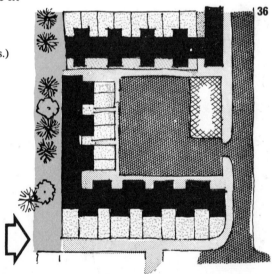

36

37

38

39

35 South Passmores, Harlow. Garages are attached to the houses, with hard-standings at their side. There is a turning space at the head of the court. On the opposite side of the terraces are private gardens, with landscaped open space beyond.

36 Laindon, Basildon. A covered car port combined with open parking space. In this layout some private gardens are on the garage court side.

37, 39 Houses in a garage court layout at Hayesford Park, Bromley. **(37)** Entry from the path side. This terrace has no enclosed private gardens. **(39)** The garage court side. Grassed strips and a paved drive-in for each garage enable cars to back out without danger to pedestrians in the court.

38 View in a garage court at Paradise Row, Henley-on-Thames. The garages are incorporated in the terrace of houses and there are small enclosed private gardens on the other side.

The garage court house

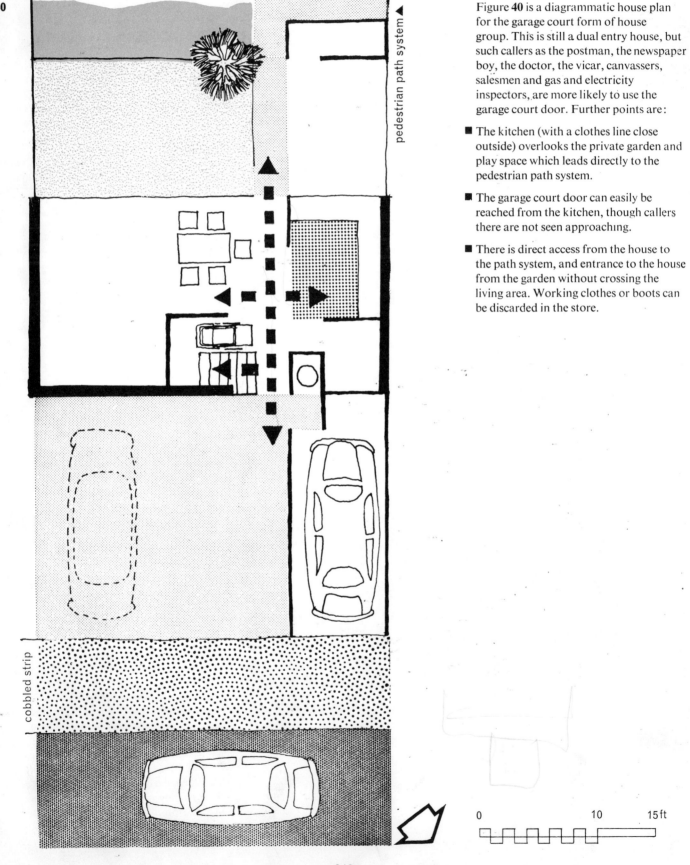

40

pedestrian path system ▲

cobbled strip

Figure **40** is a diagrammatic house plan for the garage court form of house group. This is still a dual entry house, but such callers as the postman, the newspaper boy, the doctor, the vicar, canvassers, salesmen and gas and electricity inspectors, are more likely to use the garage court door. Further points are:

■ The kitchen (with a clothes line close outside) overlooks the private garden and play space which leads directly to the pedestrian path system.

■ The garage court door can easily be reached from the kitchen, though callers there are not seen approaching.

■ There is direct access from the house to the path system, and entrance to the house from the garden without crossing the living area. Working clothes or boots can be discarded in the store.

0   10   15 ft

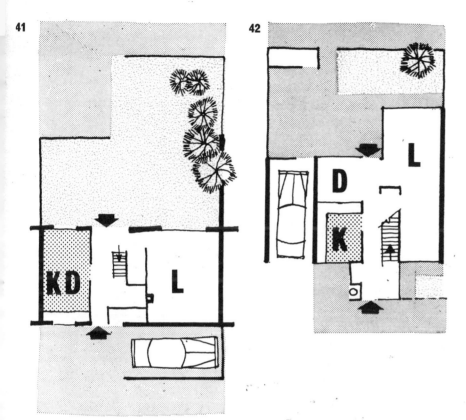

Variations on the basic house plan

41 South Side, Cumbernauld.
A dual entry house with through hall.
The garage is attached. The dining-kitchen looks out both ways, and callers at either door can be seen. Pedestrian entrance through private open space.

42 Ravenscroft Close, West Ham.
A 4-person house with dual entry and built-in garage.

43 Paradise Row, Henley-on-Thames.
A dual entry patio house. The service entrance is combined with the car port. Visitors enter from the path side. A walled garden gives complete privacy.

44 Warley, Essex. A car port, combined with an outdoor store, provides the house with a sheltered entrance.

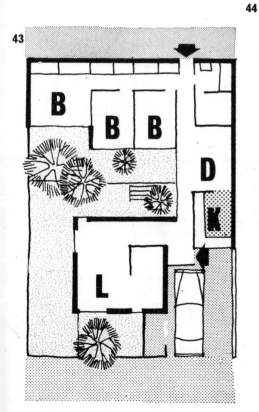

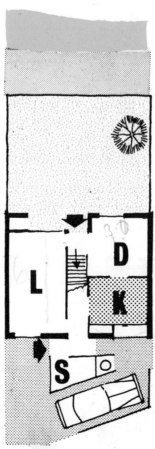

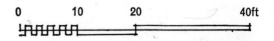

6C   The pedestrian forecourt

In this type of house group the head of the vehicle cul-de-sac is extended to form a paved area or forecourt across which pedestrians can move freely, as it is connected to the main path network. (Figures 16 and 17.)

Houses are entered from this forecourt: on their other side are enclosed private gardens, which may have a rear entrance. Garages are grouped at the nearest access point to the houses, and there should be generous provision for casual parking and plenty of turning space.

Goods may be taken or carried across the paved area, but the distance should not be too long. This involves some co-operation on the part of tradesmen and local authority services (for refuse collection, etc.).

Children can play on the paved area under supervision from the windows of kitchens or main rooms. Large areas in permanent shadow should therefore be avoided.

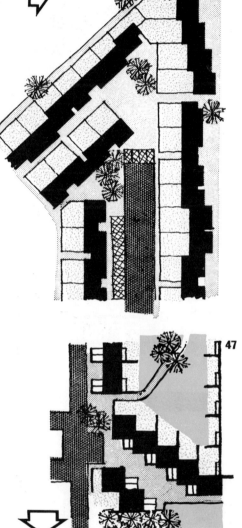

45   A pedestrian forecourt at Vanbrugh Park, Blackheath.

46   Clement's Area, Haverhill. A variation of the pedestrian forecourt layout in which terraces of houses flanking the forecourt are all orientated either to south or south-west.

47   Passmores, Harlow. A proposed scheme in which staggering of the houses increases privacy and gives a sense of enclosure.

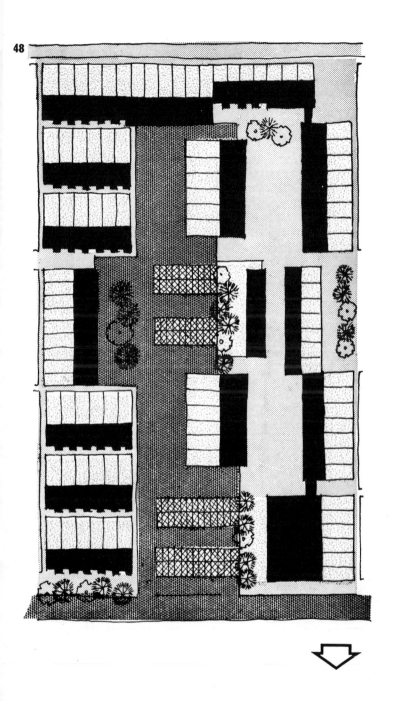

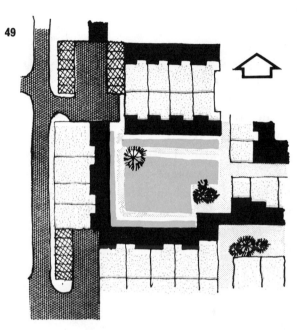

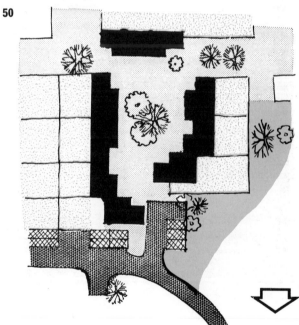

48 Hook. A pedestrian forecourt
project for the once-proposed new
town, with grouped garages and
generous parking bays. The spacious
forecourt is on the west side, and on the
east side a pedestrian passageway
arrangement as described on page 255.

49 The pedestrian forecourt becomes
a close at Bracknell.

50 Andover, Area 11. A typical
example from the scheme for the
expanded town.

The pedestrian forecourt house

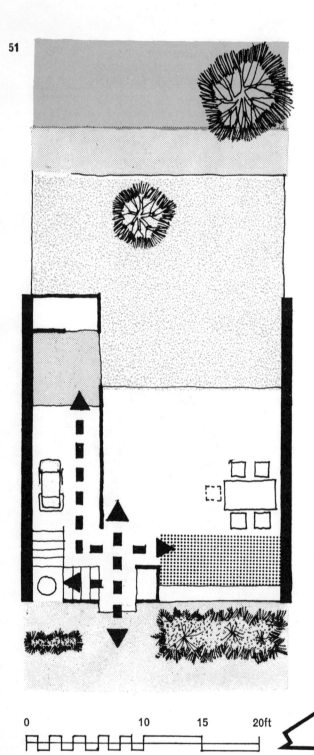

51

The diagrammatic plan (Figure **51**) has the door opening on to the pedestrian forecourt and used by all callers and visitors. There is easy access through the store to the garden behind. The kitchen window looks out on to the forecourt, so that an eye can be kept on children playing there.

There can be a garden gate for materials to be brought into the garden, otherwise all goods, from parcels to furniture, are taken or carried to the one door from the vehicle access point. Complete privacy is provided by the enclosed space or garden behind.

0   10   15   20ft

Variations on the basic house plan

52 Aldershot. Single entry patio house for 4 to 5 people. The entrance hall leads straight through the house to the garden.

53 St. Dials, Cwmbran. A dual entry house, with both doors on the fore-court side. The dining area leads through to the garden.

54 A narrow-fronted house designed for the London County Council Brandon Estate, Southwark, and schemes at Spring Walk, Stepney, and Pier Road, North Woolwich. Passage to the garden is through the living-room. The garden has a back gate giving on to a path.

55 Andover, Area 12. Another dual entry house, designed for the town expansion scheme, with the two entries on the forecourt side.

56 Hackney Wick. A single-storey patio house for 7 people with circulation straight through the house to the private court without going through the living area.

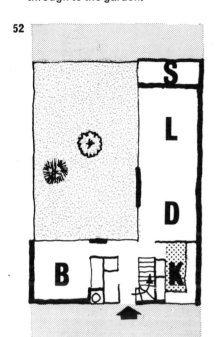

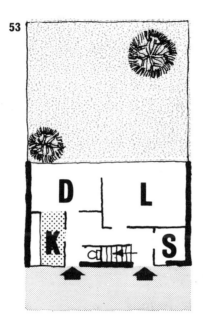

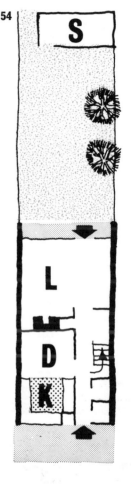

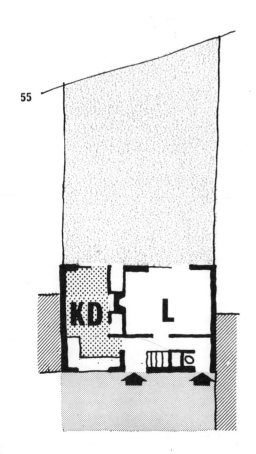

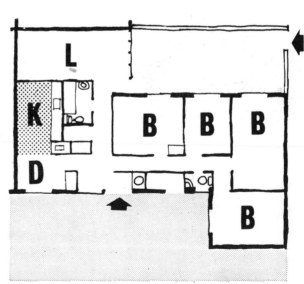

0   10   20   30   40   50ft

6Ca The pedestrian link

This is a development of the pedestrian forecourt. (Figures **18** and **19.**) The court is narrowed to become in effect a pedestrian link between two vehicle access points. Its length is limited by the maximum reasonable carrying distance for goods from the access points, which in these schemes has been set at about 300 ft. Like the forecourt, this link is directly connected with the main path system.

As before, cars are accommodated in grouped garages or car parks at the vehicle access points.

House types are single entry and basically the same as for the pedestrian forecourt; but they need also to be 'blind side' (i.e. with no ground floor windows on the pedestrian way, except possibly a kitchen window). This keeps passers-by from looking into living-rooms.

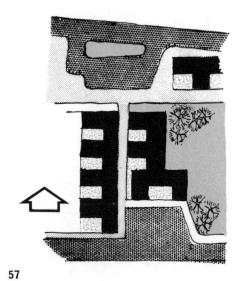

57

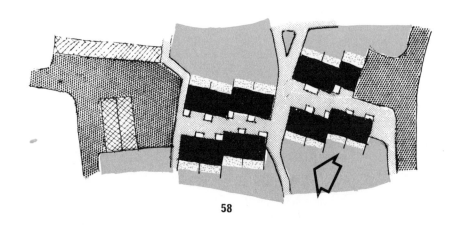

58

57 Inch View, Prestonpans, East Lothian. A covered pedestrian way linking two vehicle access points on the perimeter road. Courtyard houses are stepped up a 10° slope, and the continuous stepped roof-line allows for a form of clerestory lighting.

58 North Stannington, Sheffield. Informal grouping of short terrace blocks along a pedestrian way between vehicle access points and crossed by the main pedestrian spine.

6Cb The pedestrian passageway

In this higher density version of the pedestrian forecourt type of house group (Figures **20** and **21**), the forecourt becomes a pedestrian passageway.

All living-rooms face south or west. The houses are entered from the passageway and need to be 'blind side' to give privacy not only from passers-by but from overlooking as well.

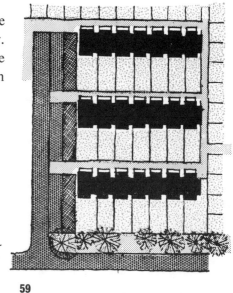

59

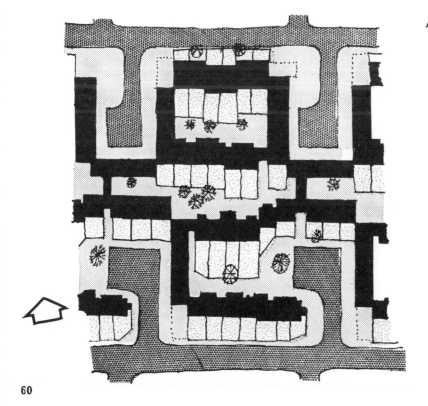

60

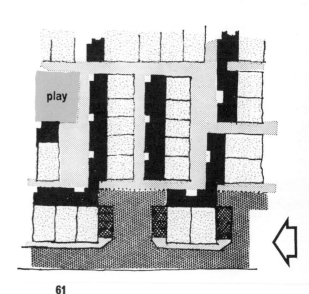

61

59 Seafar, Cumbernauld. 'Blind side' terrace houses. This particular type of layout needs high fences round each garden to ensure privacy, without cutting off sunshine or giving the housewife a feeling of isolation.

60 A group from the Greater London Council scheme at Yeading Green, Hayes, featuring a modified form of pedestrian passageway. Irregular width and change of direction make for variety and interest.

61 A group from Winklebury, part of the expansion of Basingstoke. Care has been taken to provide good sight lines for vehicles turning in from the main cul-de-sac or leaving. The close network of passageways opens at intervals to provide safe internal play spaces.

The pedestrian link or passageway house

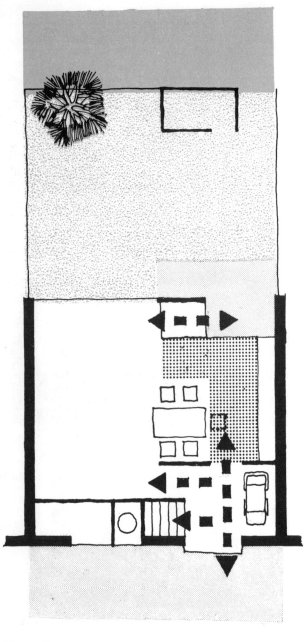

62

As the diagrammatic plan shows (Figure **62**) this type of house is 'blind side', so that passers-by cannot look in. The door, which serves all callers, opens on the pedestrian way.

All main rooms overlook the garden, and the landscaped open space beyond, and should be placed to receive all the sunlight possible.

The kitchen opens directly on to the garden.

0   10   15   20ft

63

64

65

63 Seafar, Cumbernauld. The pedestrian link has a flight of steps between vehicle access roads on two levels.

64 Another pedestrian link from Seafar, Cumbernauld, with a main pathway at intermediate level running through at right angles.

65 Burntisland, Fife. A passageway with steps and ramp.

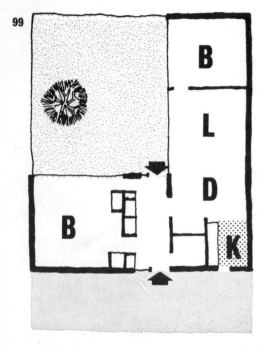

99

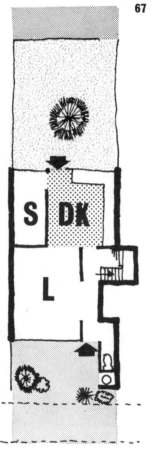

67

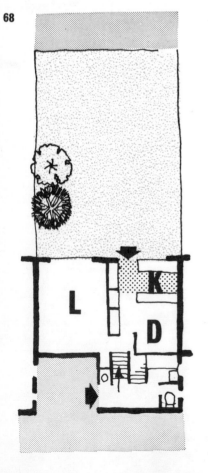

68

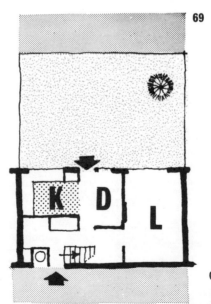

69

Variations on the basic house plan

66 Inch View, Prestonpans, East Lothian. A 'blind side' patio house, entered from a covered pedestrian link. The entrance hall leads straight through to the patio.

67 Laindon, Basildon. An interlocking terrace house for 4 to 5 people. A small entrance court prevents the living area being overlooked from the passageway. Access to the garden is from the dining-kitchen.

68 Orchard Hill, Lewisham. A 5-person terrace house on two levels with one of the entrances from a small court off the passageway. All rooms face south.

69 Carbrain, Cumbernauld. A 'blind side' terrace house with a wide frontage.

0   10   20   40ft

6 The grouping and design of houses

Bibliography

BLACHNICKI (Henryk) *and* BROWNE (Kenneth)
Over and under; a survey of the problems of pedestrian/vehicle segregation. *Architectural Review, 1961, Vol. 129, May, pp. 321-336.*

BRUNNER (Christopher)
Cities—living with the motor vehicle. Paper...at the Friends' Meeting House, London, 18th February 1960...British Road Federation, 1960. *Gratis*

BUCHANAN (Colin Douglas)
Standards and values in motor age towns; fifth Rees Jeffreys triennial lecture. *Town Planning Institute Journal, 1961, Vol. 47, December, pp. 320-329.*

COPCUTT (Geoffrey)
Car parking in Cumbernauld. *Architects' Journal, 1960, Vol. 132, December 15, pp. 862-867.*

DAVIES (Anthony B.)
Planning for the motor vehicle at Basildon. *Architect and Building News, 1959, Vol. 216, November 11, pp. 425-427.*

INSTITUTE OF LANDSCAPE ARCHITECTS
The urban scene—design for pleasure and hard wear in the landscape. Report of a symposium held at the RIBA, May 24th, 1960. The Institute, 1960. *2s 6d*

LONDON COUNTY COUNCIL
The planning of a new town; data and design based on a study for a new town of 100,000 at Hook, Hampshire. LCC, 1961. *£2 10s 0d*

MINISTRY OF HOUSING AND LOCAL GOVERNMENT
Homes for today and tomorrow. Report of a sub-committee of the Central Housing Advisory Committee. (Chairman: Sir Parker Morris, LL.B.) HMSO, 1961. *4s 0d*

MINISTRY OF TRANSPORT
Traffic in towns (the Buchanan Report); a study of the long term problems of traffic in urban areas; reports of the Steering Group (Chairman: Sir Geoffrey Crowther) and the Working Group (Chairman: Colin Buchanan). HMSO, 1963. *£2 10s 0d*
   Specially shortened edition. Penguin Books, 1963. *10s 6d*

PEDESTRIANS' ASSOCIATION FOR ROAD SAFETY
A pedestrians' bill of rights; a practical policy for safer towns. The Association, 1961. *2s 0d*

RITTER (Paul)
Planning for man and motor. Pergamon Press, 1964. *£5 5s 0d*

RITTER (Paul)
The Radburn idea in Great Britain. *Housing Review, 1960, Vol. 9, January-February, pp. 19-21.*

RITTER (Paul)
Radburn planning; a reassessment. *Architects' Journal, 1960, Vol. 132, November 10, pp. 680-684, November 17, pp. 719-723, November 24, pp. 765-769, December 8, pp. 836-842; 1961, Vol. 133, January 12, pp. 51-54, January 26, pp. 142-147, February 2, pp. 176-180, February 9, pp. 211-216, February 16, pp. 249-254.*

SIMONDS (John Ormsbee)
Landscape architecture; the shaping of man's natural environment. Iliffe, 1961. *£4 15s 0d*

STEIN (Clarence S.)
Toward new towns for America. *Town Planning Review, 1949, Vol. 20, October, pp. 202-82; 1950, Vol. 20, January, pp. 319-418.*
Includes a description of Radburn.

STEPHENSON (Gordon)
The Wrexham experiment. *Town Planning Review, 1954, Vol. 24, January, pp. 271-295.*

TURNER (Robert)
Garages in residential areas. *Town Planning Review, 1959, Vol. 30, July, pp. 145-160.*

Index

261

CONSTRUCTION LIBRARY,
Liverpool Polytechnic.
Victoria Street, L1 6EY